Praise for *Ghostland*

An NPR Best Book of the Year
A *Shelf Awareness* Best Book of the Year

"Dickey takes an erudite tour of haunted America and tells us repeatedly that the meaning of ghost stories lies not in what they claim about the occult but in what they inadvertently say about the anxieties and prejudices of the teller and the larger society. . . . His analytical and reportorial talents are evident. . . . Part of the special delight of *Ghostland* is its many informed asides, revealing Dickey's long hours of spading up obscure facts and quotes. . . . A bravura performance of storytelling, in an elegant prose style throughout that does not sacrifice intelligence for readability."
—*Los Angeles Times*

"For a relatively young nation, America is overrun with spirits. Mr. Dickey visits with Salem's witches, spectral lights at a Nevada brothel, and the eccentric widow who designed the sprawling, never-finished Winchester Mystery House . . . [to] suggest that by analyzing them we can learn a great deal about ourselves."
—*The Wall Street Journal*

"Dickey neatly dissects not just the historical, but the visual and atmospheric elements that evoke a haunting . . . As he wends his way through the landmarks and their histories, Dickey thoroughly and convincingly explores the many underpinnings of ghost stories and hauntings—as manifestations of our collective guilt, anxieties, obsessions, and historical losses; and as practical schemes for money-making, land acquistion, or controlling groups of people."
—*Huffington Post*

"Colin Dickey's essays explore facets of the world that we might overlook, take readers to uncharted spaces, and delve into bizarre corners of history."
—*Vol 1. Brooklyn*

"A stunning work of architectural theory and a spellbinding collection of true-crime tales and historical drama."
—*The Atlantic*

"Engrossing . . . Dickey's book is not so much about spooks and goblins, but about tales of them that we tell, and why. Its purpose isn't to scare, but to intrigue—and on that level, it may well keep you up late."

—*Seattle Times*

"Dickey is one of the sharpest and most erudite writers around, and his new book makes for a perfect Halloween read."

—*Men's Journal*

"Colin Dickey is a mad genius, and reading one of his books is as close to a look at his brilliant brain as we will get without use of a bone saw."

—*BookRiot*

"You wouldn't expect to read about brothels, human psychology, Victorian architecture, even a suburban Toys R Us, and come out the other side with an entirely different understanding and appreciation for ghosts. But Colin Dickey's writing is just that good. *Ghostland* is strange and unsettling in the best possible way."

—Caitlin Doughty, *New York Times* bestselling author of *Smoke Gets in Your Eyes*

"Always fascinating, sometimes horrifying. *Ghostland* is a remarkable portrait of the ways that the walking dead—or our beliefs in them—wander through, and shape, American history."

—Deborah Blum, author of *The Poisoner's Handbook*

"Spine-tingling . . . A truly creepy travelogue that's a must-have for Halloweeen."

—*BookPage*

"Come for the ghosts, stay for the history."

—*Booklist*

"Dickey pops sensationalist bubbles by observing the underlying racism, sexism, and classism associated with many hauntings' long-told tales. By exposing historical inaccuracies and sociological calumny, the work treats readers to a better understanding of the socioeconomic and political milieu in which these myths gained acceptance, ultimately providing a richer, more nuanced narrative. Sophisticated readers with gothic sensibilities who enjoy literary histories, social commentary, and authoritative travelogs will find this a worthy title."

—*Library Journal*

PENGUIN BOOKS

GHOSTLAND

Colin Dickey grew up in San Jose, California, a few miles from the Winchester Mystery House, the most haunted house in America. As a writer, speaker, and an academic, he has made a career out of collecting unusual objects and hidden stories all over the country. He's a regular contributor to the *Los Angeles Review of Books* and *Lapham's Quarterly*, and is the coeditor (with Joanna Ebenstein) of *The Morbid Anatomy Anthology*. He is also a member of the Order of the Good Death, a collective of artists, writers, and death industry professionals interested in improving the Western world's relationship with mortality. With a PhD in comparative literature from the University of Southern California, he is an associate professor of creative writing at National University. He lives in Brooklyn, NY.

www.colindickey.com

GHOSTLAND

An American History in
Haunted Places

Colin Dickey

PENGUIN BOOKS

PENGUIN BOOKS
An imprint of Penguin Random House LLC
375 Hudson Street
New York, New York 10014
penguin.com

First published in the United States of America by Viking Penguin,
an imprint of Penguin Random House LLC, 2016
Published in Penguin Books 2017

ISBN 9781101980200 (paperback)

THE LIBRARY OF CONGRESS HAS CATALOGED THE HARDCOVER EDITION AS FOLLOWS:
Names: Dickey, Colin, author.
Title: Ghostland : an American history in haunted places / Colin Dickey.
Description: New York : Viking, 2016. | Includes bibliographical references
and index.
Identifiers: LCCN 2016044006 (print) | LCCN 2016044819 (ebook) | ISBN
9781101980194 (hardcover) | ISBN 9781101980217 (ebook)
Subjects: LCSH: Haunted places—United States.
Classification: LCC BF1472.U6 D53 2016 (print) | LCC BF1472.U6 (ebook) | DDC
133.10973—dc23
LC record available at https://lccn.loc.gov/2016044006

Printed in the United States of America
1 3 5 7 9 10 8 6 4 2

Set in LTC Cloister
Designed by Nancy Resnick
Illustrations © Jon Contino

For Nicole

The main work of haunting is done by the living.

—JUDITH RICHARDSON

Ghostland lies beyond the jurisdiction of veracity.

—NATHANIEL HAWTHORNE

CONTENTS

AUTHOR'S NOTE

This book is not about the truth or falsity of any claims of ghosts. There are questions there—fascinating to some, problematic or uninteresting to others—about physics and metaphysics, theology and superstition, the natural and the supernatural, but all those questions ultimately end up circling back on themselves. As Samuel Johnson mentioned to James Boswell more than two hundred years ago, "It is wonderful that five thousand years have now elapsed since the creation of the world, and still it is undecided whether or not there has ever been an instance of the spirit of any person appearing after death." There is no amount of proof that will convince a skeptic of spirits, just as no amount of skeptical debunking will disabuse a believer. As Johnson remarked regarding the paranormal, "All argument is against it; but all belief is for it."

This book instead focuses on questions of the living: how do we deal with stories about the dead and their ghosts, and how do we inhabit and move through spaces that have been deemed haunted? These are questions that remain whether or not you believe in ghosts. Even if you don't believe in the paranormal, ghost stories and legends of haunted places are a vital, dynamic means of confronting the past and those who have gone before us. Ultimately, this book is about the relationship between place and story: how the two depend on each other and how they bring each other alive.

GHOSTLAND

ANATOMY OF A HAUNTING

New York, NY

August 1933, a summer's day in Manhattan's Lower East Side. There are children playing outside on East Fourth Street; they are wild, they are shouting and running through the street, trying to gather up the last of the season before the fall sets in. There is nothing unusual about any of this. Then the door swings open at 29 East Fourth Street, and an old woman emerges onto the stoop overlooking the street, waving her arms wildly and shouting to the children to be quiet. The children and the adults all recognize her: Gertrude Tredwell, who's lived in the house for more than ninety years, born there in 1840, five years after her father purchased it. She is enraged; she tells them they are being far too noisy, they must calm down. The children quiet, turning toward the high staircase that leads to Gertrude's front door, looking up with fear at the old woman, who, satisfied, returns indoors and shuts the door.

There's nothing unusual about any of this—except that Gertrude Tredwell has been dead now for several weeks.

It is not the last time Gertrude Tredwell will be seen at the house on East Fourth Street. In the months after her death, the house falls into the hands of a distant cousin; since by now most of the old merchant houses of lower Manhattan are gone, he decides to preserve the house as a museum, first opening it to the public in 1936. Over the years there are dozens of sightings of odd and inexplicable things happening *in the house. In the early 1980s tourists come across the house and ring the bell. A woman in period costume tells them politely that the museum is closed for the day, and could they please come back at another time. Later, when they call the house to get the hours, they are told that the museum was in fact open when they came by and that, furthermore, none of the staff ever dresses in period costume. Gertrude has also been seen inside the house, sometimes humming, sometimes playing the piano— always appearing as a frail, petite woman in period costume.*

Nor is she alone. A visitor to the house in the summer of 1995 claimed that while upstairs she had a lengthy conversation with an older gentleman in a tattered suit and a heavy wool jacket smelling of mothballs, who talked to her of what the house was like to live in. After listening to him for a few minutes, she turned away for a moment, and when she looked back, he was gone. Later she identified the man she'd seen from photographs: Samuel Lenox Tredwell, Gertrude's brother, who'd died in 1921.

Ghost stories like these mean more than we are usually prepared to admit. If you want to understand a place, ignore the boastful monuments and landmarks, and go straight to the haunted houses. Look for the darkened graveyards, the derelict hotels, the emptied and decaying old hospitals. Wait past midnight, and see what appears. Tune out the patriotic speeches and sanctioned narratives, and listen instead for the bumps in the night. You won't need an electronic device to capture the voices of the dead; a patient ear and an open mind will do. Once you start looking, you'll find them everywhere.

"We tell ourselves stories in order to live," Joan Didion once wrote, and that is just as true of ghost stories: we tell stories of the dead as a way of making sense of the living. More than just simple urban legends and camp-fire tales, ghost stories reveal the contours of our anxieties, the nature of our collective fears and desires, the things we can't talk about in any other way. The past we're most afraid to speak aloud of in the bright light of day is the same past that tends to linger in the ghost stories we whisper in the dark.

Ghost stories are as old as human civilization, appearing in the earliest written epics and throughout the ancient world. In one of his letters the Roman writer Pliny the Younger describes a house haunted by a ghost "in the form of an old man, of extremely emaciated and squalid appearance, with a long beard and disheveled hair, rattling the chains on his feet and hands." The house remained vacant until the philosopher Athenodorus rented it; his first night he waited up for the ghost, writing in his study, until the apparition appeared.

Athenodorus, according to Pliny, was not in a hurry and, when confronted by the ghost, "made a sign with his hand that he should wait a little, and threw his eyes again upon his papers." Eventually the philosopher allowed the ghost to lead him out of the house into the yard, where the ghost vanished. The next morning Athenodorus dug up the spot where the ghost had disappeared and found the remains of a skeleton in chains. He gave the long-neglected corpse a proper burial, and the haunting ceased.

Ghosts bridge the past to the present; they speak across the seemingly insurmountable barriers of death and time, connecting us to what we thought was lost. They give us hope for a life beyond death and because of this help us to cope with loss and grief. Their presence is the promise that we don't have to say goodbye to our loved ones right away and that—as with Athendorus's haunting—what was left undone in one's life might yet be finished by one's ghost.

Perhaps this is why, even without centuries-old castles or ruined abbeys, the United States is as ghost-haunted as anywhere else in the world—perhaps even more so. You'll find ghosts in the stately plantations of the South, in the wilds of the Plains states, in the ornate hotels of California, in the wooden colonials in the Northeast. They roam the streets of rust-belt cities like Detroit and Buffalo, and they haunt the gothic cities of the South. You'll find them in abandoned mining towns and in the bustling metropolis of New York City.

According to one poll, 45 percent of Americans say they believe in ghosts, and almost 30 percent say they've witnessed them firsthand. Though this belief lies outside the ways we normally explain the world— contradicting science and complicating religion—it's a difficult belief to shake. That we continue believing in ghosts despite our rational mind's skepticism suggests that in these stories lies something crucial to the way we understand the world around us. We cannot look away, because we know something important is there.

The Merchant's House Museum in lower Manhattan has stood alone against the din and rush of the city; it has stood for one hundred eighty years and might stand for that many more. Within, walls continue upright, bricks meet neatly, wood floors give gently underfoot, and spirits gather.

The house was bought by Seabury Tredwell in 1835, when he retired. Owner of a large hardware firm, he had eight children altogether, the last of whom, Gertrude, was born there in 1840, when Tredwell was sixty. Gertrude never married—she had one suitor, but her father disapproved of his Catholicism—and so she lived out her life in the house on Fourth Street, her siblings dying one by one until only she remained. Over time she focused her energies on keeping the house exactly as Seabury had intended it, maintaining its nineteenth-century charm until she died, at the age of ninety-three, in 1933. Her cousin turned the house into a museum, and the ghosts, they say, came quickly thereafter.

The Merchant's House is a prime example of a grand old American haunted house. Its exterior is stately, refined, with a touch of frayed elegance. Its front door welcomes even as it seems to be hiding something. Inside the floors creak without warning, without any sense of someone there. The old wood is thick with the humidity, as if the walls and floors still breathe. It is the oldest brownstone in New York with the furniture of its original owners still intact. All around it are gleaming glass-and-steel towers of the modern age, bustling with life still being lived.

It is easy to feel as though you're stepping back in time as you walk in the steps of those long gone. And it's easy, in such a well-worn house, to feel that something is not quite right: an invisible presence, a trace of something that doesn't belong. Through the years guests have reported feeling cold spots or seeing strange, wispy streaks of light, some of which have been captured on film. Paranormal researchers have conducted EVP (electronic voice phenomena) sessions in the house, turning on a tape recorder and asking questions to an empty room, playing back the tape later in hopes that the ghosts will have answered back. Several EVPs from the house have recorded bits of faint, muddled noise that some claim are voices speaking from the beyond.

But these events alone are easy for a skeptic to brush aside and discount. A paranormal event without a story is tenuous, fragile. What makes it "real," at least in a sense, is the story, the tale that grounds the event. That sense of the uncanny, of something not-quite-right, of things ever-so-slightly off, cries out for an explanation, and often we turn to ghosts for that explanation. Just as an oyster turns a speck of dirt into a pearl, the ghost story doesn't make the feeling disappear, but can transform it into something more stable, less unsettling.

Long before the word "haunting" became associated with ghosts, it meant simply "to frequent," in the way teenage kids haunt a park or drunks haunt a bar. A house like the Merchant's House Museum is haunted, then, by use and by habitude, by grooves worn into the floors and walls—as though you could map out the daily patterns of the people who lived here by analyzing these signs of wear.*

The ghosts at the Merchant's House emerge not only out of the uncanny feeling we get from creaking wood and antiquated architecture but also from the stories about its onetime inhabitants that are told and retold over the years and embellished where necessary to heighten the drama. Tales of Gertrude emphasize that she never married; that after her father

---

*This usage of the word "haunting" predates its associations with ghosts by several centuries, according to the *Oxford English Dictionary*, and it's not until Shakespeare that ghosts also begin to haunt.

disapproved of her only suitor, she promised him she'd stay single and live in his home. The spinster who honored her father's wishes even after his death, Gertrude seems tragic, bordering on the pathological. Even before her death, she haunted this house—an emotionally stunted recluse, unable to let go of her attachment to her father.

Her brother Samuel, by contrast, is described as a "black sheep," someone who never amounted to much and was disinherited by the family. This is a tad unfair; Samuel followed in his father's footsteps as a merchant, specializing in china and crockery, though he was not the success his father had been. He was indeed written out of Seabury's final will, mainly due to debts Samuel had incurred in the wake of the Civil War. (Seabury instead left a trust in Samuel's daughter's name.) But the legends of the Merchant's House exaggerate the tensions and family drama, relying on melodramatic caricatures. The sight of Samuel's ghost is far more exciting and menacing, after all, if he has come back from the grave to claim his rightful inheritance.

A spinster and one who seemed to resist time in a place as restless as New York City, Gertrude Tredwell embodies a set of ideas—and anxieties—about women, domesticity, and modernity. Likewise, in the ghost of threadbare Samuel Tredwell we have a story of disinheritance and filial failure that reflects how we as a culture treat men who don't live up to certain concepts of masculinity. Add to this the overbearing portrait of Seabury himself, and what the Merchant's House offers is an uncanny portrait of the American family, one that frustrates our basic assumptions about how a father and his children should act.

Instead of, or perhaps in addition to, the supernatural, old buildings are haunted by their memories: memories of those who once inhabited them, and the memories we bring to them. We're conditioned, after all, to conflate memory and physical space. At the same time that Pliny was writing his tale of Athenodorus's haunted house, Cicero and Quintilian were developing a technique for remembering great quantities of information, known as a "memory palace." Rather than memorizing information directly, one imagines a house and "places" different parts of it in different rooms. With a speech, for example, one's first point is placed in the entry-way to the home, the second point in the first room, and so on. To remember the speech, the orator simply has to "walk" through the house in her or his mind, picking up each aspect of the speech as she or he moves through the building. The technique suggests the degree to which memory is spatial or at least primed to work spatially: our brains are hardwired to think in terms of place and to associate psychic value or meaning to the places we inhabit.

Just as imaginary houses may be used to help us remember things, real physical houses may have their own memories—or at least memories we project onto them. A haunted house is a memory palace made real: a physical space that retains memories that might otherwise be forgotten or that might remain only in fragments. Under the invisible weight of these memories, the habits of those who once haunted these places, we feel the shudder of the ghost.

Ghosts, historian Thomas W. Laqueur writes, are "a representation of the unrepresentable: the dead who were somewhere." In a world where nearly every moment of our lives is photographed, recorded, and documented, the gaps in the past still beckon us. Searching for ghosts can be an attempt to reconstruct what is lost. By sifting through time for stories that have been misplaced or forgotten, we listen to the voices that call out to be remembered. Our ghost stories center on unfinished endings, broken relationships, things left unexplained. They offer an alternative kind of history, foregrounding what might otherwise be ignored.

Ghost stories are a way of talking about things we're not otherwise allowed to discuss: a forbidden history we thought bricked up safely in the walls. They cover over the gaps and in the process help us assuage our anxieties, providing a rationale after the fact. Just as Gertrude Tredwell's life has informed the ghost stories that now circulate around her, so, too, does the legend of her ghost make meaning out of her life. Those aspects of a life that are discontinuous, fragmented, or unexpected, are made whole through the ghost story.

In her study of the ghost stories of the Hudson Valley in New York, Judith Richardson describes how one ghost in particular has changed shape through the decades to suit different needs of different eras. For more than two centuries residents of the village of Leeds have reported seeing a spectral apparition of a ghostly horse galloping down the main road, dragging behind it a young woman. The story, in its most basic form, has to do with a cruel master who wickedly killed a young servant girl as punishment for some minor transgression. When she was invoked by writer Miriam Coles Harris in her 1862 novel, *The Sutherlands*, the ghostly victim is a slave of African and Native American descent; Harris used her as a parable in the vein of *Uncle Tom's Cabin*, castigating not only the institution of slavery but Northern whites for their complicity. In 1896 the same ghost appears in Charles M. Skinner's *Myths and Legends of Our Own Land*, but now she is a white European immigrant, reflecting Skinner's interest in class differences and labor warfare. Contemporary retellings of the story, though, lack these politically charged details; in a 2002 book containing the Leeds legend, for example, the slave's ethnic heritage is unmentioned and the class divide is downplayed. Her master is indeed cruel and callous, but he's portrayed nowadays as a singular figure of evil rather than a representative of a corrupt ruling class.

Paying attention to the way ghost stories change through the years—and why those changes are made—can tell us a great deal about how we face our fears and our anxieties. Even when these stories have a basis in fact and history, there's often significant embellishment and fabrication before they catch on in our imagination, and teasing out these alterations is key to understanding how ghosts shape our relationship to the past.

We like to view this country as a unified, cohesive whole based on progress, a perpetual refinement of values, and an arc of history bending toward justice—but the prevalence of ghosts suggests otherwise. The ghosts who haunt our woods, our cemeteries, our houses, and our cities appear at moments of anxiety and point to instability in our national and local identities. A ghost story is what Freud called "the return of the repressed," when something we'd rather forget returns in another form—such as the famous "Freudian slip" (what he himself called a parapraxis), revealing what we've hidden deep in our subconscious.

Our country's ghost stories are themselves the dreams (or nightmares) of a nation, the Freudian slips of whole communities: uncomfortable and unbidden expressions of things we'd assumed were long past and no longer important. If American history is taught to schoolchildren as a series of great, striding benchmarks, the history of America's ghost stories is one of crimes left unsolved or transgressions we now feel guilty about. They offer explanations for the seemingly inexplicable, address injustices after the fact, and give expression to our unstated desires and fears. They can also, just as easily, mold reality to our preconceived notions and cover over a messy reality in favor of well-worn clichés and urban legends. Ours is a forward-looking country that can have trouble sometimes reckoning with the past and the actions of our ancestors, and the spirit world has become yet another arena in which the shameful chapters in America's history, including slavery and the genocide of the American Indians, are addressed and relitigated. Uncomfortable truths, buried secrets, disputed accounts: ghost stories arise out of the shadowlands, a response to the ambiguous and the poorly understood.

I spent several years traveling the country, listening for ghosts. There was no shortage of stories to choose from: there is not a city, town, or village in this country that isn't crammed with spirits. I started with places that were renowned for their ghosts, places that had caught on in the popular imagination, whose legends seemed particularly resonant. I looked for ghosts whose stories spoke to some larger facet of American consciousness while still being rooted in a specific building.

In some cases it wasn't always clear to me at first why I was drawn to a particular place. Sometimes simply being in a strange building—spending the night in a haunted hotel, for example—was enough to leave me with a feeling that I wanted to know more. Much of this book involves not just listening to ghost stories but listening also to architecture: how a building can feel alive and unsettling due to its age or a quirk in its construction. Any building whose construction is a little bit off, as often as not, has spirits swirling about it. The language of ghosts, it seems, has become an important (if abstract) way of talking about architecture and place.

Cities and historic sites across the United States clamor to have the most ghosts per cubic inch, the most frenetic paranormal activity, so they can earn the label "most haunted." Any major city in this country offers some kind of ghost tour in which you can hunt for cold spots or EMF vibrations or otherwise find proof of the supernatural. The phenomenon has come to be known as dark tourism, a vibrant industry in its own right. Ghost tours are popular with tourists, explains geographer Glenn Gentry, because they "allow access to dissonant knowledge, dirty laundry, back stage." They are the celebrity gossip of history, the salacious underbelly of the past, and we're drawn to them because the standard history often obscures as much as it reveals.

In a quest to find this other history—the one obscured, forgotten, and ignored—I've interviewed ghost hunters and psychics, local historians and preservationists. I've read academic treatises and cheesy guidebooks, compared the legends to the historical record, trying to unearth the genealogy of the specific ghosts and how we came to love telling the specific stories. What makes a place haunted? When is a creaking floorboard more than just a creaking floorboard? And what is behind the ghost stories that we tell? A spinster locked in a decaying mansion, a slave on a plantation whose soul won't rest—what are they trying to say to us from beyond the grave?

The answers aren't confined to houses but cower in hotels and prisons, on bridges and in graveyards. Though houses are more likely to be haunted than any other place, other kinds of buildings have their own stories to tell. This book moves from the private space of the home to progressively more public spaces—to businesses, to civic spaces, and finally to whole cities. What secrets do towns harbor? Why do ghosts linger when buildings empty of living people?

Examining our country's local ghost stories—where they came from, how they've evolved, how they're recounted—may tell us a great deal about things we thought were long settled and in the past.

I

THE
UNHOMELY

houses and mansions

My wife and I began searching for a house in 2008, precisely when the real estate market was crashing, just as those first waves of foreclosures and short sales were hitting the market. We were finally able to afford houses whose prices had been ridiculously inflated only six months earlier. Occasionally we went to those open houses with smiling real estate agents and bowls of candy, where owners had recently landscaped or repainted, but we could never seriously consider any of these homes. The ones that mattered had lockboxes, were abandoned or in the process of being abandoned—houses that reeked of disrepair and despair.

We spent the summer touring nearly every distressed property in the neighborhoods east of Hollywood—Los Feliz, Silverlake, Echo Park, Atwater Village—looking for a home. There were, of course, the hoarding houses: homes we couldn't enter because of the high stacks of magazines and newspapers or other safety hazards, where we could only peer in through the windows. Far more common, though, were the malformed do-it-yourself homes. Los Angeles is a zoning no-man's-land, host to thousands of unpermitted additions and modifications, which means each house on a block of once-identical residences will look different. Dozens of bungalows in East

Hollywood were built as seven-hundred-square-foot cottages, and, over time, extra bedrooms were added, garages converted, crawl spaces enlarged into dens—often without rhyme or reason or any real sense of purpose. Living rooms were constructed behind existing bedrooms, so an exterior window would look from one room to the next; thousand-square-foot homes somehow contained four or five bedrooms, each one barely more than a closet cut from some once-sane layout; bathrooms sat in the middle of kitchens; bedrooms without windows were built into the sides of hills; doors on a second floor opened into empty air. The effect was vertiginous: you walked into a room and felt a sense of unease before you could say why.

Throughout that stifling summer, we walked into home after home that had been closed against the light but bristled with claustrophobic air. We took to nicknaming these places: the Flea House, after whatever it was that bit our agent; the Burn House, with its charred patches of wall and blackened carpets; Tony's House, after the name on the novelty license plate stuck to a bedroom door, a detail particularly creepy amid the otherwise empty gloom of the house, as though Danny Torrance would big-wheel down the hall at any moment.

It seemed impossible that anyone had called these places home. I found myself thinking of Shirley Jackson's *The Haunting of Hill House* and her description of the eponymous haunted mansion:

> This house, which seemed somehow to have formed itself, flying together into its own powerful pattern under the hands of its builders, fitting itself into its own construction of lines and angles, reared its great head back against the sky without concession to humanity. It was a house without kindness, never meant to be lived in, not a place fit for people or for love or for hope.

These homes, too, seemed without concession to humanity, but in a sense they were just the opposite. These were not the caprices of strange, wealthy men whose hubris unleashed a holy terror. Instead, they were the products of dozens of lower-class families trying to make their homes a little bigger, a little more livable, creating unworkable labyrinths out of necessity.

The feeling of moving through these spaces—particularly as we were visiting seven or eight of them in an afternoon—was indescribable. A sense of wrongness pervaded so many of these homes. In the end, the only word that seems useful for talking about the houses is one made famous by Sigmund Freud: *unheimlich*. A German word, it means literally "unhomely" or "not of the home," "unfamiliar," "eerie and ghostly"—more idiomatically translated into English simply as "uncanny."

Freud's 1919 essay "The Uncanny" is among the stranger of his well-known works. He doesn't really know where to begin with the uncanny—when it comes to the feeling, he admits, "the present writer must plead guilty to exceptional obtuseness." One wonders why he's bothering with the subject at all. Mostly he wants to contradict another psychoanalyst, Ernst Jentsch, who first attempted to define the uncanny in 1906, thirteen years before Freud's essay. Jentsch posits the sensation of the uncanny as stemming from a kind of cognitive uncertainty, where one is unclear as to whether an object or figure or person is inanimate or somehow alive.

Freud, unconvinced by Jentsch, begins by surveying dictionaries, copying out as many different definitions of "uncanny" as he can. What finally catches his attention is the fact that *heimlich*, in addition to meaning "homey" or "familiar," can also mean "hidden, locked away." He finally seizes on Friedrich Schelling's definition of *unheimlich*: "Uncanny is what one calls everything that was meant to remain secret and hidden, and has come into the open." This formulation works for Freud—he is, of course, interested in repression—but it doesn't work as well for haunted houses. What, after all, is being repressed? Jentsch's notion, of a confusion between the living and the inanimate, might work better—think of the anthropomorphized façade of *The Amityville Horror*'s house. With a haunted house, the question is: to what extent is the house itself alive, and to what extent is it inanimate?

But, really, it's the most basic definition of "uncanny"—"unhomely"—that matters. The haunted house is precisely that which should be homey, should be welcoming—the place one lives inside—but which has somehow become emptied out of its true function. It is terrifying because it has lost its purpose yet stubbornly persists. Neither alive nor dead but undead, the haunted house is the thing in between.

There are haunted structures of all kinds: churches, hotels, toy stores. There are haunted bridges and haunted alleyways, haunted parks and haunted parking lots. But in the United States, the most common—the most primal—haunted place is a house. Home ownership has always been intertwined with the American dream; we have magnified this simple property decision in part because it represents safety and security. The haunted house is a violation of this comfort, the American dream gone horribly wrong.

Even if its very construction isn't distorted, as with the homes in East Hollywood, a house can still attract ghosts, still attract stories. The French philosopher Gaston Bachelard offers a succinct and plausible non-supernatural explanation for why the structure in which we live can itself feel alive. Our houses are the places where we spend the most time, and they are, as he suggests, the places where we do the most dreaming. More than just a place of shelter, a place of comfort, or a place of privacy, the house for Bachelard "shelters daydreaming" and "allows one to dream in peace." The more elaborate a house, the more spaces it has, the more evocative it is for our dream life: "If it has a cellar and a garret, nooks and corridors, our memories have refuges that are all the more clearly delineated." It is in the corners and crevices—the places just off the main traffic corridors—that our dreams, like dust bunnies and forgotten toys, accumulate and our imagination begins to run wild. "Every corner in a house, every angle in a room, every inch of secluded space in which to hide ourselves," Bachelard notes, "is a symbol of solitude for the imagination; that is to say, it is the germ of a room, or of a house." Live in a house for any length of time, and you make it your own memory palace.

Such places in which we're actively dreaming, he suggests, become so associated with those dreams that the building itself seems to vibrate psychically: "The places in which we have *experienced daydreaming* reconstitute themselves in a new daydream, and it is because our memories of former dwelling-places are relived as daydreams that these dwelling-places of the past remain in us for all time." As Vladimir Nabokov once put it, "When we concentrate on a material object, whatever its situation, the very act of attention may lead to our involuntarily sinking into the history of that object." Just by lingering in a house, you could say you end up sinking into its history.

Houses seem to live, in other words, because we spend so much time living in them. Buried inside the word "inhabit" is *habit*: a way of being, the patterns and repetitions of life. One's habits and one's surroundings are engaged in a constantly changing, ever subtle dance. Houses are designed with certain patterns of behavior in mind, even though those patterns sometimes change faster than architecture can keep up. And of course everyone will use a house differently, leave different patterns of wear. I spent my childhood in homes that were built as part of subdivisions—my house replicated four or five times over on the same street. Visiting one of these doppelgängers was always a vertiginous experience: everything the same and yet totally different. Cool blue walls instead of white, a nook that held a flower vase instead of a bookshelf, a room used as a library instead of a bedroom—an utterly unfamiliar landscape that I could, nonetheless, walk through blindfolded.

This is another way to make sense of that haunting sensation: to walk into a home and recognize, even if you can't name the feeling, that someone else not only lived here but adopted patterns of life completely alien to your own, whose daily ritual and marks of wear will never match your own. Haunted houses are the repository of the dreams dreamt inside them—both our dreams and those of previous occupants. This can make even the most simple of houses feel, at times, alive.

Houses outlast us; they contain more than one generation's worth of stories. They can become, in turn, repositories of family histories, for both good and ill. And though ghosts may be specific to the places they haunt, they can reflect larger preoccupations and concerns of their time and place, echoing the anxieties of a community and its people. One can treat an old house like a geologist's core sample—a physical representation of time—accruing meaning and history through the years of successive owners. To own an old home means inhabiting not just your own imagination but the imaginations of all those who've lived there before you.

The houses in this section have earned their reputations in no small part by combining all these various aspects: an odd construction, an unnamable feeling, and an anxiety made physical through a building whose past isn't entirely known or understood. Like the Merchant's House Museum in New York City, they've inverted not only the notion of what a home represents but also the very architecture of the house. In the process, they've become puzzles that seem to demand some kind of response, riddles for which there is no obvious answer.

CHAPTER ONE

THE SECRET STAIRCASE

Salem, MA

Houses of any antiquity in New England," Nathaniel Hawthorne once wrote, "are so invariably possessed with spirits, that the matter seems hardly worth alluding to." It's true: you could spend a good portion of your life cataloging the haunted houses of New England: the Captain Fairfield Inn of Kennebunkport, Maine, whose original owner, Captain James Fairfield, wanders the basement; Captain Grant's, a B&B in Prescott, Connecticut, haunted by colonial spirits; the Sylvester Knowlton Pierce mansion in Gardner, Massachusetts, haunted by Pierce, his family, and a murdered prostitute from the years when the house was used as a brothel; and of course the house Lizzie Borden occupied in Fall River, Massachusetts. The countless ghosts that linger in the stately mansions up and down New England only multiply.

Despite this glut of spirits, no place in New England has a greater reputation for being haunted than Salem, Massachusetts. Home to the most famous miscarriages of justice in America's early history, Salem hosts the spirits of the nineteen men and women executed during the witchcraft trials of 1692. Strange fax machine messages come through in the office building that now stands on the old courthouse grounds. In the apartment complex built on the old Salem jail, toasters jump up and down without warning. And in the alleyway behind the Turner Seafood Restaurant—on land that many believe once belonged to Bridget Bishop, the first person executed during the witch trials—a tree drips blood.

Here in Salem, amid all these ghosts stands the House of the Seven Gables, one of the most well-known haunted houses in the country—a first among equals. Set at the end of Turner Street, looking out over Salem Bay, the house doesn't stand out; it's no taller than its neighbors, and without the signage and the parking lot you might miss it altogether. Its distinguishing feature is its color: it's painted entirely in matte black, as though it wants to suck all the available light into itself. Its name, curiously, is a bit of a misnomer. The house does not actually have seven gables; it has nine, though not all of them are original. This architectural confusion, you could say, is just one of the many strange aspects of the house—a house that defies description down to its very name.

The house started small, built by John Turner, a wealthy sea captain and merchant, in 1668. Through the years and generations, the building was enlarged several times, then pared back, as it passed to Turner's son and then his grandson John Turner III. Bankruptcy forced John III to sell the property, and it came into the hands of Susanna Ingersoll, who, among other things, was the aunt of Nathaniel Hawthorne. By the time Ingersoll bought it, the house had apparently already been nicknamed the House of Seven Gables, though by then it had, at best, four gables. The house, during the years, has gone through so many various additions and renovations, such that its shape, at least up until the early twentieth century, was never truly stable.

It was Ingersoll who first encouraged a young Hawthorne to write about Salem when he complained to her about a lack of subject matter. "Oh there are subjects enough," she replied and, gesturing to an old piece of furniture by the fireplace, went on: "Write about that old chair. You can make a biographical sketch of each old Puritan who became in succession an owner of the chair." Ingersoll's prompting led Hawthorne to one of his first writing projects, a children's book in 1840 called *Grandfather's*

Chair. A decade later, riding high on the sudden success of his novel *The Scarlet Letter,* Hawthorne returned to Ingersoll for further inspiration. This time he turned to her house.

At the center of Hawthorne's gothic romance *The House of the Seven Gables* is a house with a buried past that continues to affect its modern-day inhabitants, a house that seems somehow evil in ways we're hard-pressed to define. Its construction isn't quite right: it's "a rusty wooden house," its seven gables facing toward various points of the compass, with a "huge, clustered chimney in the midst." What's more, the book's narrator tells us, it's curiously anthropomorphic: "The aspect of the venerable mansion has always affected me like a human countenance, bearing the traces not merely of outward storm and sunshine, but expressive also, of the long lapse of mortal life, and accompanying vicissitudes that have passed within."

It's true that the house, which still offers regular tours, can feel unsettling. Walking through its rooms you feel the discomfiting effects of its low roofs, its tight rooms, and its misshapen layout. The centuries-old wood timbers seem, perhaps, to bow and breathe. Convincing yourself the house is alive is not terribly difficult.

For his novel, Hawthorne concocted a backstory to explain his fictional house's unsettling presence. The house's origins are tainted. It was built on fertile land owned by a man named Matthew Maule. The avaricious Colonel Pyncheon, desiring the property, fabricates an accusation of witchcraft against Maule, which results in Maule's execution and allows Pyncheon to easily acquire the land, on which he builds his massive, sprawling mansion.

But Pyncheon's house, despite its splendor, is cursed, and the night the colonel hosts a gala to celebrate its completion, he's found dead at his desk, blood dripping from his mouth. Nor is the colonel the only ghost of the mansion; his great-granddaughter Alice, who had "grown thin and white, and gradually faded out of the world," has come to haunt the House of the Seven Gables: "a great many times,—especially when one of the

Pyncheons was to die,—she had been heard playing sadly and beautifully on the harpsichord." In this landscape of greed and calamity, ancestral curses and mournful ghosts, Hawthorne turned the oddly built house on Turner Street into a rival of the abandoned castles of Europe's gothic novels.

Though Ingersoll's own house lacked the melodramatic origins of Hawthorne's invention, ghost stories have become so firmly associated with the house that, as one historian suggests, they "form a patina, a part of the thing itself." While the management doesn't go to great lengths to play up its haunted past—there are no ghost tours, and the tour guides seem uneasy if you press them for stories—its odd construction and subsequent reputation have nonetheless attracted numerous stories, usually involving Susan Ingersoll or Hawthorne. One former visitor to the house sent a photo to the Web site graveaddiction.com, which collects paranormal testimonies, where supposedly in one of the upper windows you can see "what appears to be a teenage girl peering back out! No, the closer you magnify it the more it becomes apparent that it is an older woman complete with sunken eyes and hair!" (I've looked and can't see anything myself.) There is another photo that has become particularly famous, of the house's exterior fence, in which supposedly the ghost of Hawthorne's son, Julian, can be seen—though everyone I've shown the image to agrees it's a shadow or, at best, a raccoon.

Many of the ghost sightings and other mysterious incidents revolve around the house's bizarre hidden staircase, its most enduring architectural feature. Just to the left of the main fireplace is a small door, one that could perhaps lead to a wood closet but in fact opens onto a strange, winding, claustrophobic staircase. Twenty steps that haphazardly curl around the house's main chimney ascend to an attic—a short but oddly perilous journey.

It is here, on this staircase, that many guests to the house have reported feeling the presence of ghosts. Visitors describe feelings of vertigo, an inability to breathe, and a pressing need to flee the house. "I began to feel . . .

as if I was on a high mountain top where the oxygen becomes less. I felt sort of dizzy and off balance in all directions," one visitor wrote on Grave Addiction. Another tourist reported that while he was climbing the hidden staircase, "I heard a woman's voice RIGHT next to my ear whisper a 'Shhh, Shhh' type of sound. I thought it was my girlfriend trying to spook me, so as I turned my head to say 'knock it off,' I saw she was still 3 to 4 feet behind me." Another writer later recounted in detail how

> as we moved through the house, I suddenly became aware of a disquieting "presence" around me. I felt it at first when we went to a dining area, and it grew stronger once we went up a cramped brick-lined stairway into the attic. Later, after we stood outside, I mentioned to my sister that I felt odd—"displaced," if that makes sense. . . . Something touched me when I was in that house—plugged into my subconscious somehow. I don't know what or who . . . but I've come to believe that a piece of "it" attached itself to me.

How long has this spectral presence haunted this mysterious staircase? Does it date from 1692, during the town's infamous witch trials, or perhaps even earlier? Did a young Nathaniel Hawthorne feel it, and did this presence haunt him when he set out to immortalize his aunt's home as the most famously haunted house in American literature?

The nation was still young when Hawthorne began writing, but he could already draw inspiration from Puritan New England's buried past and hidden legacy. Salem has long embodied a contradiction in the bedrock of American consciousness: upright piety mixed with hypocrisy, sober religion mixed with violent hysteria. Hawthorne's own great-great-grandfather John Hathorne was one of the judges who presided over the Salem witch trials of 1692, and Nathaniel had grown up knowing about the family legend—that one of Hathorne's victims had cursed him and his descendants.

Certainly Salem was a place ripe for haunting, and Hawthorne would repeatedly return to wrongs unavenged in his hometown to propel the more gothic aspects of his fiction. This is the recurring structure of a classic ghost story, after all: the ghost remains because it cannot believe the perverse normality of a world that has gone on living, that has forgotten whatever personal tragedy happened here. The carpets are cleaned, the furniture is sold, and the house continues with new inhabitants, the ghost alone keeping vigil over whatever once took place.

With *The House of the Seven Gables*, Hawthorne took a house that, by accident of haphazard and evolving construction, had acquired a gothic patina and imbued it with the history of Salem—transforming the house into a microcosm of not only the town's rise and fall but also its hidden secrets and unrighted wrongs. The goal of the novel, as Hawthorne writes in his preface, is to "convince mankind—or, indeed, any one man—of the folly of tumbling down an avalanche of ill-gotten gold, or real estate, on the heads of an unfortunate posterity, thereby to maim and crush them, until the accumulated mass shall be scattered abroad in its original atoms."

And in Hawthorne's novel, it is precisely because the house is the physical spoils of this injustice that it becomes haunted. The book pushes and pulls against the stain of the past, straining under the effort of breaking free of it. There is only one way to escape this curse, according to Holgrave, the novel's young hero: we must tear down old houses altogether. Holgrave, a daguerreotypist (the technology was brand new then, suggesting a cutting-edge man of the future), opines that we shall soon live to see the day "when no man shall build his house for posterity." He instead imagines a country in which "each generation were allowed and expected to build its own houses," a simple change that would ameliorate most of society's ills. "I doubt whether even our public edifices," he concludes, meaning capitols, courthouses, and other government buildings, "ought to be built of such permanent materials as stone or brick. It were better that they should crumble to ruin once in twenty years, or there-abouts, as a hint to the people to examine into and reform the institutions which they symbolize." As the ill-gotten remnants of the past, the build-ings that have borne witness to the sins of the fathers, the houses we in-herit must be destroyed. If we want to truly be free of the past, we must first start by destroying our ancestral homes.

Holgrave's proposal is seductive, and certainly each generation dreams of remaking itself anew without the baggage of the ones that have come before. But even though architecture embodies the past, the past is more than the buildings we leave behind, and even cities that are famous for demolishing old buildings in favor of the new—Los Angeles, New York, Las Vegas among them—have not escaped their pasts.

Holgrave's dream of a world free of property inheritance stands in stark contrast to the actual context of the witchcraft crisis, which was far more about real estate and land acquisition than we normally assume. While we mainly associate the Salem witch trials with hysteria, religious fervor, and scapegoating, scratch the surface some and one finds property disputes and shady transfers of property and money.

One of the first girls who claimed to be afflicted, twelve-year-old Ann Putnam, initially accused the servant Tituba, as well as two other women, Sarah Good and Sarah Osborne. At the time Osborne was involved in a property dispute with Putnam's parents. Osborne's first husband had died owning a fair amount of property; he wanted to leave some of it to his sons, who were second cousins to Putnam. Osborne and her second hus-band wanted to keep all her first husband's property for themselves. This dispute was ongoing when Putnam accused Osborne of visiting her as an apparition and "pinching and pricking" her "dreadfully."

Ann Putnam would a few weeks later also name Rebecca Nurse as a tormentor. Like Osborne, Nurse was involved in land disputes with the Putnams. While some of the women accused during the crisis were marginalized—servants, widows, or otherwise impoverished women with-out community support—Nurse was a well-respected figure in the community, pious and well liked by many. What was happening in Salem was no longer the traditional model of witchcraft persecution, in which primarily the defenseless were targeted. It was now clear there was money to be made and land to be gained.

Among the most rapacious players in this drama was the Essex County sheriff, George Corwin, who'd quietly begun seizing property and assets of those convicted of witchcraft. One of the richest citizens to be accused of witchcraft, Philip English, managed to flee Salem to avoid trial, but after he disappeared, Corwin seized his house and other assets, roughly 1,500 pounds' worth. In the case of John and Elizabeth Proctor, Corwin didn't even wait until they were convicted and began removing their property while they were still awaiting trial, leaving nothing for their children. On December 12, 1692, a new law—meant explicitly to protect Corwin— allowing the seizure of property and land of those convicted of witchcraft was passed. The situation got so out of hand that the governor of Massachusetts, Sir William Phips, finally complained to William Stoughton, lieutenant governor and chief justice of the Court of Oyer and Terminer (the body empowered to try the Salem witches), that Stoughton "by his warrant hath caused the estates, goods and chattles of the executed to be seized and disposed of without my knowledge or consent." (After Corwin's death, supposedly, Philip English put a lien on his corpse, seizing the sheriff's body and refusing to relinquish it until Corwin's relatives paid him what little was left of his estate.)

In Hawthorne's novel, at least there is the possibility of justice, as Pyncheon's avarice leads in short order to his death. Hawthorne attempted to blend what he called "romance" and the "novel": despite his general adherence to realism, supernatural elements creep in. For one, Hawthorne implies that the accused wizard Matthew Maule is, in fact, capable of damning Pyncheon. As Maule faces his accuser from the gallows, he turns to Pyncheon, "with a ghastly look, at the undismayed countenance of his enemy," crying, "'God will give him blood to drink!'" before he dies—a phrase that haunts the novel when Pyncheon is found dead of unknown causes, blood spilling from his mouth.

In this Hawthorne borrowed a bit from history: while Sarah Good awaited execution on the gallows, she defiantly told one of her accusers, the Reverend Nicholas Noyes, "you are a lyer; I am no more a Witch than you are a Wizard, and if you take away my Life, God will give you Blood to drink." According to the nineteenth-century historian Thomas Hutchinson, Noyes did ultimately die, in 1717, of a hemorrhage, which was seen by some as Good's prophecy fulfilled. The popular narrative of Salem, perhaps, also partakes of a blend of fact and fiction and a sneaking suspicion that the ghosts of Salem are in fact capable of supernatural vengeance. Perhaps it's true that ghost stories arise from an injustice un-avenged, but perhaps it's also true that part of what keeps such injustices alive in our consciousness is the titillating possibility that they were not entirely unjust.

This may explain why we have returned so many times in the past three hundred years to Salem, trying again and again to make sense of what happened there. Numerous theories have been advanced as to what happened in Salem: everything from actual witchcraft to petty juvenile delinquency, from hallucinations induced by ergot poisoning to an out-break of encephalitis. Some of these theories fit better than others, but the theories—and the books—keep coming, as though the question itself can never be fully answered, as though the itch can never fully be scratched.

The House of the Seven Gables was in bad shape when Caroline Em-merton bought it in 1908, for the measly sum of $1,000. Emmerton, a philanthropist from a wealthy Salem family, had long been involved with the settlement house movement—a program that helped provide educa-tion and other social services to impoverished and immigrant children—and in the old house on Turner Street, she saw a unique opportunity. By restoring the ruined house to its former glory, she could revitalize a piece of Salem's past and use revenue from tours to fund the town's Settlement chapter.

Emmerton had first seen the house when it was owned by Henry and Elizabeth Upton. "My first visit to the House of Seven Gables was in 1879 or 1880, when I was still a young girl," she later recalled. "I went there with a party of young people and I will remember the thrill that the gaunt old house gave me when I first caught sight of it." She and architect Joseph Everett Chandler went to work, ultimately spending more than ten times what she'd paid for the house on its restoration.

By then the house no longer had anything close to seven gables; what's more, it wasn't even clear where those seven gables had once been. When Emmerton bought the property, the house was T-shaped, with only three gables, though remnants of another set on the south wing were visible. Emmerton and Chandler quickly found traces of another by studying the beams in the attic. In her account of the restoration, Emmerton speaks of reconstructing the seven gables as something of a puzzle and a mystery—tracking down old plans of the house in stacks of probate court records, divining the shape of the old house through traces left in the woodwork. She decided that the seventh and final gable must have been over the back portion of the house, which had been torn down long ago and thus could give no clues.

Only after she'd rebuilt this back portion with its gable did Emmerton discover court records showing the seventh gable over the kitchen instead. Subsequent restoration work further revealed that the house at one point had an eighth gable, over a second-story porch. She couldn't find evidence that the house had ever had just seven gables, and it certainly didn't by the time she got done with her restoration. "To console me my friends suggested that Hawthorne called his novel 'The House of Seven Gables' because that title was more pleasing and prosaic than the 'House of Eight Gables' would have been."

Though Emmerton stressed that she was careful to not let the book influence her restoration, Hawthorne's novel persisted as a shadow about the building, she claimed, forcing her and Chandler to second-guess every move, to seek clues where none existed, to add restorations that might not have been true to the house itself.

And then there is its crooked spine: the curling, amorphous, and anomalous staircase that curls around the central chimney, snaking skyward as if it might draw out the bad spirits from the house. Emmerton claimed that the secret staircase was rediscovered by Upton, who found on it a "pine-tree sixpence and a book" in 1888 while he was renovating the chimney. She writes that, while she was still a young girl, he showed her the staircase and the book: "It was a religious book, a prayer book or a hymn book, and very ancient." When the secret staircase was built and why, Emmerton didn't know for sure, but in her narrative she weighs—and dismisses—several possibilities, including that it was built for smuggling ("Of what use for smuggling is a secret stairway unless it leads to a secret room where goods could be stored . . . ?") or that it was used as a hiding place against Indian raids ("Hiding places would hardly avail against Indians whose practice it was to set the house on fire").

Her best guess was that it had been built by John Turner II, in the fateful year of 1692. Five minutes away was the house of Philip English, who fled after he was accused of witchcraft. When he finally returned, he found his house ransacked, and Emmerton suggested that he built a safe room of sorts in case of future incidents and that this gave Turner the idea to build his own secret hiding place. "Can there be any doubt that the arrest of Mrs. English would make John Turner anxious for the safety of his sisters?" Emmerton asks. "Can there be any doubt that he began to plan to protect them, and whatever plan he hit upon a temporary hiding place in the house would probably be needed. I believe that he built the secret staircase for that purpose—a recent addition to the house giving him the opportunity."

If Emmerton is correct, then the House of the Seven Gables preserves traces of the witchcraft crisis in its very DNA. Hawthorne's use of this house was no accident, for no other building remains as haunted by those terrifying months. And yet the seemingly most important detail—the staircase itself—appears nowhere in the novel.

Why doesn't the novel mention the staircase? If it was so central to the house's construction and well known by its inhabitants, and if it influenced Hawthorne's conception of his own gabled house, why does it never appear in the book? There does not appear at first to be any clear answers for such a pressing question. "Thinking it over," Emmerton writes, "I have been wondering if Hawthorne did not come across in some way, in an old letter, perhaps, some allusion to the secret staircase which he made use of in the first draft or outline of his romance, but on showing it to Miss Ingersoll encountered her strong objection to anything which should arouse the interest of the curious in her house." Perhaps the hidden staircase was meant to stay hidden, a feature known only to the house's inhabitants, like some family secret bricked up in the walls.

And yet, Emmerton insists, it exists, it influences the novel, it exerts its force on both readers and those who move through the house. "For it seems to me that we feel the absence of the secret staircase in the story just as we feel the absence of a bit of a picture-puzzle that has been lost and has left an unfilled place in the picture."

A few years ago the management of the House of the Seven Gables admitted the truth: the staircase was built not by Turner or Ingersoll, nor by smugglers or freedom fighters or witches, but by Emmerton and Chandler themselves when they first restored the house in preparation for giving tours. Hawthorne made no mention of it because in his day it didn't exist; the door on the first floor that opens to the staircase did, in fact, originally lead to the wood closet.

Reading Emmerton's explanations for the staircase in light of this information reveals a remarkable bit of mythmaking in which she suggested that the staircase deeply inspired the novel while at the same time offering a reason why Hawthorne didn't mention it. Hers is also a remarkable effort of literary criticism, turning the staircase into a hidden presence that works on the novel—an absent presence, an architectural ghost haunting a novel about a haunted house.

And she ensured that the house would remain an enduring attraction, above the other colonial revivals and period museums dotting New England. Over the years the tour script has changed every so often regarding the origin and meaning of the staircase, and it remains adaptable to any number of plausible explanations. What Emmerton and Chandler seem to have understood is that the simple addition of an anomalous element to a house's construction immediately opens up vertiginous possibilities. The secret staircase, simply by virtue of not being immediately self-explanatory, renders the entire house even more uncanny. Its meaning, then, can shift with the times. The Underground Railroad, the witch trials, smugglers, the Indian wars—it can evoke and encompass all these aspects of history simply because it has no real apparent meaning.

The ghosts of Salem linger in strange ways. Most of the nineteen men and women executed in 1692 were pardoned in the early eighteenth century, but six women—Bridget Bishop, Susannah Martin, Alice Parker, Ann Pudeator, Wilmot Redd, and Margaret Scott—went without exoneration for more than two centuries. Not until 1946 was a bill to clear their names introduced in the Massachusetts legislature, and it failed. It failed again when reintroduced in 1950, and in 1953, and in 1954. It took a change in the bill to get it finally passed, in 1957: the six women would be pardoned, but the legislation would also absolve the state of Massachusetts of any legal or financial obligation to the victims' descendants. Which is to say, whatever gains had been gotten by Sheriff George Corwin and his ilk, no matter how ill gotten, they would not be righted.

The town seems caught between past and present, like a doubly exposed negative. By the end of the nineteenth century, various Salem businesses (including a fish company, a popcorn factory, and a bicycle company) had begun using the nickname "Witch City" to sell their wares, and by the 1930s the town itself had begun to see itself as a tourist destination. In 1971 the TV series *Bewitched* filmed a few episodes in Salem and shortly thereafter a Wiccan named Laurie Cabot arrived in Salem. She opened a "Witch Shop" selling witchcraft supplies and trinkets and quickly attracted a following. Dubbed the "official witch of Salem" by Massachusetts governor Michael Dukakis in 1977, Cabot more than anyone changed the modern face of Salem, turning it into a mecca for those interested in both the pagan practice of Wicca and the Disneyfied image of witches with their black conical hats and broomsticks.

But what does any of this have to do with 1692? The people executed by the Court of Oyer and Terminer, no matter what else they were, almost certainly were not witches, neither pagan witches nor supernatural servants of Satan. They were devout Christians, wrongly accused; if anything, the condemned would have the same antipathy toward the modern Wiccans as their accusers. Hawthorne's confusing blend of romance and novel, fact and fantasy, has come to embody how we treated the victims of Salem's executions. We see them as innocent victims, and yet throughout pop culture we have repeatedly returned to the idea that they were also, paradoxically, somehow supernatural, actual witches. Twentieth- and twenty-first-century pop-culture depictions of Salem—not just *Bewitched*, but the recent TV series *American Horror Story*, with its coven descended from Salem, J. K. Rowling's *History of Magic in North America*, which asserts that a "number of the dead were indeed witches, though utterly innocent of the crimes for which they had been arrested," and of course the show *Salem*, in which the town is the scene of an actual metaphysical battle between witches and Puritans—treat the victims of 1692 as actual witches capable of working spells and magic.

These confusions lie at the heart of Salem, and they're what keeps the town going. It is undeniable that these days the Salem witch trials mean, for the city and its inhabitants, money. The town is overrun on Halloween with tourists, despite the fact that neither Wiccans nor Puritans celebrate the holiday. Salem, with its broom-riding-witch logo on its police cars, has turned tragedy into spectacle. The same unresolved questions that drive scholars to understand the town's past also fuel its kitsch popularity.

In a town suffused with kitsch, nonsense, and a few tasteful memorials, the House of the Seven Gables wants none of it; tour guides do not bring up haunting and are encouraged to downplay it if asked. The eponymous house of Hawthorne's novel is presented simply as a historical museum. And yet a big feature of its allure remains the hidden staircase, an architectural feature built originally to beguile tourists.

The ghosts of Salem, and of the House of the Seven Gables, are a product of ambiguous commemoration. We know Salem—we know it to be a tragedy, we hold it up as a cautionary tale about mass hysteria and persecution—and yet we're also confused: we conflate the dead with actual witches, we attribute actual supernatural powers to those killed, we revisit their deaths for comedy and entertainment. Above all, we fail to apply the lessons we've supposedly learned from 1692, for by no means was this the last time in American history when a powerless minority was scapegoated, persecuted, and killed by an ignorant mass. We recall the events of Salem, but we can't quite remember why they matter.

And so the ghosts remain—they walk the streets, haunt the buildings that have been erected over their hanging grounds. They keep alive the events of 1692 without forcing a reckoning. What remains is barely more than a whisper in the dark or a strange presence on the staircase.

CHAPTER TWO

SHIFTING GROUND

St. Francisville, LA

In her book *In the Devil's Snare*, historian Mary Beth Norton argues that one pressing fact lay behind the witchcraft trials and drove the hysteria: the judges and magistrates overseeing the trials were all military and civil leaders who had failed repeatedly to keep Essex County safe from Native American attacks during King Philip's War and "unable to defeat Satan in the forests and garrisons of the northeastern frontier, they could nonetheless attempt to do so in the Salem courtroom." The witchcraft trials might have begun with a group of teenage girls, but Norton argues that the town's leaders quickly seized on this outbreak as a means of exonerating themselves for past shortcomings: they were the ones on trial, and they acquitted themselves.

Norton's theory reminds us that the Puritans who settled New England were not simply religious zealots but were also actively, constantly engaged in territorial warfare—with the French, with the Wabanaki and other indigenous groups, and with one another. The ghosts haunting Salem must include the casualties of those land wars alongside those falsely accused of witchcraft. As Hawthorne puts it, this curse goes to the very bedrock of the town's foundations: "The pavements of the Main-street," he writes in one sketch, "must be laid over the red man's grave."

Salem, of course, is far from the only place in the United States whose pavements are laid over the graves of indigenous people. There's nowhere in this nation that wasn't already inhabited before Europeans arrived, and there's no town, no house, that doesn't sit atop someone else's former home. More often than not, we've chosen to deal with this fact through the language of ghosts.

Fifteen hundred miles to the south, just off Louisiana State Route 61, stands the Myrtles Plantation. Hemmed in by giant oaks that drip Spanish moss, the low-slung plantation sits at a remove from the road, the lace ironwork delicately enclosing the portico beneath the row of symmetrical gables along its second floor. It was built in 1796 by David Bradford, a lawyer from Pennsylvania who'd taken a prominent part in the tax revolt known as the Whiskey Rebellion in the early years of the republic. With a warrant out for his arrest, Bradford fled the nascent United States for Spanish-owned territory, establishing his home in what is now St. Francisville, Louisiana. Even though the Myrtles has undergone expansions and renovations over the centuries, it has none of the haphazard feel of a building like the House of the Seven Gables: everything seems neatly ordered and in its place.

Look closely, though. The keyhole to the front door is upside down, a detail added by Ruffin and Mary Catherine Stirling, who bought the house in 1834 and nearly doubled its size. Based on a folk belief that ghosts who lived in the trees would try to enter the house at night via keyholes, an upside-down lock was a means to confuse the ghosts and keep them out.

Over the years, at least ten murders have taken place on the grounds of the Myrtles, including three Union soldiers who were shot while trying to ransack the plantation during the Civil War; and William Drew Winter, the man who married the Stirlings' daughter Sarah—shot in 1871 on the portico, and who still roams the house.

The most well-known ghost is that of a slave named Chloe, whose story is beloved by guests and a highlight of the plantation's tours. When Bradford's son-in-law, Judge Clark Woodruff, lived on the plantation, in the early nineteenth century, he took a shine to a young slave girl—a light-skinned mulatto no more than thirteen or fourteen—whom he brought into the house and made his concubine. As the master's mistress, Chloe had far more freedom than the other slaves on the plantation and was allowed to come and go throughout the house as she wished. She used this freedom to eavesdrop on Woodruff, who caught her one day with her ear pressed against the door while he was doing business. As punishment, Woodruff cut off Chloe's ear—and from then on she wore a green turban to hide her deformity.

Chloe was sent to work in the kitchen but, desperate to win back her lover and owner, concocted a plan to redeem herself. She would secret a mild poison (boiled oleander leaves) into a cake she baked for Woodruff's children, Mary Octavia, James, and Cornelia Gale—just enough to sicken them—then she would swoop in and nurse them back to health, proving her worth and earning her place in the Woodruff household once more. But the plan backfired horribly—the oleander didn't just sicken the children; it killed them outright, along with Woodruff's wife, Sarah, who also ate the cake.

It didn't take long for Woodruff to discover who had murdered his family; Chloe had run to the slave quarters in hopes that she would be safe there, but her fellow slaves turned her in. Woodruff ordered his slaves to hang Chloe and afterward to throw her body in the river. Killed violently and denied a proper burial, Chloe now stalks the grounds of the Myrtles Plantation, talking to guests, wandering the hallways, and appearing in photographs—always wearing her green turban.

Melodramatic and tawdry, Chloe's story is also, depending on whom you talk to, either mostly or wholly fictitious. None of Woodruff's family died from poisoning—his wife, Sarah, and his children James and Cornelia Gale all died of yellow fever just over a year apart from one another in the early 1820s, and Mary Octavia lived until 1889. None of the records of the plantation have turned up a slave named Chloe. This is unsurprising: Chloe's tale plays up several basic stereotypes common to American folklore and reads more as an amalgamation of stock characters than the story of a real person. It has strains of both the Jezebel figure, a sexually precocious slave who disturbs the natural order of the nuclear household, seeking to supplant the white wife; and the "mammy" figure, a motherly slave who earns her spot in the white household by loving and caring for the master's children. Appearing in some versions as notably light-skinned, Chloe, as historian Tiya Miles points out, also conforms to the cliché of the "tragic mulatto": a woman, alluring because of her mixed-race heritage, who seeks entrance into white society but is rebuffed by her white lover. The lack of clear details or historical substantiation means that the legend of Chloe is adaptable: each person who tells her story can borrow from the various stereotypes as needed, emphasizing different aspects over others to suit the telling.

Frances Kermeen had never heard of Chloe or any of the other ghost stories surrounding the plantation when she bought it in 1980, hoping to turn it into a bed and breakfast, but she soon found herself beset by paranormal events of all kinds. During the ten years she owned the plantation, among other things, she saw candelabras float through the air and balls of light hovering about her, smelled inexplicable perfumes whose source could not be found, heard footsteps in the middle of the night and voices that called her by name. Chloe appeared to guests and spoke to them, and the ghost of Clark Woodruff made amorous advances toward young women staying at the plantation. Amid this flurry of activity, a new spirit appeared: a young Native American woman, who would appear naked in the courtyard beneath a weeping willow tree. Reportedly, once spotted, she will turn to face you, holding your gaze for a moment before blurring slightly as she fades away.

This last ghost, Kermeen implied, might hold the key to the Myrtles Plantation and its host of spirits. Writing in 2005, she offered a few different explanations for the surfeit of ghosts at the Myrtles Plantation. One was an Indian burial ground located beneath the parking lot. This land, so her story goes, was sacred to the Tunica, a small Indian band famous throughout the Mississippi River Valley during the Colonial period. Adept at making salt (then a highly prized commodity), the Tunica were sought out by both Spanish and French colonialists as trading partners. According to Kermeen, when Bradford set out to build his plantation, he sought out a hill above the surrounding swamps, inadvertently choosing land sacred to the Tunica, who used hills for their burial sites. It was this ill-fated decision that started all the trouble.

The Anglo fascination with Indian burial lands stretches back at least to the eighteenth century. The Revolutionary poet Philip Freneau was one of the earliest to approach these sacred lands with a mix of exoticism and foreboding. In his 1787 poem "The Indian Burying Ground," he saw the spirits of vanquished Indians still hunting, feasting, and playing:

> Thou, stranger, that shalt come this way,
> No fraud upon the dead commit—
> Observe the swelling turf, and say
> They do not lie, but here they sit.

Be wary of the Native burial ground, Freneau warns us, for life still moves there.

In the 1970s this idea reappeared in the country's imagination, turning malevolent and becoming the foundation for a series of horror movies and stories of haunted houses. Its popularity stems almost entirely from Jay Anson's 1977 massive best seller, *The Amityville Horror*, and the genre-defining horror film based on it. Anson's book, advertised as a true story, was based on testimony from George and Kathleen Lutz, who claimed to have undergone a harrowing experience in the Long Island, New York, hamlet of Amityville. When the Lutzes bought their dream home, they knew it had been the site of six murders: in October of 1974, twenty-three-year-old Ronald DeFeo, Jr., shot his father, mother, two sisters, and two brothers in the house. Deciding not to let this factor influence their decision, the Lutzes bought the house just over a year later. But a host of unexplained occurrences took place as soon as they moved in: George began waking up every morning at 3:15, the time that the DeFeo murders had happened, and the Lutz children began sleeping on their stomachs, the same pose in which the DeFeo victims had been found dead. The children began acting strangely and claimed to see a pair of red eyes hovering outside their bedroom. In less than a month, the Lutzes abandoned the Amityville home, leaving their possessions behind.

According to Anson, while George and Kathleen Lutz were trying to find out why their new home was so haunted, a member of the Amityville Historical Society revealed to them that the site of their home had once been used by the Shinnecock Indians "as an enclosure for the sick, mad, and dying. These unfortunates were penned up until they died of exposure." Anson further claimed that "the Shinnecock did not use this tract as a consecrated burial mound because they believed it to be infested with demons," but when paranormal researcher Hans Holzer and psychic medium Ethel Johnson-Meyers investigated the Amityville house, Johnson-Meyers channeled the spirit of a Shinnecock Indian chief, who told her the house stood on an ancient Indian burial ground.

None of this has held up under any kind of scrutiny: the Shinnecock lived some fifty miles from Amityville, and according to Ric Osuna (who spent years unearthing the facts about Amityville), the nearest human remains that have been found to date are more than a mile from the house. Nor would the Shinnecock—or any other Native people—have treated their sick and dying in such a callous, brutal fashion. But then, the entire *Amityville Horror* narrative was, it now seems likely, an elaborate hoax: in 1978 the Lutzes sued two clairvoyants and several writers working on alternative histories of the house, alleging invasion of privacy. In the course of the trial, William Weber, Ronald DeFeo's defense attorney, claimed that the entire story had been concocted by him and the Lutzes and that he had provided the couple with salient details of the DeFeo murders to substantiate their account.

This sensationalized portrayal of Native burial rites shouldn't be entirely surprising. What is surprising, then, is how quickly the trope of a haunted Indian burial ground took root and spread throughout the rest of American culture. Haunted Indian burial grounds have appeared in *Poltergeist II*, in Stanley Kubrick's adaptation of Stephen King's *The Shining*, and in countless lesser-known films, novels, and TV episodes. It's a legend that's become so ubiquitous that it's something of a cliché, showing up these days as often as not as a punchline in comedies, appearing everywhere from *South Park* to *Parks and Recreation*.

Stephen King's 1983 novel *Pet Sematary* is a particularly striking version of this narrative, in part because he describes in great detail the nature and function of the burial ground. Louis Creed, the protagonist, has moved his family out to rural Maine to take a job as a doctor at the local university. When his daughter's cat is hit by a car on the nearby highway, his new neighbor Jud Crandall takes him to a Micmac burial ground that has the power to bring the dead back to life. They bury the cat, which returns the next day, alive but changed: mean and smelling of death and foul earth. After Louis's two-year-old son is killed on the same highway, Louis, overcome with grief, attempts to resurrect him in the same manner, with predictably horrific consequences.

At the time the book was published, it was quite topical, as scholar Renée Bergland points out: during the years that King was writing *Pet Sematary*, the state of Maine was involved in a massive legal battle against the Maliseet, Penobscot, and Passamaquoddy bands of the Wabanaki Confederacy. Beginning in 1972, the tribes sued Maine and the federal government over lands to which they were, by federal law, entitled, which amounted to 60 percent of the area of the state. Long inhabited by non–Native Americans in Maine, the land in dispute was home to over 350,000

people who would have needed resettlement had the tribes been successful. Once it became clear that their claim had merit, the government
scrambled to find a settlement that wouldn't involve the displacement of
large amounts of nonindigenous residents, ultimately awarding the three
tribes more than $81 million, much of that earmarked to purchase unde-
veloped land in Maine, along with other federal guarantees.

All this history lies in the background of King's novel. Early on, Louis
is exploring the wilderness that is his backyard with his family and his
neighbor Jud, when his wife, Rachel, exclaims, "Honey, do we *own* this?"
(a question that will become fraught as the novel progresses). Jud answers
Rachel, "It's part of the property, oh yes"—though Louis thinks to himself
that this is not "quite the same thing." This tension between holding the
deed to a piece of property and true ownership of the land continues
throughout the book.

Jud repeatedly invokes the very real land disputes happening in Maine
at the time, though in King's book it is the Micmac people fighting for
land in Maine (an odd distortion: the Micmac people were never part of
the Wabanaki Confederacy and lived primarily in Canada, not Maine).
"Now the Micmacs, the state of Maine, and the government of the
United States are arguing in court about who owns that land," he says at
one point. "Who does own it? No one really knows, Louis. Not anymore.
Different people laid claim to it at one time or another, but no claim has
ever stuck." Jud stresses that the power of the land predates the former
owners: "The Micmacs knew that place, but that doesn't necessarily mean
they made it what it was. The Micmacs weren't always here."

In her account of the Myrtles Plantation, Kermeen follows a similar
logic. As she discusses the "sacred Indian burial ground" beneath the
house's parking lot, she hypothesizes that "the Indians chose that spot
because it already possessed mystical qualities. The house was reportedly
haunted long before a previous owner paved over the graveyard to make
a parking lot." As King does with his pet cemetery, Kermeen attempts to
attribute power and mystery to the Tunica burial ground while at the

same time downplaying the tribe's agency and ownership—they, too, were simply temporary lodgers on a land with its own autonomous power.

The narrative of the haunted Indian burial ground hides a certain anxiety about the land on which Americans—specifically white, middle-class Americans—live. Embedded deep in the idea of home ownership—the Holy Grail of American middle-class life—is the idea that we don't, in fact, own the land we've just bought. Time and time again in these stories, perfectly average, innocent American families are confronted by ghosts who have persevered for centuries, who remain vengeful for the damage done. Facing these ghosts and expelling them, in many of these horror stories, becomes a means of refighting the Indian Wars of past centuries.

King's novel, like the legend of the Myrtles Plantation, works by playing off a buried, latent anxiety Americans have about the land they "own." If you're willing to see this conflict over land as the basis of many of our ghost stories, then it won't be surprising that so much of America is haunted. There's precious little land in the United States that hasn't been contested, one way or another, through the years. Americans live on haunted land because we have no other choice.

The land of lower Louisiana is constantly shifting. A floodplain of the meandering Mississippi, the land has evolved and sometimes disappeared without a trace as the river changed course. The land on which New Orleans stands didn't even exist five thousand years ago. At the end of the last ice age, some eighteen thousand years ago, glaciers that had come down as far as Cairo, Illinois, began to melt and recede, sending a deluge of water down the Mississippi's alluvial plain. The water was loaded with sediment accumulated from farther north, and it carried this sediment down the Mississippi Embayment (the low-lying basin that runs from Illinois south) until it hit the Gulf of Mexico, where the water slowed and deposited its sediment. Over time, this sediment built up and became the Mississippi River delta—a process of accumulation that was still under way until very recently. While Louisiana had mostly reached its current state by the time the French found it in the early 1700s, the topographical changes continued into the nineteenth century. One visitor to New Orleans, Captain Basil Hall, wrote in 1828 of coasting along "past small sandy islands, over shallow banks of mud," and on through Lakes Borgne and Pontchartrain, "whose Deltas are silently pushing themselves into the sea, and raising the bottom to the surface."

The constant evolving of the land around the Mississippi delta is anathema to human habitation, and civilizations that don't make their mark through massive earthworks and geologic engineering—as New Orleans has—are easily erased by the constant flow and flux of the river and its mud. Finding archaeological material is difficult, since geographical clues in missionaries' reports or oral histories often no longer correspond to contemporary landscapes.

But the clues are there, if you look closely enough. In 1968 a guard at the Louisiana Penitentiary in Angola began hunting around at the former Trudeau Plantation, a swath of swampland on the east bank of the Mississippi, near the prison. Leonard J. Charrier was not a trained archaeologist, but he understood the land of Louisiana and, in particular, how the course of the river could change over the years. Using historical documents that he researched in his spare time, and comparing those against the changes in the meander of the river, he was able to make a stunning discovery: a lost burial ground.

Using a metal detector, Charrier located the grave of a Tunica chief, Cahura-Joligo, as well as more than a hundred other graves. He excavated hundreds of objects from the fields of the Trudeau Plantation and, having nowhere else to put them, began stockpiling them in his house. Jeffrey P. Brain, a curator at Harvard's Peabody Museum, was alerted to Charrier's find and in 1970 traveled to visit him and his priceless artifacts. Objects from the burial grounds were on every piece of furniture, in every closet and cupboard, and covering the floor so thoroughly that only small walkways were left. One walk-in closet had been filled with a four-foot-high pile of kettles, muskets, wire, and other ephemera.

Charrier loaned the objects to Harvard while he haggled over the price, but when Harvard asked for some kind of document from the landowner renouncing any claims to the Tunica artifacts, Charrier stonewalled. A series of lawsuits ensued, involving Charrier, Harvard, the state of Louisiana, and the squabbling heirs of the Trudeau Plantation, each claiming a right to a share of the artifacts that had become known as the Tunica Treasure.

The only parties unable to enter into litigation were the Tunica themselves, because the tribe wasn't recognized by the United States. The Tunica-Biloxi Tribe had been fighting since the 1920s for federal recognition, but a continual stumbling block had been a lack of clear evidence that the tribe had a history. In a curious twist of fate, Charrier's discovery remedied this problem, proving beyond doubt that the Tunica had inhabited southern Louisiana; as a direct result, in 1981 the tribe was granted federal recognition. Now it, too, could pursue a claim for the artifacts. After more than a decade of ongoing litigation, the Tunica-Biloxi Tribe was finally granted possession of the Tunica Treasure, now housed in a cultural center in nearby Marksville.

Not everyone, of course, was satisfied by this outcome. "I found the thing," an embittered Charrier told the *New York Times* when it was all over with, "I spent many an hour digging it up, and if I hadn't, the Mississippi River would have taken it from us all."

The land where the Trudeau Plantation once stood is almost twenty miles from the Myrtles Plantation, and the claim that the Myrtles Plantation has anything to do with the Tunica ground that Charrier excavated is demonstrably false. But in the wake of the long-running legal dispute over the Tunica burial ground and the war between the heirs of the Tunica tribe, Harvard, and the federal government, rumors began to circulate that the Myrtles Plantation itself stood atop this contested land, the treasure and its fraught ownership becoming part of the lore of the house.

Over time the Tunica burial ground and the Myrtles Plantation have fused together, one becoming part of the story of the other. Alongside the fictitious story of the slave Chloe and the dozen unsubstantiated murders that supposedly took place on the Myrtles' property, the plantation has accrued these legends and allowed them to settle, like sediment, about its foundations. Today the plantation is a popular spot for tours and ghost hunts and has parlayed its history into a successful destination for seekers of the paranormal. Like the ground beneath the property, over the years these stories have shifted and changed with the tides and with the tastes of tourists, changing subtly with the landscape.

If you listen closely, the ghost stories of the Myrtles Plantation say more about the tellers than they do about the supernatural. A slave abused by her master, who in response turns murderous; the Indian ghosts whose burial lands have been disturbed—all of these stories, in one way or another, respond to history. Ghost stories like this are a way for us to revel in the open wounds of the past while any question of responsibility for that past blurs, then fades away.

CHAPTER THREE

THE ENDLESS HOUSE

San Jose, CA

It's hard to know where San Jose, California, starts, where it ends, and what distinguishes it from the dozens of adjoining small suburbs that stretch northwest to San Francisco and northeast to Oakland. The city—if you can call it that—is a labyrinth of repetition, a nonspace, a suburban blur that spreads northward from the Santa Clara Valley into two fingers of land: one the San Francisco peninsula, the other the East Bay. Individual hamlets like Santa Clara, Sunnyvale, and Cupertino overlap, their individual downtowns long dried up and replaced by shopping malls and office parks that distort any real sense of geography.

Urban sprawl isn't unique to San Jose, of course, but the city has a miniature allegory of itself in the form of a sprawling, formless Victorian mansion that sits in its very center. If there is a central monument to San Jose now, it is this labyrinthine, inscrutable house in the heart of the city. Tours leave every twenty minutes, lasting roughly two hours, every day but Christmas. During the course of the tour guests walk over a mile, mostly staying inside the house. This is the Winchester Mystery House, just off Interstate 280, facing the major thoroughfare now named for it, Winchester Boulevard, next to a Cineplex and across the street from two massive shopping malls. It is what many have called the most haunted house in the world.

Implacable, anachronistic, unchanging. Holding its secrets within.

The basic facts of how the house got started are clear enough. In 1862 Sarah Pardee married William Wirt Winchester, the son of a successful shirt manufacturer who would go on to found the Winchester Repeating Arms Company. Sarah and William's only daughter died in infancy in 1866, and William died of tuberculosis fifteen years later. In 1885 the wealthy widow moved to the Santa Clara Valley, where she bought an eight-room farmhouse and began work on enlarging it. It grew massively; by the time she died in 1922, it had 160 rooms and sprawled in every direction. At one point it was even larger, but much of it was damaged by the 1906 earthquake, including a seven-story tower, which she never repaired or rebuilt. Many of the rooms remain unfinished, as though the builders simply walked off the job the day Sarah Winchester died.

Opened to the public the year after her death, the house became immediately famous, working its way into American culture in unlikely ways. Author Shirley Jackson grew up not far from San Jose, and the mansion features briefly in *The Haunting of Hill House*: as Dr. John Montague describes the features of Hill House, he claims its builder, Hugh Crain, "expected that someday Hill House might become a showplace, like the Winchester House in California." Ten years later, the Winchester house was used as the inspiration for Disneyland's Haunted Mansion: Walt Disney wanted a haunted mansion but nothing that was derelict or in ruins, so he turned to the immaculate Victorian façade of the Winchester house. Stephen King claims he first heard the story of the house in a *Ripley's Believe It or Not* comic when he was a kid and remembered it for years after. King's *Rose Red*—a television miniseries from 2002 about a team of paranormal researchers who investigate a massive, sprawling maze of a house—was the closest direct work of his to be based on the Winchester house, but one finds traces of it throughout his other work as well, from *'Salem's Lot* to *The Shining*. And then there's the artist Jeremy Blake, who shortly before his suicide produced a trilogy of short films based on the Winchester house. In them, the façade of the house is merged with shifting, kaleidoscopic colors, images from 1950s cartoon westerns, and the suburban landscape of San Jose. The effect of the films is unsettling in the extreme as Blake's work draws out a latent foreboding in the Victorian eaves and gables of the house. "There's the psychological aspect of the place," he said at the time, "the neurosis and mad logic and creativity all flowing together in this crazy quilt of rooms. It gets unbelievably twisted."

The legend of the house, which has been told so many times that most people take its veracity for granted, begins with the death of Sarah Winchester's daughter and husband. Believing her family to be cursed, Winchester went to a famous Boston psychic named Adam Coons. During a séance, Coons told her that her family was being haunted by the ghosts of all those killed by Winchester rifles, particularly the Native Americans who had been killed by the "gun that won the West," and that the only way to keep them at bay would be to begin building a house that was never to be finished, an endless work in progress. And so Winchester came to San Jose, bought an eight-room farmhouse, and hired crews to build onto her house, literally twenty-four hours a day, seven days a week, for the rest of her life. When she died in 1922, all work immediately stopped: rooms were left unfinished, nails were left half driven into walls. This is the story Stephen King remembers: "At one séance, Sarah Winchester asked the medium, 'When will I die?' . . . The medium replied, 'When your house is done.'"

This story of the endlessly deferred completion of construction as a means to stave off death reinforces the notion of a woman whose superstition and gullibility led her to create a house beyond the bounds of sense or competence. Nightly séances were conducted in a blue room in the center of the house, from midnight until 2 a.m., when Winchester would summon ghosts to instruct her on the next day's construction and how to keep herself safe from evil spirits. Among the house's signature features is a staircase that ascends half a flight, makes a ninety-degree turn to the left, then ends directly at a wall, as though to trick ghosts who might be pursuing the solitary heiress. These are the prime selling points of the Winchester Mystery House: the dead-end staircases, the trapdoors and false rooms, the labyrinthine network of traps and detours. All of which were meant to confuse the ghosts haunting Winchester, creating a private maze that only she knew and understood, in which she could feel safe from these forces of malevolence.

Winchester managed this incredible building feat due to her extreme wealth: because of her stock in the Winchester Rifle Company, Sarah Winchester's income, the tour guides explain, was around $1,500 a day, somewhere north of $32,000 in today's dollars. As such, she bought lavishly and could afford to be eccentric. An early stop in the tour is the so-called Million Dollar Storeroom, which holds several priceless works of Tiffany glass that Winchester had specifically commissioned. The room conveys opulent wealth, but the message is clear: these things belong in a palatial mansion, not a madwoman's house. A crazy person should not have had access to them.

Among the Tiffany pieces is one with an intricate, stunning spiderweb pattern, made with thirteen semiprecious stones. Winchester's fascination with the number thirteen is a well-established aspect of the lore surrounding her life—there are thirteen bedrooms, thirteen bathrooms, thirteen windows in certain rooms—and her triskaidekaphilia is presented as more proof of her morbid eccentricity. It was, supposedly, in the thirteenth bedroom of her mansion that Winchester died, on

September 5, 1922, attended by her improbably named physician, Dr. Euthanasia Meade.

As compelling as this narrative is, there are several problems with it. People talk of the "staircases" that go nowhere, but there's only one—most likely an uncorrected architectural mistake. The fascination with the number thirteen is also a later concoction. No record of a Boston psychic named Adam Coons exists (though Euthanasia Meade was certainly real), nor is there any definitive evidence that Sarah Winchester ever visited a psychic. The story of the ghosts of the Winchester Rifle's victims is almost certainly invention as well. Nor do most people know that Winchester owned several other spectacularly average homes and that most of her later years were spent in her home in Atherton, some miles away, or that she spent very little of the last seventeen years of her life in the Winchester Mystery House, which she called Llanada Villa ("house on flat land"). The blue room in the center of the house, where she supposedly conducted séances each night at midnight? This was her gardener's bedroom.

Still, questions remain. If this story is mostly, if not entirely, false, then what is the real story—why is the house so large, why did she keep on building, and why doesn't it have any kind of observable order or plan? Why tell this lie instead of the truth, and why did it take such firm root in our psyches? How did it come to obliterate nearly all traces of the true story, and why does it remain so alluring?

Sarah Lockwood Pardee was born in 1839 in New Haven, Connecticut, into an upper-middle-class family. (Throughout her life she was called not Sarah but Sallie, after her maternal grandmother.) The third-youngest of six children, all but one of them girls, she grew up amid the Golden Age of New England industrialism. The wizard Eli Whitney had just moved his factory to nearby Hamden, and all around New Haven mill towns like Lowell and Lawrence, Massachusetts, thrummed with life. Sarah's father, Leonard, was a woodworker by trade and established himself as an expert craftsman of the ornamental flourishes that came to define Victorian architecture.

Among those who were rising on the wave of American industrialism was the Pardees' neighbor Oliver Winchester. He had arrived in New Haven from Baltimore in 1845, virtually penniless but determined to make a name for himself. Possessed of an ideal combination of business acumen and mechanical understanding, within ten years he had reversed his fortunes. Using an innovative design for the production of men's shirts, he and his business partner, John Davies, founded the Winchester and Davies Shirt Manufacturing Company, which would in a few short years transform into a juggernaut of industry.

From 1850 to 1860, Leonard Pardee, building homes the barons of industry could now afford, increased his income tenfold, to $15,000 in assets (roughly a million dollars today). But he had a problem: too many daughters in an age when women were mainly thought of as a financial liability. He gave his children a strong education—they learned foreign languages, art, and music—and then set about marrying off his girls. The second to reach the altar, Sarah married her childhood neighbor William Wirt Winchester in 1862. It was a simple ceremony that belied the wealth of the two families: there was a war on, materials were sparse, and it was not a time for ostentation. The week that William and Sarah married, there were battles in Louisiana, Missouri, and Virginia. It had been a year since the first battle of Bull Run had awakened the United States to the horror of battle, and in a few weeks the Second Battle of Bull Run would grind up another eighteen thousand soldiers. By then, death had reached all corners of the North and the South.

Most of the Pardees and Winchesters stayed out of the war, being rich enough to spend the $300 for a deferment. (Sarah's brother served in the first Battle of Bull Run but chose not to reenlist when his initial three-month appointment was up; her brother-in-law Homer Sprague was the only member of her near family to see sustained conflict.) If anything, though, Oliver Winchester wanted more involvement in the war. In 1857 he had bought the failing Volcanic Repeating Arms Company from Horace Smith and Daniel B. Wesson, two designers who had invented a promising but as-yet-unsuccessful rifle that could fire multiple shots without the cumbersome and complicated reloading process of most rifles. (Smith and Wesson, of course, would found another arms company, bearing their names, that would find a great deal more success.) Winchester knew that a repeating rifle, a rifle that one could reload in a matter of seconds rather than minutes, could change the landscape of war forever, and he was convinced that the U.S. Army needed to adopt it. He took one of his most valued mechanics from his shirt factory, Benjamin T. Henry, and worked with him to improve on Smith and Wesson's idea.

Despite its obvious advantages, the resulting Winchester Repeating Rifle, nicknamed "The Henry," failed to make an impact on the war. Some individual soldiers purchased them, but the army never adopted the rifles wholesale; by the end of the Civil War, repeating rifles made up only 1 percent of all weapons used in battle. At the time, William saw his father's venture into weapons as an interesting side project; the real family fortune still lay in shirts. By then William was the secretary of Winchester and Davies, and he and Sarah had built themselves a comfortable life—one ideally suited for a child. On June 15, 1866, Sarah gave birth to a daughter, whom they named Annie, after William's sister, who had recently died in childbirth.

The delivery was fairly uneventful, but almost immediately Annie seemed to deteriorate before their eyes. A doctor diagnosed her condition as marasmus, a deficiency in which the body cannot process calories or manufacture its own protein. Normally marasmus results from severe malnutrition, but Annie was not lacking in food; her body simply could not process it. In an utterly cruel irony in a nation that had recently undergone such deprivation, Annie, born to one of the few families well off enough to provide handsomely for their child, was dying of want.

Annie Winchester died on July 25, a mere forty days old. William returned to his job at Winchester and Davies, but his father's other business was rapidly changing. The Henry rifle had finally begun to take off, and with it, the Winchester Repeating Arms Company. By securing lucrative contracts with foreign militaries, Oliver Winchester was able to keep his company thriving even through a postwar depression. By 1869, with the completion of the transcontinental railroad, the rifle assumed a new purpose: the company began aggressively marketing it as *the* best weapon for frontier self-defense. In time the Winchester rifle would earn the nickname "the gun that won the West," becoming synonymous with America's westward expansion and the Indian wars.

As the West became increasingly important to the company's fortunes, Winchester established offices in San Francisco, and in 1870 he sent William and Sarah to the Bay Area to oversee their installation. In portraits of the couple taken during that trip, William looks haunted, hollowed-out; his eyes hold a haggard allure, fixed deep into the distance. The tuberculosis that plagued him most of his adult life is not quite visible, but he seems fragile. Sarah, on the other hand, seems to face the camera head-on, even from a three-quarters profile. She exudes, if not beauty, then a vitality and a quick-wittedness, an awareness of the world around her and a desire to reshape it.

When people speak of the deaths in Sarah Winchester's family that drove her to build her house in San Jose, they mostly mean the deaths of her infant daughter and her husband, as if these two events happened coterminously. In fact, they took place sixteen years apart. Annie died in 1866, and Sarah continued to live on in New Haven until the mid-1880s. She and William never had another child, but by the few extant accounts, they lived generally happily and comfortably during that time.

Then in early 1880 Sarah's mother died, and in the winter of that year, her father-in-law, Oliver Winchester, died, followed by her husband less than a year later from tuberculosis. A few years later, she lost another close relative. By the mid-1880s Sarah Winchester found her family life decimated.

But when she moved to San Jose, she didn't come alone: she came with two sisters and their families. Why San Jose? Sarah and her husband had visited San Francisco in the 1870s, and found it quite pleasant, but the real reason has to do with her brother-in-law Homer Sprague, who in 1885 was appointed president of Mills College, in Oakland. When he and Sarah's sister Antoinette (Nettie) moved to the Bay Area, both Sarah and another sister, Isabelle (Belle) Merriman, and her family all moved together. In San Jose they would re-form their family, and Sarah, who had married into money and had the most stable fortune, would build a home to house them all.

In those years after the Gold Rush, the San Francisco Bay Area promised much. San Francisco's population grew at around 8 percent a year during the 1860s and 1870s, from 135,000 people in 1867 to 233,700 in 1880, and they were still coming in droves, thanks to the railroad. Most came seeking not gold but the "life-giving Nature" of the West; as one unnamed physician of the time put it, "Nor is sickness that scourge of humanity here to harass and hinder us in our pursuits. The general salubrity of California has justly become a proverb. The surgeons of San Francisco have remarked that wounds heal here with astonishing rapidity, owing, it is supposed, in a great measure, to the extreme purity of the atmosphere."

People afflicted with all manner of disease came to California, but consumptives most of all; stories were told of tubercular cases, or "lungers," as they were known, miraculously healed simply by breathing the dry, warm air of the West. According to one historian, by 1900 one-fourth of all migrants to California were tuberculosis patients who had come for their health and ended up staying. And so as Sarah Winchester joined the disease train to the San Francisco Bay Area, she was followed by her husband's killer, the White Plague.

She settled in the small but ambitious rural community of San Jose. Always in the shadow of its neighbor to the north, San Francisco, San

Jose by then had begun to try to distinguish itself. It could boast of its great Electric Light Tower, built in 1881 for $5,000. Straddling the intersection of Santa Clara and Market streets, the tower was 207 feet high, topped with six carbon arc lamps that provided 24,000 candelas of light—so bright, one could read by its light over a mile away. "For the first time the citizens of San Jose realized that they had the wonder of the nineteenth century," the *Daily Herald* proclaimed, "that they lived in the only city lighted by electric light, supported by a tower, which like the Colossus at Rhodes, stood astride her two principal streets." Local cops preferred working the beat around the tower, because migrating ducks would often fly into it and fall, electrocuted, dead to the ground, and the cops could pick up the dead ducks and sell them to restaurants.

Despite this welcoming beacon of progress and light, most people reaching the Santa Clara Valley found a city adrift. "California was a hotbed that brought humanity to a rapid, monstrous maturity," the *Annals of California* reported in 1855, "like the mammoth vegetables for which it is so celebrated." People everywhere "lost their brains," which is to say, they went insane. Suicides by strychnine and arsenic were common, including that of a woman named Claude Lorraine, who'd lost a sock containing $500, and a man named Riley, who botched a suicide attempt in January of 1884, told the police he was tired of life and wanted to die, and apologized for not making a "better job of it." Newspapers referred to suicide as "solving the Great Problem," as in the headline that ran in the July 13, 1885, *San Jose Daily News*: "STRYCHNINE: Margaret Risley Solves the Great Problem." The Great Problem was life; the solution was death.

Sarah Winchester's original idea was to enlarge her house so that it could comfortably fit her family. But her brother-in-law Homer Sprague's tenure at Mills College ended almost before it had begun, and within a year he and Winchester's sister Nettie moved to North Dakota for a different university job. Meanwhile, her sister Belle Merriman and her family had moved to San Francisco, leaving only their daughter Marion, whom Sarah all but adopted. The goal of building a great house for herself and her siblings' families ended almost immediately.

And yet Winchester kept building. She initially hired at least two architects but quickly dismissed them, preferring to do most of the work herself. Most of what we know about her building methods come from two surviving letters written to her sister-in-law Hannah Jane (Jennie) Bennett in 1898. They speak not of a madwoman beset by spirits but of a woman experimenting with the construction and design of her house. "I am constantly having to make an upheaval for some reason," she writes on June 11. "For instance, my upper hall which leads to the sleeping apartment was rendered so unexpectedly dark by a little addition that after a number of people had missed their footing on the stairs I decided that safety demanded something to be done so, over a year ago, I took out a wall and put in a skylight." Despite what you're told on a tour of the house, she did not employ workers twenty-four hours a day, seven days a week; when she found that the plaster she wanted couldn't be set in the heat of summer, she dismissed her workmen in order to wait for cooler weather, and she writes, "then I became rather worn and tired out and dismissed all the workmen to take such rest as I might through the winter." Her fatigue is a constant refrain. "If I did not get so easily tired out I should hurry up things more than I do," she wrote, "but I think it is better to 'go slow' than to use myself up. Just having the furnace man here and going over all the details with him used me up completely for a day or so."

There's a passive-aggressive quality to Winchester's building: she was nominally getting her house ready to entertain guests, particularly family from New Haven, who were accustomed to houses of a certain size, but then continually begged off guests under the pretense that the house was never quite done. "I hope some day to get so situated that I shall feel that it would not be an imposition on my friends to invite them to visit me," she says, more than ten years after she began improvements on her house.

At some point the perpetual building seems to have become a pretense to keep her family away.

This is one, perhaps uncharitable, way of looking at the house. Another perspective is that at some point the building ceased to be a means to housing her family and became an end unto itself. We are not used to seeing Sarah Winchester as an architectural pioneer, but she was. At the time she began work on her house, most would have seen the phrase "woman architect" as a contradiction in terms. Perhaps the most famous female architect of the early twentieth century, Julia Morgan, had not yet applied to École des Beaux-Arts, in Paris. When she did, in 1897, the school had only recently begun allowing female applicants. Particularly recalcitrant was the architecture school: Morgan had to apply three times before they were willing to admit a woman. The second time she nearly made it, but according to one judge her score was lowered because "they did not want to encourage young girls." Morgan would go on to define the architecture of the San Francisco Bay Area in the first half of the twentieth century before being hired by William Randolph Hearst to design many of his buildings, including, ultimately, Hearst Castle in San Simeon, California.

It's tempting to compare Winchester's house to Morgan's work—two female architects at the dawn of the twentieth century. But the tendency to judge the house by other architectural models or too closely through the lens of its creator is to miss the thing itself. Without any overall or grand design, without any intention of a unified effect, the Winchester mansion sprawls and flops in a dozen different directions, moving like a coral reef. Its aesthetic, its beauty, is precisely in its lawlessness. The house is, in a way, a form of automatic writing, a stream of consciousness made spatial.

For many visitors this is also what makes the house so unsettling. The Winchester house can feel endless, much larger on the inside than it is on the outside. This is something you find in Shirley Jackson's Hill House, and you find it in the disorienting space of Disney's Haunted Mansion (only from an aerial view do you understand that nearly all of the ride happens not in the house itself but in an adjacent warehouse space, giving you the sense that the tiny mansion you enter goes on forever inside). The disturbingly endless house appears repeatedly in horror novels, from Poe's House of Usher to the eponymous structure in Mark Z. Danielewski's *House of Leaves*, built elegantly around the unsettling fact that the house in question is slightly larger inside than it is outside. And this is to say nothing of the numerous gothic novels that feature secret passageways, where the endlessness isn't supernatural, including the estate in H. P. Lovecraft's "The Rats in the Walls." If houses are supposed to be places of security, then most terrifying is the idea that they might go on forever, that they might be labyrinths.

But this isn't the only reason the Winchester house has captured the imagination of so many. Add to this another kind of haunting, the one popularized by Charles Dickens in his 1861 novel *Great Expectations*, a novel involving the spinster Miss Havisham, living alone with a young girl named Estella in a massive mansion. Everything in her house is frozen in time: place settings are covered in cobwebs and dust, but readied as though at any moment the dinner party might begin again. As Pip tells us,

> I began to understand that everything in the room had stopped, like the watch and the clock, a long time ago. I noticed that Miss Havisham put down the jewel exactly on the spot from which she had taken it up. As Estella dealt the cards, I glanced at the dressing-table again, and saw that the shoe upon it, once white, now yellow, had never been worn. I glanced down at the foot from which the shoe was absent, and saw that the silk stocking on it, once white, now yellow, had been trodden ragged. Without this arrest of everything, this standing still of all the pale decayed objects, not even the withered bridal dress on the collapsed form could have looked so like grave-clothes, or the long veil so like a shroud.

Here, too, we find a fictional story ready to be transposed onto Sarah Winchester, complete with the young girl, played by Winchester's niece, Marion Merriman. The spinster in perpetual mourning, time standing still, the perpetual sense of arrested decay—none of this had much to do with Winchester, but from outward appearances it was a perfect fit, and it offered a ready-made explanation of what went on behind closed doors. Ghosts, you could say, flock to women left alone.

On Friday, March 29, 1895, an unsigned article titled "Strange Story: A Woman Who Thinks She'll Die When Her House Is Built" was published in the *San Jose Daily News*, with the subheading "A Magnificent Mansion on the Saratoga Road Near San Jose—A Maze of Turrets and Towers." The legend of Sarah Winchester, widow in perpetual mourning, superstitious kook whose wealth was squandered in a deluded quest to keep the spirits at bay, truly originates here.

"The first view of the house fills one with surprises," the article proclaims. "You mechanically rub your eyes to assure yourself that the number of the turrets is not an illusion, they are so fantastic and dream-like. But nearer approach reveals others and others and still others." With a mixture of wonder and a tinge of horror, the anonymous *Daily News* writer taps directly into the idea that the house may literally be endless:

> How it is possible to build on an already apparently finished house and preserve its artistic appearance through so many changes is a query that nobody can answer, but the fact remains that it has been done. From every point of view new towers appear, and one has to make a circuit of the building to see all of these, for every addition to the many that is made has one or more separate roofs, and every roof is elaborated into a tower or resolved into a dome.

From there, the article gets down to business.

> Ten years ago the handsome residence was apparently ready
> for occupancy, but improvements and additions are constantly
> being made, for the reason, it is said, that the owner of the
> house believes that when it is entirely completed, she will die.
> This superstition has resulted in the construction of a maze of
> domes, turrets, cupolas and towers, covering territory enough
> for a castle. Although no part of the structure is over two
> stories high, the house is large enough to shelter an army.

As the article continues, it lays out the story that has come to be associated
with Sarah Winchester, which has remained almost entirely unchanged in
over a century.

> As fast as new rooms are finished—and they are all made
> with the very latest and most modern of accessories—they are
> furnished with the utmost elegance and closed, to be used
> hardly at all. Mrs. Winchester and her niece live alone in the
> great residence, and its doors are closed to all but a few. The
> tap, tap, tapping of the carpenters' hammers never disturbs
> them in their many and luxurious quarters, which are far re-
> moved from the sound as if it were somebody else's house that
> was being built.

Here one finds, arising almost *ex nihilo*, the entire mythology all at
once: A building somewhat anachronistic, no longer fully in use. A
woman, arrested in time, living in the past, unable to move forward and
rejoin the stream of humanity. A house that never ends, that's built as a
labyrinth, that is uncanny in the way it uses familiar domestic elements
while upending them in a strange, discomfiting way.

One last element that would have been on the minds of readers of that original article might have contributed to the vicious rumors that began to spring up around Sarah Winchester. Two years earlier, on May 5, 1893, the United States suffered its worst economic shock in decades, one that would lead to a depression that would be eclipsed only by the Great Depression of the 1930s. By 1895 unemployment had gone from 4 percent to 14 percent; there were more than 500 bank failures and 1,600 business failures. Henry Adams saw the panic of 1893 as a conspiracy from Wall Street, by that "dark, mysterious, crafty, wicked, rapacious, and tyrannical power to rob and oppress and enslave the people." According to H. P. Robinson, the editor of *Railway Age*, writing in 1895, "It is probably safe to say that in no civilized country in this century, not actually in the throes of war or open insurrection, has society been so disorganized as it was in the United States during the first half of 1894; never was human life held so cheap; never did the constituted authorities appear so incompetent to enforce respect for the law."

In this context of social upheaval, in a city like San Jose, already teetering on the edge, we find Sarah Winchester—a recluse, a woman, someone who gave to charity but did so anonymously, who had no real social circle to stand up for her. She made an easy target, and the slurs of insanity, the echoes of Miss Havisham and her own pathological mourning—these things all clung to Sarah Winchester because she appeared to those around her as a gaudy reminder of the haves versus the have-nots. She was the 1 percent, and the city resented her for it. And so it punished her through gossip and myth.

At any other point in time, in any other place, and with any other person, any other structure, none of these stories would have gelled quite in this way. Sarah Winchester's house is unique not because of its architecture or because of the motivations for its construction but because it was vulnerable to a series of resentments that converged in a singular moment in history.

Defenders were few and far between. Two years later an article titled "Only Gossip: No Truth in the Story of the Winchester Palace" appeared in the *San Jose Evening News*, arguing that the myth was the "result of rural rumors." The article quoted an "acquaintance" of Sarah Winchester's, who said bluntly that the "story about Mrs. Winchester being superstitious, and believing that she is going to die when the house, or rather all additions are completed, is all nonsense. She is not superstitious, but is an unusually sensible woman. She has erected a magnificent home. She has made many improvements on the first plans. It may be that building is a fad with her, and if it is, she is able to satisfy it, for she is a woman of ample means." This acquaintance, not satisfied, went on quite pointedly:

> We are constantly inviting people of wealth to locate in Santa Clara valley. Mrs. Winchester is one of the most desirable settlers we have ever had. If people who come here with fortunes are inclined to spend it, I do not think it is wise to circulate reports that they are "cranks" merely because they do not get "thick" with the neighbors. . . . Mrs. Winchester is a lady of refinement and culture. . . . If she wants to build a castle on her premises near Campbell, she should be permitted to do so without ascribing her motives to foolish superstitions. If people of wealth who settle in Santa Clara are to be ridiculed when they spend their money lavishly, we might as well put up the bars. . . . After awhile the lady might not want to have a nail driven about the place for fear that someone would run off to a newspaper with a cock-and-bull story. This would be the means of preventing the circulation of a large amount of money among builders and furnishers and that is why we encourage people of wealth to locate in Santa Clara valley. We want industries developed, improvements made and this valley beautified.

The article was indeed a corrective to the urban legends of the reclusive Winchester, but it was curiously couched in the language of civic investment, encouraging the wealthy to relocate to the Santa Clara Valley.

The house was either the work of a rich, mentally unstable widow or a potential source for local jobs and investment. The story of Sarah Winchester's house, built on the fortune of the rifle that "won the West," is always, one way or another, the story of money.

After her death, her numerous real estate assets were sold off one by one. Of all her holdings, including the houses and vast plots of land she owned throughout the valley, the Winchester house itself was, according to her lawyer Samuel Leib, "appraised as of no value." Gargantuan, sprawling, beautiful, as salable real estate the house was worthless: too odd, idiosyncratic, lavish, and useless to be sold to another buyer. At an auction of the property, no one bought it; the only interested party was a man named John H. Brown, who didn't have the money to buy the house but offered to lease it, with an option to buy it later.

Brown had come a long way: from an amusement park called the Crystal Beach Resort on the Canadian side of Lake Erie. There he had invented one of the earliest roller coasters: a ten-mile-an-hour ride called the Backety-Back, which in June 1910 had killed a woman who'd somehow been thrown from its slow-moving car. Brown relocated his family to California, where he heard of the Winchester house and the rumors regarding its construction. Among Crystal Beach's other attractions was a "house of mystery" that Brown had seen draw large crowds. According to historian Mary Jo Ignoffo, who put together a biography of Winchester, it was Brown who took the rumors of the Winchester house and reinvigorated them, building a mythology around it and offering tours. As attitudes toward America's westward expansion and manifest destiny changed, so, too, did the role of the Winchester rifle in the tour, now emphasized as the gun that had killed untold Native Americans, all of whom were now haunting the widow who'd profited from the murder weapon. As with the Myrtles Plantation, vengeful American Indians have loomed large in the script.

Among those who took a tour in those first years was Harry Houdini, who had spent much of his professional career by that point debunking psychics and disproving supernatural phenomena. Yet when he got to the Winchester house, his attitude seemed to change completely. After his visit, he did not speak of the folly of superstition or of Winchester being crazy or duped by disreputable psychics. After repeating the story that by then had been accepted as gospel, Houdini went on: "The whole thing is beautifully inlaid because the woman wants the workmen to take plenty of time. Never was there such a marvelous place."

After the great debunker gave his seal of approval to the tourist attraction that Sarah Winchester's house had become, its business grew steadily. Over the years her former employees and friends made attempts to correct her story; when she died, Leib's son and business partner Roy commented that she was "as sane and clear headed a woman as I have ever known, and she had a better grasp of business and financial affairs than most men." Testimony from her many employees over the years mattered little, though; what mattered, then as now, was the story that taps into those larger social and cultural trends, perfectly embodied by such an architecturally unsettling house.

The legend of Sarah Winchester depends on a cultural uneasiness to which we don't always like to admit. An uneasiness about women living alone, withdrawn from society, for one. An uneasiness about wealth and the way the superrich live among us. And, perhaps largest of all, an uneasiness about the gun that won the West and the violence white Americans carried out in the name of civilization.

These may be unconnected anxieties, but they're brought together in this story of a rich woman alone, haunted by the American Indians killed with her father-in-law's gun. It's a compelling story, perhaps, because it's one in which Sarah Winchester is punished for these transgressions—driven mad by guilt, unable to join society, her money wasted and misspent. Winchester herself had little documented guilt about the role of the rifle in American history, but we've projected shame on her nonetheless, as though we can quarantine such thoughts in the mind of someone long dead so the rest of us can go about our days unburdened, enjoying the California sun.

CHAPTER FOUR

THE RATHOLE REVELATION

Georgetown, NY, and Bull Valley, IL

Sarah Winchester may not have designed her house with guidance from the spirit world, but if there is a house that *was* indisputably built by someone influenced by the dead, it is Timothy Brown's in Georgetown, New York, about thirty-five miles southeast of Syracuse. Brown had not yet begun building his house when, he later explained, his dead sister, Mary, presented him with a vision one morning. She offered up several types of house and invited him to pick the one that suited him. From that point on, the spirits guided him in its construction. As the Spiritualist journal *Banner of Light* later related, Brown "found that if he put his chisel in the wrong place his arm had no power to use the mallet or strike a blow, but when his chisel was rightly placed the blows were freely dealt."

The house that Brown and his spirits built still stands, a remarkably odd and beautiful structure from the 1860s. It might have been an unremarkable square house but for the fringe of scalloped wood that hangs from its eaves, an ornamental design of wooden lace that drips down as though the roof is melting. The wooden lace adds a richness of detail and a depth of character to the house that begs for closer inspection. Rather than constructing an A-frame roof to keep snow from building up, as was customary, Brown built his roof with a unique funnel that leads to a central drainpipe. (This might have led to the leak that severely damaged the interiors when the house was left vacant in the mid-2000s.)

Ghosts are the quintessential unwanted guests: like pests or dry rot, they do not belong. When homeowners discover ghosts on their property, they will do anything in their power to excise or exorcise them. Usually, that is. For there is a long history of Americans doing exactly the opposite: people who've tried to populate their houses with the paranormal, to *welcome* spirits in and make them feel at home. Timothy Brown saw himself as part of a larger movement—Spiritualism—and his house stands as a monument to the great American passion for communing with the dead that held fast in this country (and elsewhere) for the better part of a century.

America's popular fascination with ghosts began in 1848, in a small house in upstate New York, where two sisters, fifteen-year-old Margaret and twelve-year-old Kate Fox, revealed that they had been communicating with the spirit of a dead man in their basement. The house had been thought haunted before the Foxes moved in, and almost immediately after they arrived, they were tormented by loud, unexplained sounds, doors closing by themselves, and objects that inexplicably moved. Beset by this unexplained activity, the sisters found that they could talk to the resident spirit by rapping on the wall and floor; it would answer questions with knocks, indicating that he knew the girls' ages as well as other pertinent information.

One neighbor recorded his experience with the Fox sisters' ghost:

I then asked if Mr. ——— [Naming a person who had formerly lived in the house] had injured it [the spirit], and if so, manifest it by rapping, and it made three knocks louder than common, and at the same time the bedstead jarred more than it had done before. I then inquired if it was murdered for money, and the knocking was heard. I then requested it to rap when I mentioned the sum of money for which it was murdered. I then asked if it was one hundred, two, three, or four, and when I came to five hundred the rapping was heard. All in the room said they heard it distinctly. I then asked the question if it was five hundred dollars, and the rapping was heard. . . . I then asked it to rap my age—the number of years of my age. It rapped thirty times. This is my age, and I do not think anyone about here knew my age except myself and my family.

Soon the Fox sisters were touring the region, displaying their abilities to communicate with the dead while others rushed to get in on the act. Within a year there were more than a hundred spiritual mediums in New York City alone, and in Philadelphia there were another fifty-some "private circles." Popular contacts included not just lost loved ones but historical figures: Thomas Jefferson and Benjamin Franklin, as well as Francis Bacon, Enlightenment-era mystic Emanuel Swedenborg, Daniel Webster, and Shakespeare. The dead communicated through table rappings, by moving objects about the room, and by automatic writing, in which mediums scribbled on paper until words began to emerge. There was no shortage of means of reaching the dead, and the growth of Spiritualism was exponential: by some estimates, there were as many as eleven million Spiritualists in the United States by the end of the 1850s.

At least some of Spiritualism's appeal lay in its social aspect: it was a means of bringing together a community over a shared grief or curiosity, in an intimate and emotionally intense setting. In Georgetown Timothy Brown and his wife held annual gatherings for Spiritualists in the house that became known as Brown's Temple, and, as *Banner of Light* concluded, "his wonderful persistence has well-nigh conquered the prejudices of his doubting neighbors, and the structure stands *a striking edifice of the power of will concentrated on one object, and of the guiding inspiration, as he firmly believes, of spiritual beings in the life beyond.*" It is without a doubt a testament to the power of a self-trained carpenter, a genuinely artistic achievement.

And it is also, based on contemporary reports, a testament to one way in which Spiritualists could ingratiate themselves with a community, which may further explain Spiritualism's widespread appeal.

Which is not to say that the new religion wasn't controversial; the word "Spiritualism" first appeared in print in 1853 in a book by skeptic John Ross Dix, in which he referred to Spiritualism as one more "paroxysm of humbug" afflicting America. In spite of its many detractors, the movement only grew in ensuing decades. When Margaret Fox publicly confessed in 1888 that she and her sister had faked the original rapping incident, many Spiritualists denounced her, and she was forced to recant her confession a year later.

Spiritualism's explosion and massive popularity was never the result of a single event; rather, a confluence of obsessions and cultural needs all came together in the 1850s. Preceding the movement was another homegrown philosophy: Transcendentalism, which caught fire in the American imagination in 1836 with the publication of Ralph Waldo Emerson's essay "Nature." In it Emerson emphasized a personal revelation free from organized religion, in which one could seek direct access to the divine through solitary contemplation of nature. His teachings would inspire some of the seminal works of American literature, including Henry David Thoreau's *Walden* and Walt Whitman's *Leaves of Grass*.

The Transcendentalists often viewed Spiritualism with a skepticism bordering on outright hatred. Emerson called it the "rathole revelation" and claimed that the adepts of Spiritualism "have mistaken flatulence for inspiration." His disdain was shared by, among others, Herman Melville, who parodied Spiritualism and its "table-rapping" sessions in a short story, "The Apple-Tree Table," in which a family believes a table to be possessed by spirits, only to discover that it's infested with bugs. "I hate this shallow Americanism," Emerson proclaimed in an 1859 lecture, "which hopes to get rich by credit, to get knowledge by raps on midnight tables, to learn the economy of the mind by phrenology, or skill without study."

Like it or not, Emerson and his fellow Transcendentalists had laid the groundwork for the kind of personal revelation Spiritualism promised. Emerson himself, after all, wrote in his essay "Nominalist and Realist," "It is the secret of the world that all things subsist and do not die, but only retire a little from sight and afterwards return again," as if agreeing with all those mediums reaching out across the grave into the spirit world. The basic tenet of Transcendentalism was that one need only open up an extra-sensory perception to access the divine all around us. If Emerson could find God in the forest, why couldn't a medium find departed loved ones in a darkened room?

Spiritualism took fast hold of the American consciousness at the same moment our attitudes toward death were changing. The early half of the century had seen a war between religion and science over how to handle the dead body and when dissection was permissible. Burial reformers pushed the importance of sanitary corpse disposal, and so families, many of whom were used to keeping vigil with a loved one's body for several days after death, saw these bodies removed from their care at a rapid rate. Suddenly bereft of this final communion due to medical and sanitation laws, families turned to Spiritualism as a means of continuing that conversation, seeking in séances a closure that had been denied them.

For Spiritualists, there was no hell, and there were no evil spirits; rather, the spirit world existed on a continuum with the world of the living: in the afterlife, the dead were at peace in a place known as Summerland. Spiritualism offered hope and comfort, not just because it put the living in touch with the longed-for dead but because it did so without the intermediaries of organized religion. In the world of Spiritualism there was no vengeful God who damned infants who died before baptism, there was no predestination condemning you to Hell no matter your actions. The harsh Calvinism of the Puritans had given way to an afterlife without pain or judgment, and one that anyone could access. Spiritualists, despite nominally maintaining their Christian faith, began to downplay the role of Jesus himself, since without a judgmental God or Hell, there was no longer a theological need for a savior to die for their sins. Death instead was simply part of a natural process, overseen by a benevolent deity.

This new DIY religion brought with it an additional attraction: since the spirit world was accessible to all, Spiritualists saw little need for the men who traditionally controlled organized religion. In short order Spiritualism became dominated by women: for one thing, they were generally acknowledged to be superior mediums, and many saw in Spiritualism an antidote to the patriarchal misogyny of traditional religion. In volume 3 of *History of Woman Suffrage*, edited by Elizabeth Cady Stanton, Susan B. Anthony, and Matilda Joslyn Gage, Spiritualism was singled out as "the only religious sect in the world . . . that has recognized the equality of woman."

Among the many reasons Transcendentalists like Emerson might have viewed Spiritualism with skepticism may lie in how it took a philosophy authored by men and transformed it into a women's movement. Spiritualism tended to valorize traits that were elsewhere labeled as women's psychiatric diseases, including convulsions, incoherent babbling, open displays of sexuality, and other violations of Victorian decorum. Behavior that would have then been diagnosed as nervous sensitivity and hysteria were exactly the kinds of traits that made for good mediums. In an age when male-dominated religious and medical institutions were working overtime to contain, train, diagnose, and treat all women who didn't fit an established mold, the Spiritualists, Stanton, Anthony, and Gage noted, "have always assumed that woman may be a medium of communication from heaven to earth, [and] that the spirits of the universe may breathe through her lips." Spiritualism offered a radical inversion, according empowerment and respect precisely to those who refused or were unable to toe the line.

Early suffrage meetings were heavily populated with mediums and trance speakers; in some places it was difficult to find suffragists who *weren't* also Spiritualists. Spiritualism had given many of these women practice and confidence in speaking to groups with authority; by allowing others (the dead) to speak through them, American women began to speak for themselves in greater numbers. Spiritualism was only one of many factors and social movements that drove women's suffrage, but it was a vital and important one.

As Spiritualism became associated more and more with a rejection of patriarchal religion and traditional marriage, women's rights, and other subversive agendas, the backlash became increasingly vehement. The contemporary attitude toward Spiritualism as a particularly ridiculous belief stems in no small part from the misogyny with which it was attacked in the second half of the nineteenth century. It has been subsequently consigned to the dustbin of that century's excesses and ridiculous fads, alongside phrenology, animal magnetism, and the temperance movement, but Spiritualism-influenced political agitation led to lasting reform: the Nineteenth Amendment to the U.S. Constitution, passed in 1920. Since women gained the vote, however, Spiritualism's importance as a women's movement has more or less been forgotten or downplayed. Its influence waned as the nineteenth century drew to a close, and after a brief resurgence in the wake of World War I, Spiritualism was absorbed by the broader, more diffuse field of parapsychology. As a movement with clear leaders and well-articulated beliefs, it had mostly died out by the end of the 1920s.

The movement itself may be gone, but Spiritualism's penchant for using the latest technological advances to communicate with the dead has found a resurgence with modern paranormal enthusiasts and ghost hunters. Ghosts have become a business of gadgets. Amazon.com is filled with gadgets for the paranormal investigator: KII meters, which measure electromagnetic field variations; portable motion sensors; "ghost boxes," which sample FM frequencies randomly in search of voices from the beyond; and all manner of digital recorders rebranded as EVP recorders, claiming to offer superior paranormal recordings ("Get Ready to Converse with Spirits!" boasts one such device, which retails for $119.85).

Ghost hunting is a thriving, growing business, thanks to a glut of

reality TV shows that have emerged over the past decade: starting with
Syfy's *Ghost Hunters* in 2004, in which a crew of investigators travel to
reputedly haunted locations to trot out gadgetry in search of definitive
proof of the hereafter. Add to this the popularity of ghost tours in historic
downtowns throughout the country and museums like Merchant's House,
which have increasingly added ghost tours as part of their public outreach.
You could say that Spiritualism, now practiced at Halloween and on reality TV shows, is back from the dead.

During his speech on the mysteries and virtues of Sarah Winchester's
house, Harry Houdini mentioned a curious room without corners, built
by a man he claimed to know from "the East": "This fellow had been
taught by spiritualists. He built himself a perfectly round, tower-like
room, so that when the devil came for his soul he wouldn't be able to find
a corner in which to catch it." Houdini went on to claim that Winchester's
supposed séance room was similarly built: "There is a séance room without corners, so that the spirits won't hurt themselves coming in and out.
Mrs. Winchester has a vast wardrobe of variously colored robes, and she
uses a different robe for each spirit."

Houdini was wrong: there are no round rooms in the house, and the
one currently claimed to be her séance room is certainly rectangular. But
he did not originate the idea that Spiritualists built rooms and houses
without corners, and lately this fascination has become attached to one
house in particular: the George Stickney House of Bull Valley, Illinois.

Far outside Chicago, a distant suburb barely deserving of the name,
Bull Valley was untrampled wilderness when George Stickney went there
in 1835. He helped found the nearby town of Nunda, Illinois, building its
first school and serving as the town's school director as well as its road
commissioner. In 1839 he met and married Sylvia Beckley, ten years his
junior, and brought her with him to the hardscrabble wilds of Illinois,
where they settled down to raise a family.

They began construction on their home not far from Nunda in 1849, on land that would eventually be incorporated as part of Bull Valley, finally finishing it in 1865. The house's rounded corners—which punctuate its otherwise unremarkable Italianate style—are often held as evidence of the Stic_kneys' Spiritualist beliefs, though there does not appear to have ever been any kind of codified building regulations, rounded corners or otherwise, for spirits. Certainly Brown's Temple did not feature circular rooms or rounded corners.

The notion of round buildings being built to prevent the devil from catching you in a corner has a longer lineage, one that predates both Spiritualism and George Stickney, and it was used sometimes to account for the curious design of barns built by Quakers and Shakers. While it's not clear where this superstition might have originated, the rounded barn has much more prosaic origins. Scotsman J. C. Loudon's *Encyclopaedia of Cottage, Farm, and Villa Architecture and Furniture*, first published in 1833, notes that cows and horses are approximately half a foot narrower at their heads than they are at their hindquarters, which means that the most economical shape for a stall is a wedge. A circular barn with wedge-shaped stalls can house the same number of animals as a rectangular barn in three-quarters the amount of space, with the added benefit of making it easier for the farmer to feed all the animals from the center.

There is a Chinese folk belief that evil spirits—*kuei*—can travel only in straight lines, a belief that supposedly accounts for the curved eaves on Chinese roofs, and which might have at some point filtered into the American consciousness, leading to the supernatural association with round barns and houses. And so a practical, if unusual, design becomes associated with a foreign folk legend about the devil, which then gets repurposed as part of the narrative of the new, burgeoning Spiritualist movement, and this in turn gets attached to an ordinary house in rural Illinois. The legend stuck, the stories began to accumulate, and over the years the house's reputation made it the target of vandals and bored teenagers. And so the building's current owner, the village of Bull Valley, has been trying its best to downplay the myths associated with the Stickney House. In 1995 the village clerk, Phyllis Keinz, who worked in the building, told the *Chicago Tribune* that the closest thing to ghosts in the house are the birds that sometimes get into the attic. Local politician Virginia Peschke, of the Stickney House Restoration Committee, told the paper, "There's never been anything to those stories, which we believe were just made up by local kids. And we feel the stories have contributed to a lot of the terrible vandalism the house has suffered." Peschke said she'd interviewed several previous residents of the house, and none had ever complained of ghosts. "The house is out in the middle of nowhere," she added, "and they were always bothered a lot more by vandals than any ghosts." One former resident, Devona Edinger, who was born in the Stickney House and lived there for a few years, confirmed this: "It's just something creepy that kids like to say about the place."

More than a century later, the house remains, having been passed down through various owners until it was eventually deeded to the village of Bull Valley. Now it sits by itself, a squat two-story building that houses the Bull Valley Police Department and the village clerk. The Stickney House, like Sarah Winchester's mansion, may have little or nothing to do with Spiritualism, but the fact that we impute a Spiritualist motive to anomalous houses like these attests to the strange grip the movement has on our imaginations. The more unusual the house, the more likely it'll cause unease among its neighbors and the more we seem to require some kind of story to explain its construction. That several of our eeriest, most inexplicable houses are misattributed to Spiritualism suggests how little we know about the movement, aside from Hollywood depictions of wild-eyed mediums and table sessions.

The Stickney House's reputation for ghosts nowhere matches the House of the Seven Gables or the Winchester Mystery House, but among locals it has long been considered haunted. Presumably a house built to welcome good spirits at some point brought in a few bad ones, and since the 1970s stories have circulated about its strange energy. In a 2011 post to the Web site trueghosttales.com, a woman named Carri Williams wrote about an experience with the Stickney House. Her brother had been killed on the highway near the mansion in 1984, and she had thought little of it until a few years later when, driving to school one cold January day, she saw a tall, hooded man dressed in a black robe "walking toward a group of pine trees in the snow. There were no houses around. . . . I did not understand why someone would be walking in the bitter cold like that. I did not think nothing of it until I realized the man dressed in the black robe was headed for Bull Valley and he was walking in the direction toward where my brother had died in a car accident and near the Stickney Mansion." Later, Williams claims, she realized that this was not a man but some kind of spirit, and "an evil one" at that.

Whatever one makes of this story, it's hard to connect it to the house's actual history: no terrible murders were committed within its walls, nor is there any record of a single horrible event that might give rise to an evil spirit. Perhaps this malevolent spirit might account for the fact that only three of the ten Stickney children lived past infancy, but then, child mortality rates in the nineteenth century were high everywhere. It's just another of many stories that imply, more or less, that by dabbling in Spiritualism, the Stickneys invited ghosts to this corner of Illinois—ghosts that haven't ever left.

Meanwhile, Brown's Temple has vanishingly few stories of ghosts attached to it. In 2009 it went up for sale, and money manager turned spiritual healer Madis Senner attempted to buy the house, with hopes of restoring it to its former glory. In a YouTube video, he discussed the floating orbs (mysterious balls of light that sometimes appear floating in videos and photos) that many people find on photographs of the house but went on to say that it "is a divine place that has been a sacred site for thousands of years." Rather than view it as a haunted place that inspires fear, Senner suggested instead that one should "put fear aside, and you may well encounter the divine there."

The walls of Brown's Temple retain the imprint of Spiritualism in its very architecture. And if it is truly haunted, then it is haunted not by ghosts or evil spirits so much as by an idea that has vanished; a building left behind, without the animating spirit that inspired its construction.

Spiritualism, like Transcendentalism, is woven inextricably into the fabric of American consciousness: much of what we now accept as our canonical culture was influenced by Spiritualism—in ways we'd perhaps like to forget. Not only were some of America's great literary masters (including Walt Whitman and Mark Twain) believers in ghosts, but inquiries into the afterlife drove the philosophy and teachings of William James, the founder of American psychology. But Spiritualism ultimately was not an institutional religion by and for "great men" like Whitman and James; it was a messy, homespun set of beliefs that were embraced and spread mainly by women, and so American history has downplayed it as aberrant and foolish rather than accept its place in our national psyche. As a political and social movement, Spiritualism has become a ghost itself, a legacy of feminist liberation and belief without dogma that still haunts the land.

Spiritualism might have lost its influence by the end of the 1920s, but it may be more accurate to say it simply went mainstream. The percentage of Americans who identify as spiritual but not religious has been creeping ever slowly up in recent years as people turn away from organized churches and seek their own spiritual paths. Meanwhile, our belief in ghosts remains high; according to one study, 73 percent of Americans believe in life after death, and 20 percent believe in communication with the dead. While these people may not call themselves Spiritualists or spend their Friday nights clasping hands around a table, it's clear that they have adopted a similar belief system: a focus on personal revelation unmediated by dogma or doctrine, and a belief in the perseverance of the soul beyond death, a spirit that is still somehow apprehensible by the living. Belief in a spiritual realm may now be depoliticized, divorced from the radical social agenda that once went hand in hand with Spiritualism, but it remains vitally alive nonetheless. One can dismiss Spiritualism as unscientific, as wishful thinking, as hucksterism, or as any number of other things, but it was—and continues to be—anything but fringe.

CHAPTER FIVE

THE FAMILY THAT WOULD NOT LIVE

St. Louis, MO

It is, quite literally, a dark and stormy night. A summer storm has settled over St. Louis: gray-black clouds turning the air yellowish and electric, the rain pulsing down in waves. The sprint from the parking lot to the front door of the Lemp Mansion—no more than fifty feet—leaves you soaked. The thunder is following on the heels of the lightning; it is right above us. In the bar the stained-glass portraits of William Lemp, Jr., and his first wife, Lillian Lemp—the Lavender Lady—flicker to life from the lightning outside with disturbing frequency, the accompanying thunder coming fast afterward. It is the perfect night for a ghost hunt: the air already electric, everyone already a bit on edge. In his portrait, William Lemp looks prematurely old; the glass artist has added shading to his face to give the appearance of three dimensions, but the result instead is that he appears haggard, black pits around his eyes, deep creases in his skin.

As if he knows he's going to die.

Unlike the House of the Seven Gables' management, the owners of the Lemp Mansion seem quite content to capitalize on the building's reputation. Ghost hunters come here regularly to take tours, use KII meters and ghost boxes, and record for EVPs and orbs. I'm here for one such tour,

led by a local ghost-hunting group. I'm also here to spend the night, since
the Lemp Mansion operates as a bed-and-breakfast—though I won't be
able to get into my room until 11 p.m. My room, the Elsa Lemp Suite, is
itself part of the tour: the most haunted room in this most haunted house.

The Lemp family story should be remembered as your classic
rags-to-riches success story: Johann Adam Lemp emigrated to America
from Germany in 1838 and within a short time had grown a prosperous
business selling beer. At the time the only beers available in America were
strong English ales, and Lemp, along with John Wagner in Philadelphia,
is credited with introducing the lighter, German-style lager beer that has
since become ubiquitous in the United States. Lemp's beer caught on
quickly, particularly in the German immigrant community of St. Louis,
and by 1850 he was shipping four thousand barrels of beer annually. Prior
to electric refrigeration, Lemp had found that the natural caverns beneath
St. Louis provided a stable and year-round cool environment, which allowed him to ramp up production without fear of spoilage. His success
was mirrored by constant rivals Eberhard Anheuser and Adolphus
Busch, whose Budweiser beer would play second fiddle to Lemp's Falstaff
brand well into the early twentieth century. Johann died in 1862, but the
company soldiered on under the direction of his son, William, who continued to grow the brewing juggernaut, which, by the dawn of the twentieth century, seem destined to endure forever.

The first suicide in the Lemp Mansion happened in 1904. Three years
earlier, William's twenty-eight-year-old son, Frederick, who had been
groomed to take over the family business, died suddenly from heart failure, leaving William distraught. When William's closest friend, Frederick Pabst (of the blue-ribboned Pabst Brewing Company), died a few years
later, on January 1, 1904, it sent William over the edge: he shot himself in
the head just over a month later in the mansion the family had occupied
since 1876. William's successor, William Jr. (Billy), lacked his father's head
for business; he spent lavishly, and the business floundered. His marriage
to Lillian fell apart, and the couple's messy divorce in 1906 made head-

lines. But the real crippling blow to the Lemp brewing empire came in 1919, with the passage of Prohibition. Billy shuttered the company without notice, and within two years both he and his sister Elsa had killed themselves. The family retired from the public eye, out of the beer business for good, almost forgotten, until another of William Sr.'s eight children, Charles, followed in the footsteps of his father, brother, and sister, killing himself with a revolver on May 10, 1949. (Tradition holds that Charles shot his dog before himself, though this is nowhere mentioned in the police reports of the incident.)

Charles Lemp was the only one to leave a note, which read simply, "In case I am found dead, blame it on no one but me." But most have instead chosen to blame a curse of some kind, a curse under which the Lemp family suffered, unable to shake the fate that awaited each in turn. In the Haunted Lemp Mansion board game, players move through the mansion while collecting various strategy cards; if a player collects both a "revolver" card and a "bullet" card and then happens to land on a "suicide" space, he's out of the game—an oddly tasteless reference to the gruesome series of tragedies that repeatedly befell the House of Lemp.

Unlike the Winchester Mystery House, with its sprawling, formless labyrinth of rooms; the George Stickney House, with its rounded corners; or the House of the Seven Gables, with its secret staircase, there is nothing particularly odd—architecturally speaking—about the Lemp Mansion. It is large, to be sure, and stately, but its outer construction is straightforward, and its rooms are laid out in a fairly sensible order. Its additions over the years increased its size, but its overall shape and appearance don't suggest anything out of the ordinary.

And yet the mansion itself—far more than the neighboring brewery, the caves below the city where the fabled Falstaff beer was once stored, or the other homes the Lemps have owned through the years—remains inextricable from the family and its curse. This is how we tend to think of old, august families that have lasted through the generations: there should be one central, ancestral home, a single estate that embodies the bloodline.

It's an idea ingrained in the very word "house," with its dual meaning as both building and family. And like Edgar Allan Poe's House of Usher, the House of Lemp seems to have failed. In Poe's story "The Fall of the House of Usher," house and House are conjoined so tightly that when Roderick Usher's sister, Madeline, seems to rise from the grave to carry off her brother (the last surviving member of the Usher family) to his own death, the house itself collapses, supernaturally torn asunder, and crumbles into the swamp just as the narrator escapes. But unlike the house of Usher—and despite the tragedies and calamities that have befallen its occupants—the Lemp Mansion still stands.

The rain is deluging the streets outside, and we gather in one of the dining rooms on the first floor, where there are light snacks and infrared camcorders. My friend Elizabeth has joined me for this tour, and we wait along with the other guests—there are maybe twelve of us total—who range from college age to mid-forties, and altogether we are a fair enough cross section of the general population. It's hard to read the faces of the other people on the tour, or discern their interest in ghosts or this house. As we settle in and munch on our celery sticks and slightly stale cookies, the guide gives us a brief rundown on the history of the house. In our hands are ordinary camcorders to which infrared rigs have been attached, and we're instructed how best to hold them so our arms won't get tired, as well as other basic tips, such as don't pan too fast through a room or the image will blur, and don't look through the viewfinder while going up or down stairs or you'll get vertigo.

After the guide finishes with the instructions, we gather our equipment and head toward the stairs. You feel a bit dizzy, but you tell yourself it's probably because you're looking through the infrared camera's viewfinder too much. Your feet feel a bit unsteady, but that's probably because, after more than a hundred years, the staircase and the floors have begun to slope slightly as the foundation of the house has become uneven. All your hairs are standing on end—probably, you tell yourself, from the storm outside. It's time to go upstairs.

Ghost hunts without technological devices these days are almost unheard of; one could almost say that ghosts don't exist without the technology that records them. But though the devices have gotten more complex, the spirit world has long been intertwined with technology. Four years before the Fox sisters' rapping, Samuel F. B. Morse demonstrated the first use of the telegraph; despite its very straightforward technical workings, here was a machine that could send and receive disembodied messages over great distances—as though they'd come from another world. The parallels between Spiritualism and telegraphy were immediately drawn, and early publications, such as the *Spiritual Telegraph*, attested to this very simple analogy: just as the telegraph could send and receive over great distances, the Spiritualist could send and receive across the divide of life and death. The raps of the Fox sisters, after all, were themselves a form of Morse code. Media and medium were two sides of the same coin.

It's not that a belief in ghosts began in 1848, of course, but the Spiritualist revolution reformulated *how* we believed in ghosts. No longer were they purely emanations of terror; now a direct communication with the dead could be established through technology. This has largely continued through all subsequent technological advancements: nearly every major communication technology has sooner or later been appropriated by ghost seekers.

There is photography, of course: pioneered just prior to the telegraph, it came into its own in the second half of the nineteenth century and became one of the prime means of documenting ghosts (though from the very beginning the veracity of spirit photos was questioned by skeptics). Radio and television, too, were seen as receptors for spirit messages from the beginning, with ghosts frequently discerned through static and failed connections. The introduction of consumer magnetic tape recordings in the 1940s and '50s spurred yet another revolution in communicating with

ghosts; with recording now significantly cheaper and more portable, analog tape (with its added bonus of tape hiss and other audio imperfections)
put the voices of the dead in the hands of the masses.

In the late 1950s Swedish painter and documentary filmmaker Friedrich Jürgenson decided to record birds singing in his garden; while playing
back the recording, he unexpectedly heard on the tape the voice of his
dead mother calling his name. He spent years making further recordings
and researching the technique before publishing *Radio Contact with the
Dead* in 1967. Jürgenson's work was followed and greatly expanded by
Latvian psychologist Konstantin Raudive, who published his extensive
documentation of EVPs in his *Unhörbares wird Hörbar* (The Inaudible
Made Audible), published in English in 1971 as *Breakthrough: An Amazing
Experiment in Electronic Communication with the Dead*. Raudive reported his
lengthy experiments with EVP and transcribed some of the more disturbing communications he received. "Here is night brothers, here the birds
burn," one voice told him one night. Another came through the wire to tell
him: "Secret reports . . . it is bad here."

Raudive claimed that his work would lead "to empirically provable reality with a factual background," but skeptics point to the degree of leeway
he gave his spirit voices in their attempts to communicate. He explained
that spirits talked in multiple languages, even in the same sentence; that
they could speak in languages they hadn't known in life; and that they
sometimes spoke backward. Considering all these allowances, it's not terribly surprising that Raudive could discern so much chatty conversation
from the dead. If you're looking for spirit voices, you can find them in just
about any string of gibberish or noise if you listen hard enough.*

Perhaps it's less important *whether* one believes than *why* he believes.
Jürgenson used EVP as many Spiritualists did: to contact lost loved ones,

---

*As the media theorist Jeffrey Sconce put it in his *Haunted Media* (p. 87), "Such difficulties
testify either to the genuinely mysterious complexity of spiritual communications or to the
number of allowances Raudive was willing to make to convince himself of the reality of such
communications."

to be reassured that they were okay and in a better place. The search for ghosts often takes this form: of a kind of mourning, a working through of grief and loss. We look for the ghosts of those whose deaths we have not yet gotten over, as though we need their blessings to let them pass on.

There is no sense of grief or loss—at least nothing outwardly visible—in any of the people climbing the Lemp Mansion's stairs with me. If anything, the vibe is of veiled thrill seeking and vague curiosity. Near the top of the stairs is the Elsa Lemp Suite, where I'll be staying the night in a few short hours. Elsa was the youngest of William Sr. and Julia Lemp's eight children, born in 1883, when Julia was forty-one years old. Elsa married the vice president of a metal company, Thomas Wright, in 1910, but by all accounts the marriage was troubled. After losing their only daughter in childbirth, Elsa filed for divorce in 1919, citing mental anguish and abandonment. After their separation, Elsa, the wealthiest woman in St. Louis, changed her will to write Thomas out of it entirely. But just thirteen months later they were reunited and they remarried on March 8, 1920. Twelve days later Elsa killed herself with a single self-inflicted gunshot wound to the heart.

The unassuming suite that bears her name, hers when she was a child, looks out to the north, with St. Louis spilling out before it. But though Elsa succumbed to the same "curse" as did her brothers and father, you will not find her ghost here. She died in her own home, at 13 Hortense Place, some seven miles from the Lemp Mansion. The ghosts that haunt this room date from a period in the mid-twentieth century when the house was used as overflow housing for a local pediatric hospital. The spirits of terminally ill children, they've been known to engage in mischievous behavior: pulling at the sheets while guests are trying to sleep or tugging at their legs as if they were by their feet.

Nearly every room in the house, it turns out, has a story. In Charles Lemp's bedroom, sometimes small items will move about the room without warning. In another bedroom, a smell of raw sewage sometimes emanates from nowhere, indicating that the spirits of the house don't like you. Through the hallways roams the spirit of a young child whose identity has never been completely verified. A shadowy figure lurks in the basement, and an unknown man has been seen sitting down for a meal in the first-floor dining room, only to vanish when approached. With this many stories, I half expect a scene out of Disneyland's Haunted Mansion, with rooms of translucent figures cavorting and mischief making—but so far, even with the spooky weather outside, we've seen nothing.

Then at some point I find myself alone in the Elsa Lemp Suite while the other guests are investigating other rooms. All the lights on the floor have been shut off, and the only way to see anything is through the infrared camera. I run the camera over the room, pausing on a small window air conditioner that's rumbling slightly under the stress of keeping the room cool. As I hold my camera on the window, a strange light moves across it, a wave of light that holds, then passes by and disappears.

It could have been car headlights passing by outside, except that I'm on the third floor and the light would have to have been coming from behind me, where there are no windows or other sources of light. No one is nearby that I can see, and no other explanation offers itself. I keep the camera focused on the air conditioner, seeing whether the phenomenon will repeat itself. For a minute I watch the machine soldier on stoically, but the light doesn't reappear and nothing else happens.

Viewing a dark mansion through an infrared lens is undeniably eerie, no matter who you are. The realm of otherwise mundane objects takes on a pall. People's irises turn ghostly white, so that the folks standing next to you—living, breathing, and very much alive—look like hollowed-out zombies. Things that are still in normal light pulse faintly in infrared; they seem like they could come alive at any moment.

It's not just the infrared; walking around the mansion, I see how the viewfinder of a camera can change the landscape. The way a camera can single out a specific object for our attention makes us presume that something specific is going to happen. The more ordinary the object and the longer the wait, the more our expectations heighten. You tense up.

Horror movie premises so often involve a perfectly innocuous object turned malevolent—a house, a toy, a child.* I discover that holding the camera for a long five seconds on an object is usually enough to make it unnerving, and I begin to question the light that I saw playing out over the air conditioner. Perhaps it was just my expectation of something, but standing alone in a pitch-black room of an old mansion, with nothing for illumination but an infrared camera, thunder rolling through the distance—it becomes unnerving very quickly.

We're now on the second floor, in one of the large middle bedrooms. Because houses were taxed based on the number of bedrooms, the Lemp Mansion, as was the custom at the time, has overly large bedrooms separated in the middle by pocket doors (once the doors were fully closed, two bedrooms could be had for the price of one). Supposedly ghost hunters have gotten strong electromagnetic pulse (EMP) readings from the center of this room, supposedly this is significant, supposedly the distant sound of a dog can be heard on some recordings. The infrared cameras, we're told, can pick up organic matter that's otherwise invisible on carpets. And sure enough, panning a camera down to the floor reveals stains in blotches and clumps. This is the room where apparently Charles Lemp shot his dog, and it's strange to look down and see beneath your feet what looks like the poor animal's blood, as though it was killed only yesterday.

But it's probably not blood: without the camera, the stains look more like ground-in dirt than spectral blood. Despite the great legends of the Lemp Mansion, it becomes clear that the terrifying experience always happens on some other tour, some other time.

---

*Among my favorites in this genre is 1983's *De Lift,* a Dutch film about a haunted, murderous elevator, with the tagline "Take the stairs, take the stairs. For God's sake, take the stairs!!!"

It's at this point that my friend Elizabeth reveals a secret: if you toggle your infrared lights on and off while standing near someone else, the interference will cause orbs and shadows to appear on the person's video. You can, in other words, create your own ghosts. The light I saw moving across the air conditioner in the Elsa Lemp Suite may very well have been this. Perhaps someone passed by me in the hallway while I wasn't looking, and some unintended interference on their part was enough to create a momentary play of light—one that I was all too ready to accept as paranormal.

No matter how hard we look, it seems, the ghosts won't materialize on demand. Why should they? Moving through these rooms supposedly haunted by the Lemp family, the other people on the tour are eagerly hunting for orbs and shadows, evidence of the ghostly presence of the Lemps and their supernatural curse. But it seems equally plausible to read their story as a history of family mental illness, perhaps a clinical depression or bipolar condition passed down through William Sr.'s genes to his doomed children, children who lacked the cultural or medical support to combat this neurological condition. The tragedies of the Lemp Mansion might have been entirely a matter of brain chemistry, attributable to nothing other than a lack of timely medical intervention.

In 1901 a man in a black suit entered a downtown jewelry store and identified himself as William Lemp, Jr. He asked for the largest sunburst diamond in the store, then told the owner, "I will take it with me now, and you may send the bill to the brewery." He pawned the diamond and was never heard from again. In 1915, according to historian Davidson Mullgardt, a woman named Mrs. Fannie Zell had herself sent flowers from Billy, Charles, and their brother Edwin Lemp to convince others that she had admirers among the rich and powerful.

And then there's the curious case of Andrew Paulsen, who appeared in St. Louis in 2010 claiming to be one of the last living descendants of the Lemp family. He had a key to the Lemp mausoleum, along with a painting by Louise Lemp (one of Billy's nieces and an established artist) and other assorted memorabilia, including housewares he claimed were from the family, which he began selling on eBay. "Our desire and passion is to let the wonderful people of St. Louis and the world know there is a Lemp descendant who is willing to share never before told stories of the famous Lemp family of St. Louis," his business partner, Cheryl Sochotsky, wrote on their Web site, Lemp Treasures. He began giving tours of sites in St. Louis and attracted admirers among those obsessed with the Lemp family.

But in short order Paulsen's story began to unravel. The woman he claimed was his mother—Anne-Marie Konta, granddaughter of Annie Lemp (Elsa's eldest sister)—died in 1973, thirteen years before Paulsen was born. As people began asking questions, he was unable to provide anything like proof that he actually descended from the Lemp family. When *St. Louis Magazine* reporter Jeannette Cooperman asked him for some kind of confirmation, he stonewalled, then threatened legal action. Why someone would concoct an elaborate fiction solely to hawk some meaningless housewares online for a few bucks is a mystery, but just one more example of someone trying to capitalize on the long, sad history of the Lemp family.

It does speak to the aura surrounding the family, which has not diminished along with their fortunes. In some ways, the dramatic ending of Poe's "Fall of the House of Usher" seems overly optimistic and convenient: with Roderick's death and the end of the family line, the house falls into the swamp and the name vanishes as well. In reality, decline is much messier, and even though the House of Lemp has lost its former glory, the house and the name still linger, drawing an odd breed of revenants along with the ghost seekers.

After the tour one of the dining room servers stops us in the hall. "Did you see anything?" she asks, excited. She has been working here for only three weeks and hasn't experienced any haunted moments, though she's hoping to. She has no doubt in her mind that the house is haunted; after all, she's seen ghosts all her life. She was seven or eight, she says, when she first saw one, on her family's land, which had once been a plantation: a young girl, pale, running, terrified, always returning near her birthday. The server didn't ever try to figure out what the story was: "I figured it wasn't my business. She wasn't hurting anyone." Her face now is full of excitement: how lucky we are to have had the chance to commune with the spirits in such a legendary place. How could we have failed to see at least one?

Spend enough time debunking the legends associated with haunted places, trying to see past it all—the marketing, the dubious electronic devices, and all the other trappings—and you sometimes forget how real, and how persistent, the belief in ghosts is for many of us. A belief that in various ways, and for various people, gives an explanation and a meaning to experiences that can't be explained away easily. A belief that can help us mourn and give us hope.

The hunt finally over, I retrieve my bags from the foyer and head back up to the Elsa Lemp Suite, hoping for a good night's sleep in the most haunted room of the most haunted mansion in the country. By now I've been awake for almost nineteen hours, having woken up at four thirty in the morning to make my flight to St. Louis. I am thoroughly exhausted, and though I toy with the idea of staying up to see what happens through the night, the truth is, I pass out in minutes. If ghosts swarmed about me that night, they did not trouble my sleep.

II

AFTER HOURS

bars, restaurants, hotels,
and brothels

ouses are by no means the only haunted places in America. Hotels, bars, bookstores, restaurants—all manner of businesses, really—also attract the supernatural. If a haunted house is unnerving because homes represent safety and security that's upturned by the presence of a ghost, the haunted business is the inverse of this: the place where *we* are the ones who don't belong—places we pass through, spending a great deal of time in without ever thinking of them as "home."

A hotel room, for example, is meant to mimic your own bedroom: bed, television, nightstand—it's all there. But it's not yours: not your bed, not your chair, not your taste in tasteful art. You're only the latest in a long string of folks who have slept on those sheets and used those towels, a fact hotels (at least the nice ones) take great pains to hide from you. Hotels are *unheimlich* in the truest sense of the word: like a home but stubbornly not.

The ghosts of the Stanley Hotel in Estes Park, Colorado, like to remind you that you're not the first to stay there. If the guidebooks are to be believed, guests have reported spectral figures in tuxedos and 1920s-era gowns moving about the hallways and ballrooms, raising champagne toasts and carousing through the night. Built in 1909 by industrialist

Freelan O. Stanley (creator, with his twin brother, of the Stanley Steamer automobile), his namesake hotel was advertised as the first to "heat, light, and cook meals exclusively with electricity" and offered opulence and mountain air to the well heeled. A four-story Colonial Revival nestled among the mountains just outside Rocky Mountain National Park, the hotel has seen its share of ups and downs over the years but has always been a popular destination for those seeking luxury in the Rockies.

The stories of the hotel's haunting are in themselves unremarkable, and the kind of thing you'd hear about in dozens of hotels across the country: mysterious children running down hallways, the piano playing itself in the dead of night. That anyone cares about the Stanley's ghosts at all is thanks to the imagination of one guest in particular and the novel it spawned: *The Shining*.

Stephen King and his wife, Tabitha, came to the Stanley the night before Halloween, right as the hotel was closing for the season. "We found ourselves the only guests in the place—with all those long, empty corridors," King writes. Alone in an old hotel, he was inspired. "Except for our table all the chairs were up on the tables. So the music is echoing down the hall, and, I mean, it was like God had put me there to hear that and see those things."

That sense of emptiness is key to a good haunting. Few things are more unsettling than being somewhere emptied out, after everyone else has left. If you've ever worked a closing shift, or as a security guard, you know the way a place can change after the doors are locked and the lights are dimmed, when the lighting so carefully designed to spotlight the latest gadgets goes slack, when the mood lighting gets moodier. It's as though you don't belong there. The Moravian Book Shop in Bethlehem, Pennsylvania—the oldest bookstore in the country, founded in 1745—has a ghost that manifests only after closing. A longtime employee, Jane Clugston, told *The Guardian* that she saw a dark figure in a back hallway of the bookstore one night as she was closing up. The figure walked into the kitchen, and Clugston followed her, only to discover that the stove and fan had been left on. "I don't know why this person, ghost, spirit drew us back there, but I guess to turn off those appliances," Clugston said. "I'd never thought of it until I told someone else and they said a ghost led you back there. But in that back hallway a lot of people have said that they've felt things and they've seen things." As with King's story of his time at the Stanley, things get eerie when the lights go down.

Once you start looking for them, you notice that haunted businesses can come in all shapes and sizes—even brightly lit, happy places that sell toys. Though I grew up near the Winchester Mystery House, the haunted spot where I spent far, far more time as a child was down the road in the opposite direction. The Toys "R" Us in Sunnyvale, California, has a long history of haunting, all of which revolves around a former ranch hand who died pining for his true love. Johnny Johnson, as he's known, worked on Martin Murphy's massive wheat plantation, on land that's now the city of Sunnyvale. He was killed in some sort of machinery accident in 1884, when the artery in his leg was severed and he bled to death on the spot where the toy store was eventually built, and now he floats amid the board games and stuffed animals, setting off remote-controlled cars and spilling basketballs.

Reports of Johnson's ghost have fluctuated since the toy store was built in the early 1970s; he was popular in the late '70s and again in the early '90s. As the landscape around it has changed through the years, the store has sat alone, unchanged by time or renovation. A stucco brick of a store, with no windows and only a few sets of doors, it might as well be an Egyptian tomb, sealed to the external world, if not for the iconic, brightly colored letters inviting children of all ages into its darkened doors. A former employee delightfully named Putt-Putt O'Brien told the *Chicago Tribune* in 1991 that she saw Johnson's ghost once. She described him as a young man, likely in his twenties or thirties. Wearing a work shirt, knickers, and a gray tweed snap-brim cap, Johnson walked past her once while she was working. She also told the paper that she'd heard horses galloping through the store.

"He's a classic case of a ghost caught in a time warp," says Sylvia Browne, a world-renowned psychic who has made her name investigating places like my local Toys "R" Us. "He's hard at work at his handyman job, tending to the Martin Murphy ranch that thrived on the same land a hundred years ago. He can't figure out for the life of him (excuse the expression) where all these loud, rambunctious children keep coming from who tear up his freshly planted vegetables, having no clue that the children are actually playing up and down the aisles of the toy store that sits there today." According to Browne, Johnson had fallen in love with his boss's daughter, Elizabeth Murphy, and was heartbroken when she married an East Coast lawyer and left for Boston. A short time later, he gravely injured his leg in the accident that killed him, and now his ghost limps through the toy store's aisles, still tending to work he believes is left undone.

Browne's fame is bound up in Johnson's, since Browne hosted a séance in the Sunnyvale Toys "R" Us in the late '70s specifically to commune with him. She had been giving psychic readings for only a few years at the time, and the ghost of Johnny Johnson—and the subsequent attention the event attracted—helped jump-start her career. In an infrared photo taken during the séance, one can see the cluster of people gathered around in a circle, their bodies colored white and gray, as one would expect of warm bodies caught in infrared. Standing at the edge of the group, a figure leans against the wall; his hands might be in his pockets, or it could be that his thumbs are hooked in his belt loops in stereotypical cowboy fashion. Unlike the warm, light bodies of the people in the foreground, the figure in the distance appears to have no body heat whatsoever—he is an almost completely black silhouette.

In an age when anyone can digitally manipulate a photograph in seconds, it's easy to dismiss how captivating such a photo could be, ostensibly offering definitive "proof" of a spirit. It helps that infrared photography is often misunderstood by the public. One might assume, for example, that the figure in back is black because he's not giving off any body heat, but infrared film isn't the same as thermal imaging and doesn't capture heat. Whoever this figure is, he's likely simply too far from any available light source to be reflecting any infrared waves back at the camera. A simpler explanation, to be sure, if also a lot less fun.

The whole event, including the mysterious photograph, was featured on the 1980s TV show *That's Incredible*, establishing the fame of both Browne and Sunnyvale's Toys "R" Us. Coming at the dawn of the syndicated daytime talk show, Browne came to popularity in a tabloid-hungry era when media outlets were more and more willing to showcase fringe beliefs in order to give their audiences something salacious. The story also gained traction because it suggested that *anywhere* could be haunted—not just creepy old Victorian mansions or derelict graveyards. Even a seemingly anodyne toy store might have a deeper story. (As if to prove the point, in the wake of Sunnyvale's fame, numerous other Toys "R" Us stores, from San Bernardino, California, to North Bergen, New Jersey, have also been known to house spirits.)

Browne went on to become a best-selling author who, by the end of her career, was charging hundreds of dollars for psychic readings and appearing regularly on *The Montel Williams Show* to communicate with the beyond. But paranormal reports involving Browne might best be taken with a grain of salt. Though she often claimed to have helped law enforcement with missing persons cases, independent analyses of her work have determined that her advice was always either too vague to be useful, of no help at all, or an actual hindrance to investigations. She developed a notorious record of being wrong, telling families that their missing loved ones were alive when they were already dead and vice versa.

She never forgot Johnny Johnson, though, and made regular trips to the Toys "R" Us to stay in touch. According to her 2003 book *Visits from the Afterlife*, she repeatedly tried to convince Johnson that he was dead and that if he wanted to be reunited with his lost love, all he had to do was "go to the light of God that was waiting for him." But Johnson had no interest in following her advice: "He got so tired of hearing it that one day he snapped at me and said, 'If you don't stop telling me I'm dead, I'm never going to talk to you again.' I decided that keeping the lines of communication open between us was better than nothing, so I've never mentioned it again."

An informal poll I took of workers at the Toys "R" Us in December of 2015 confirmed that nearly everyone who works there is aware of the ghost of Johnny Johnson, but no one I spoke to claimed to have personally seen anything of him. I myself can't recall any paranormal sightings from my childhood visits. But I would have felt differently, I think, had I stayed the night and participated in a séance, particularly a séance filmed for national television. Primed for something to happen, expectant and a little on edge, in a building you only ever see during business hours that's now darkened and newly unfamiliar—it's natural that noises and lights in the dark would take on new meaning.

Commercial spaces are designed to be navigated in a very specific way, to entice a purchase and then to facilitate customers getting out of there. There are myriad techniques, refined through decades of research, to accomplish this: fast food uses bright colors—mainly red and yellow—which work to activate hunger and grab your attention; furniture showrooms like IKEA use their layouts to guide you through a scripted experience; big-box retailers line the checkout aisles with impulse buys. Perhaps, most obviously, one thinks of casinos, where every detail is managed to create a specific kind of psychological effect once you step inside the doors. Some proponents have long argued for casino layouts that are dark and confusing, that encourage a labyrinthine disorientation so as to keep people gambling and discourage them from leaving. Others favor a bright, airy landscape with high-end decor to give players a sense that they are themselves high rollers and embolden them to spend lavishly. Either way, what's clear is the amount of energy devoted to using a building's architecture, layout, decor, music, even scent, to craft a specific, highly engineered experience.

It's when this script breaks down that we start to see ghosts. They over-run places like the RMS *Queen Mary*, built to embody the grand opulence of an age, now a struggling tourist attraction in the harbor of Long Beach, California. It's operated mostly as a hotel these days, going through a suc-cession of owners who've yet to make a profit on the enterprise. When my wife and I stayed on the *Queen Mary* one summer Sunday night, we found its ornate detail still relatively intact, including the lovely Observation Bar and Art Deco Lounge. There, deep wood fixtures are overseen by a back-lit mural of Jazz Age flappers, and plush red leather chairs offer a glimpse of an age of glamour long past. On a ship from the 1930s, designed for opulence and for more than two thousand passengers, we walked the halls encountering almost no one else except a few who did occasionally material-ize, jarringly out of place in shorts and flip-flops. Like the Stanley Hotel, closed up for the season, the *Queen Mary* seems to be waiting for some-thing, though for her the spring will never arrive.

Ghosts move into places such as these: businesses that have fallen on hard times, places where the façade has started to fall away.

CHAPTER SIX

A DEVILISH PLACE

Richmond, VA

There are ghosts everywhere in the historic Shockoe Bottom neighborhood of Richmond, Virginia. The upscale restaurant Julep's is thought to be haunted by the ghost of a gunsmith's apprentice, Daniel Denoon. His boss, James McNaught, shot Denoon over a disagreement while Denoon was climbing the stairs. The staircase his body fell down was later converted into a storage closet, but employees report hearing the thump of a body falling in it from time to time. Tiki Bob's Cantina, a bar on Eighteenth Street, is now closed, but in its heyday it was home to bikini contests, Jell-O wrestling—and the spirit of a knife-wielding fishmonger.

At the ornate Main Street train station, workmen and security guards have heard footsteps through the empty halls late at night. Next door Rosie Connolly's Pub is haunted by several ghosts: one, a woman in period dress who vanishes when confronted; another, a man often seen in the kitchen, whose past is similarly unknown. Over on East Cary Street the building standing between Fourteenth and Fifteenth streets is supposedly built on the site of a brothel that dates back to the early 1800s; on its upper floors spectral women clad in gauzy dresses wander. Staff are known to hear their names called, only to turn and find no one there.

It's hard to find a building in Shockoe Bottom that *doesn't* have a ghost story attached to it. Local historian and paranormal investigator Pamela Kinney speculates that this is because Virginia was home to the earliest settlements in North America. Which makes sense so long as we all agree that by "settlements" we really mean "settlements of Europeans." Which is to say, the kinds of ghosts you look for, and the kinds of ghosts you see, depend on your frame of reference. For when I began to tally the supernatural records of the area at the heart of Richmond, a simple fact emerged: the ghosts of Shockoe Bottom are overwhelmingly white.

This is curious, because if you walk just a little way away from the haunted bars and shops, down by the freeway you'll find the Devil's Half Acre. For decades black men, women, and children were brought here, imprisoned, and tortured while they waited to be sold to planters and speculators. Dozens of slave traders had offices here, where slave auctions were widely advertised and men came from all over the South to make their fortunes on the backs of those enslaved. Tens of thousands of men's and women's lives changed hands here in the years leading up to the Civil War; all the activity centered on Wall Street, in the heart of Shockoe Bottom. Today Wall Street is gone, replaced by the freeway, though the rest of the area remains mostly unchanged. While it's difficult to estimate how many people lost their lives in the slave pens of Shockoe Bottom, hundreds of sets of human remains have been found in the nearby slave burial ground.

We typically think of ghost stories in terms of the remnants of a terrible tragedy, a past we cannot escape, or a justice unavenged. Why, then, in a place that should be so haunted by the legacy of such a terrible injustice, the scene of countless deaths, should there be nothing but white ghosts?

Given its low elevation and proximity to the James River, the Bottom became an ideal place for trading, easily facilitating the loading and unloading of cargo. Alongside tobacco, cotton, and other goods, slavers traded men, women, and children. After the transatlantic slave trade was banned, in 1808, traffic in enslaved individuals in Richmond actually increased; after New Orleans, this was the most heavily trafficked slave trading area in the United States.

In the decades leading up to the Civil War, much of the South was sick with "Alabama Fever," the idea that any (white) person could get rich by buying frontier land and putting enslaved people to work with cotton—a fever from which Northern traders, even those who on the surface were fervently opposed to slavery, nonetheless benefited greatly.

The human capital that was lost here in Shockoe Bottom is staggering. Only New Orleans had a larger volume of human beings been bought, sold, or hired out for temporary work. What's more, Richmond was first in the nation for slavery-related price manipulation and futures speculation. It was, in other words, not just where men, women, and children were bought and sold but where the entire economic foundation of the industry of slavery was built.

The cruelty on display in Shockoe Bottom was starkly evident to foreign visitors. In 1842 Charles Dickens came to Richmond on a tour of America, and despite being taken with the city itself, "delightfully situated on eight hills," he was horrified by the barbaric acts he witnessed at Shockoe. In his *American Notes* he excoriated the men and women who profited from Richmond's slave trade, namely

owners, breeders, users, buyers and sellers of slaves, who will, until the bloody chapter has a bloody end, own, breed, use, buy, and sell them at all hazards: who doggedly deny the horrors of the system in the teeth of such a mass of evidence as never was brought to bear on any other subject, and to which the experience of every day contributes its immense amount; who would at this or any other moment, gladly involve America in a war, civil or foreign, provided that it had for its sole end and object the assertion of their right to perpetuate slavery, and to whip and work and torture slaves, unquestioned by any human authority, and unassailed by any human power.

As Dickens rightly noted, such people, when they speak of "freedom," "mean the Freedom to oppress their kind, and to be savage, merciless, and cruel."

"The exposure of ordinary goods in a store is not more open to the public than are the sales of slaves in Richmond," remarked Frederick Law Olmsted, the great architect behind New York's Central Park. While touring Richmond in the 1850s, he happened upon a commission agent's office, empty save for

> three negro children, who, as I entered, were playing at auctioneering each other. An intensely black little negro, of four or five years of age, was standing on the bench, or block, as it is called, with an equally black girl, about a year younger, by his side, whom he was pretending to sell by bids to another black child, who was rolling about the floor. My appearance did not interrupt the merriment. The little auctioneer continued his mimic play, and appeared to enjoy the joke of selling the girl, who stood demurely by his side.

Among those unfortunate enough to find themselves imprisoned in such a hell was Solomon Northup, a freed Northerner who was kidnapped and sold into slavery. As he later recounted in *Twelve Years a Slave* (later adapted into an Oscar-winning motion picture), Northup was held in Richmond on his way from Washington, D.C., where he'd been kidnapped, to New Orleans, where he'd later be sold. He described how, on reaching Richmond, he and his fellow captives "were taken from the cars, and driven through the street to a slave pen, between the railroad depot and the river, kept by a Mr. Goodin." Northup describes a surreal scene, one where "there were two small houses standing at opposite corners within the yard. These houses are usually found within slave yards, being used as rooms for the examination of human chattels by purchasers before concluding a bargain."

Northup soon found himself chained to a man named Robert, "a large yellow man, quite stout and fleshy, with a countenance expressive of the utmost melancholy. He was a man of intelligence and information." Robert had been born free, like Northup, but had been "seized at Fredericksburgh, placed in confinement, and beaten until he had learned, as I had, the necessity and the policy of silence. He had been in Goodin's pen about three weeks." Northup did not stay long in Richmond before being moved farther south, to New Orleans. By this point Virginia had less need for slave labor for its own sake, and Richmond functioned more as a market for buying and selling people, like Northup, who would end up in the South and the West.

At the center of this activity was slave trader Robert Lumpkin's jail complex. To reach his half acre of land, you had to either descend a sandy, irregular embankment from Broad Street that descended dangerously down one hundred feet to the floor of the Bottom, or enter via Franklin Avenue, an untidy, crooked lane that worked its way down. Lumpkin's house on the property was bordered by a fence that stretched ten—in some places twelve—feet high. Nearby were several squat brick buildings where he kept enslaved men and women waiting to be sold. In the center of the complex, its focal point—a nightmare of torture and misery—was the low, rough brick building that served as Lumpkin's jail.

As abolitionist minister James B. Simmons would later remember, "In this building Lumpkin was accustomed to imprison the disobedient and punish the refractory. The stout iron bars were still to be seen across one or more of the windows during my repeated visits to this place. In the rough floor, and at about the center of it, was the stout iron staple and whipping ring."

Accounts like this, from foreign observers, from the enslaved men and women who spent time here, and from the wardens themselves, helped cement Lumpkin's jail as a truly horrific place. Among the many who were whipped in it was the Reverend Armstead Mason Newman, who was taken to the jail in 1862, when he was just a child. "On the floor of that room were rings," he later recalled; his hands and feet were stretched out and tied to the rings, leaving him spread-eagled and facedown on the floor, while a "great big man" stood over him and flogged him.

Simmons referred to the complex as a "place of sighs." In its time it was known more generally—throughout the country—as the Devil's Half Acre.

In their collection of ghost stories, *Haunted Richmond: The Shadows of Shockoe*, Scott and Sandi Bergman write of Shockoe Bottom's rich and complicated history, particularly as "the epicenter of some of the most profound and tragic events in United States, Virginia, and Richmond history." But in their subsequent list of these tragic events, slavery is absent: "The area surrounding the Shockoe Valley has been the backdrop for the destruction of indigenous peoples, a revolution, the birth of a nation, foreign and domestic wars, famine, disease, floods, fires and engineering disasters, to name some of the causes of turmoil, tragedy and trauma experienced in the capital city." After recounting the ghost stories of Rosie Connolly's Pub, the bar housed in the building once known as the Railroad YMCA, the Bergmans confess, "We have been able to find very little in the way of historical details of the Railroad YMCA that might help explain the identity of the reported ghosts." And yet the land where the pub stands is steps from the former site of the Charles Hotel—where many traders, including auctioneers Benjamin and Solomon Davis, had their offices—and mere yards from Lumpkin's Jail.

Rather than explore this complicated history and whether the ghosts of Rosie Connolly's Pub might be related to the tragedy of slavery, the Bergmans tell stories mostly of mass-casualty accidents: the collapse of the Statehouse gallery in 1870 that killed sixty-two people and wounded another two hundred; the fire at the Old Richmond Theatre on December 23, 1811, that killed seventy-two; the Church Hill Tunnel Collapse in 1925 that killed four. "If a premature exit from this world is the primary reason for paranormal activity," they note, "then it is no wonder that there are so many shadows to be found in Shockoe." In Shockoe there is a hierarchy of shadows: those known to ghost hunters, whose stories are told to tourists, and those allowed to slip unseen into the fog of forgetting.

Ghost stories and haunted tales connect us to the past, to family and to our ancestors. The ghost stories of the South, particularly those that reach back to the antebellum era, establish a through line in a property or a place, giving our surroundings a depth and a richness that go beyond the present moment. As supernatural beings, spirits often come to represent some universal truth of the past. They turn space into time and can be a way of making a place stand for some transcendental value or universal ideal.

A good case in point is Thomas Jefferson, whose ghost can be found haunting his home, Monticello. There the president is heard whistling in the corridors or seen seated at his writing desk as the ghosts of his beloved mockingbirds flutter in cages around him. Tourists and workers on the property have spotted him in the entrance hall, eyeing distinguished guests, or beside his wife, Martha, at the dining room table, exuding charm and goodwill. Jefferson's ghost is not in pain, nor is he anguished by some injustice never addressed. He is serene, patriarchal, and benevolent. His reassuring presence, real or imagined, connects us to the past, giving guests a sense of what it was like to live at Monticello two hundred years ago.

Of course, Jefferson did not live there alone; Monticello was populated by slaves. Despite his love of liberty and his eloquence in defending it, and despite the myriad apologists over the years who've attempted to mitigate or downplay his slave owning, Jefferson's treatment of his slaves remains an inexcusable aspect of his legacy. He was never particularly shy or embarrassed about being a slave owner, as many others were; on the contrary, he repeatedly laid out lengthy justifications for the practice. In 1821 Jefferson lamented that "we have the wolf by the ears, and we can neither hold him, nor safely let him go"; if not for the traffic and exchange of slaves throughout the South, he worried, the enslaved would rise up and overthrow their white captors. Diffusing slaves' numbers over as wide an area as possible was the only means of keeping whites alive. "Justice is in one scale," he wrote, "and self-preservation in the other." As Tiya Miles notes in her book *Tales from the Haunted South*, the consuming horror that animated most whites was "not a fear of ghosts but a fear of black rebellion." The only way to keep alive the white world of Southern belles and elegant gentlemen was to deny the humanity of black people: their names, their identities, their families.

An advocate for liberty and equality, and yet a slaveholder, Jefferson embodies the contradiction of early America, particularly of the South. And for all its architectural beauty, Monticello bears the ineradicable stain of its origins in slave labor. Indeed, in 2002 archaeological evidence of a graveyard for Monticello's slaves was discovered at the edge of the south parking lot, some two thousand feet from the main house. Monticello does now offer tours specifically addressing the plantation's slaves, but so far no reports have emerged of any of these Americans reaching out from the afterlife.

If ghost stories depend on an ongoing oral tradition, passed from one anonymous source to another, embellished and refined through the telling, then they can only ever reflect the knowledge and the folklore of the people telling them. Does an absence of these ghost stories suggest that there is still, over a century later, a lacuna in the culture's memory, a taboo about its past, a refusal to discuss certain things? What does it mean to whitewash the spirits of a city? Does Virginia have ghosts that it is still not ready to face?

The absence of black ghosts at Monticello is not unusual; you're not likely to find them in most places in the South. The Myrtles Plantation's Chloe is a rarity, and ghosts like her are vastly outnumbered by whiter shades. There's a kind of effacement here, which in the end is not terribly surprising, since the work of slavery, after all, was to destroy the interior lives of those enslaved, marginalize their humanity, render them nothing but empty bodies. Slavers learned early on that the best way to keep the machinery of slavery in motion, and to make as high a profit as possible, was to break the individual into a series of component parts: height, age, price. In New Orleans one trader advised a new plantation owner, "It is better to buy none in families, but to select only choice, first rate, young hands from 16 to 25 years of age (buying no children or aged negroes)."

The Africans who were kidnapped and brought to the New World had, like every culture, significant ties to their ancestors and their burial grounds and derived no small portion of their identity from these kinships. Families broken apart and moved roughshod throughout the country obliterated connections to the past and to the dead. This was not unintentional; the forced migration of enslaved people, facilitated by the massive slave markets in places like Shockoe Bottom and New Orleans, stripped people of their humanity so as to maximize their profit potential.

Funeral rites, sacred burial sites, and even ghost stories—people of all stripes use these as a means of taking the sting out of death. They're how we remind ourselves that after we're gone we won't be forgotten—a relative who tends to our gravestone and brings flowers to our grave keeps us alive year after year even after we're gone. It was precisely these kinds of rituals and rites that the slaver meant to rob his victims of, stripping them not only of their life but also of their memory in death.

The goal in all these varieties of violence was to create what historian Edward E. Baptist calls "the new zombie body of slavery": the body of the slave that could work but not feel, that would not be slowed down or deterred by such human qualities as memory, longing, despair, or fear. Slavery was designed to create bodies without souls, to exorcise out of men, women, and children their spirits, so that they would function as animate and obedient bodies.

And yet slave owners were never fully invested in completely robbing these men and women of their humanity; there were always aspects of a slave's humanity that were retained for specific political and economic purposes. The most obvious example of this was the Three-Fifths Compromise built into the U.S. Constitution, which determined a state's population by counting each slave as three-fifths of a person so as to increase the South's number of elected officials in the federal government. That slave owners could not have fully dehumanized these men and women, because they were first and foremost people, is important, but it's worth recognizing that slavery's objective was to make them both present and absent simultaneously—to enslave someone was not necessarily to efface that person entirely but to render him or her a ghost.

Here, then, is a central paradox in the way that ghosts work: to turn the living into ghosts is to empty them out, rob them of something vital; to keep the dead alive as ghosts is to fill them up with memory and history, to keep alive a thing that would otherwise be lost.

Once you start looking for ghosts that aren't white, they're easy to find. As Baby Suggs tells Sethe in Toni Morrison's *Beloved*, "Not a house in the country that ain't packed to its rafters with some dead Negro's grief." In the 1930s workers under the Works Progress Administration began collecting stories of former slaves: everything from recollections of their day-to-day lives under slavery to questions about clothing, medicine, and firsthand accounts of slave auctions and mistreatment. The stories were compiled in seventeen states, from Indiana to Florida, and accelerated with urgency once it became clear that these firsthand accounts were quickly disappearing—more than two-thirds of the respondents were in their eighties when they were interviewed between 1936 and 1938. By the twentieth century America's understanding of the history of slavery had become tinged with nostalgia via folklore involving contented slaves and benevolent owners, emphasizing agrarian life—typified by Joel Chandler Harris's Uncle Remus folktales. The slave narratives collected by the

WPA, on the other hand, sought a more neutral approach. Allowed to speak in their own voices, those interviewed as part of this project offered a largely untold version of the antebellum landscape.

Interviewers were given a list of questions to ask, and one of them—number 13—asked specifically about ghosts. Could the respondent remember the songs and stories of their childhood? Had she heard any stories about "Raw Head and Bloody Bones" or any "other 'hants' of ghosts"? Had he personally seen ghosts? Answers to the question vary: some interview subjects didn't believe, some knew rumors of ghosts were just whites intimidating them, some spoke of ghosts as terrifying things, as comforting things, as exhausting things.

Jane Arrington of North Carolina told one WPA worker the story of John May, a slave who had been beaten to death by two white men named Bill Stone and Oliver May. After his death, she reported, "John May come back an' wurried both of 'em." He kept them awake, hollering and groaning all through the night, hounding them relentlessly. According to Arrington, it got so bad that other slaves became afraid of the white men, because the "ghost of John wurried 'em so bad."

Another respondent, George Bollinger, spoke of a haunted Benton Hill in Missouri, telling the interviewer, "One night we was driving through dere and we heard something dat sound like a woman just a screaming. Old man Ousbery was with me and he wanted to stop and see what it was but I says, 'No you don't. Drive on. You don't know what dat might be.'"

In these stories ghosts terrify, but embedded in the terror are cautionary tales. A woman named Florida Clayton recalled how, as a child, she and her peers would often see a covered wagon that would appear in Tallahassee, where she lived, always in some secluded spot. While the kids would be tempted to approach this mysterious wagon and investigate it, they were told by adults that inside was "Dry Head and Bloody Bones," a ghost "who didn't like children." Only as an adult did Clayton learn that the wagon was in fact owned by a slave hunter, who would steal children and take them to Georgia to be sold, and that her parents and other adults had invented the Dry Head and Bloody Bones ghost as a means of protecting them.

A man named Thomas Lewis of Indiana once described a "place where there is a high fence" that was haunted: "If someone gets near, he can hear the cries of the spirits of black people who were beaten to death. It is kept secret so that people won't find it out. Such places are always fenced to keep them secret." He then recounted a story: Two men were out hunting nearby, and their dog began chasing something, running through the fence after it. As one of the men started to follow, his friend asked, "What are you going to do?" The other replied, "I want to see what the dog chased back in there." His friend told him, "You'd better stay out of there. That place is haunted by spirits of black people who were beaten to death." Isabelle Daniel of Missouri recalled one haunted tobacco factory that no slave would go near after nightfall: "When the nights were still and the moon was full," she reported, "you could hear the ting, ting, ting, of the lever all night long and voices of the slaves crying out and complaining, and you knew there wasn't anybody there at all, jest hants."

Throughout, the WPA narratives reference "hags" and "witches" who would visit people at night, inhabit their bodies, and "ride" them all night, returning them in the morning. Silvia Witherspoon of Alabama put it succinctly: "How come I knows dey rides me? Honey, I bees so tired in de mawnin' I kin scarcely git outten my bed, an' its all on account of dem witches ridin' me." Ghosts steal one's capacity to work.

Again and again, these ghost stories revolve around a tenuous and threatened connection to the past. Ghosts will emerge at times through the breakdown of family. One woman in Tennessee saw the ghost of a woman appear before her while she was giving birth. Not recognizing the apparition, she called out, "Who are you?" The ghost replied, "Don't forget the old folks," then vanished. That was when the young woman realized that it was the ghost of her own mother. A man identified only as Uncle Louis spoke of ghosts in terms closer to melancholy than fear. Ghosts, he claimed, are "sociable," and they want to stay near living people. "When folks gets scared it hurts de haunt's feelin's an dey goes somewhere else." If slave owners and traders sought, in a very real way, to obliterate memory and history for those they enslaved, then melancholic ghosts like the ones Uncle Louis saw may themselves be in search of their own pasts.

Folklore always bleeds and blurs, and it would be overly reductive to state a hard and fast distinction between ghost stories told by whites and those told by the black community. There are, of course, stories of black ghosts that serve the same function as white ghosts—marking a location, explaining the unexplainable, commemorating an event. But what is clear is that history is not just written by the victors; it's written by the literate. The prohibition against enslaved Americans learning to read or write had the immediate purpose of denying them agency and keeping them under control, but in the long run it also meant that the stories, lives, and opinions of millions of Americans were lost to time.

Ghost stories, theoretically, should be an antidote to this. Based on oral tradition and handed down through the years, outside the purview of acceptable history, such folklore should—and often does—act as an alternative history, a record of the oppressed and forcibly illiterate, the marginalized.

But Shockoe Bottom's ghosts show that this isn't always the case, that precisely because ghost sightings are so ephemeral, and so vague, they can easily be attached to the dominant narrative and only that narrative.

"The legacy of Wall Street is a difficult history to commemorate, as it involves memories that are painful, controversial and unsettling," Jack Trammell wrote of the Richmond slave trade. "People are interested in battles, campaigns, and military heroics; they are not as interested in what those campaigns were fought over." And while I had assumed that ghost stories are one way to tell those stories that people don't want to hear otherwise, as it happens, they are just as often used to reinforce those blind spots.

Once one of the main economic engines of the South, Shockoe Bottom now feels hollowed out, devoid of life and real commerce. Far from the universities, it doesn't attract much in the way of a nightlife feel, though not for lack of trying. There are half a dozen bars, Thai food and by-the-slice pizza, a couple of vape shops, and a few nightclubs. Which is not to say that there haven't been attempts to revitalize the area. For years the mayor of Richmond had pushed a plan to build a new stadium for the city's minor league baseball team, the Squirrels, downtown on land adjacent to the Devil's Half Acre. Meant to draw new life into a faltering part of town, the plan succeeded mainly in drawing ire from preservationists and those worried that such a massive construction project would obliterate valuable archaeological traces of the city's past.

After the project was announced, an archaeological team largely funded by Richmond's Slave Trail Commission set out to uncover the Devil's Half Acre; through a careful study of old maps, they located the area where Lumpkin's complex had stood, some of it now partially obscured beneath the freeway. But in December 2008 excavation work through the damp and muddy ground by the James River Institute for Archaeology, under the direction of Matthew Laird, unearthed the remnants of the jail. While the team didn't find the expected implements of torture, such as whipping rings or iron chains, what it did find were unexpected hints of lives lived here—bits of tableware, including English china and earthenware and the remnants of a porcelain doll.

How does a city balance commerce with remembrance? The ghost stories that are told about Shockoe Bottom are not only harmless; they add a festive patina to the city's bars and restaurants, an air of mystery and glamour. They invite you to spend an evening with an ephemeral time just out of reach, to add a small bit of wonder to an otherwise average night out. What they don't do is speak to a past whose legacy can still traumatize. They don't ask the patrons of Richmond's nightlife to consider a complicated history; in particular they don't ask the city's white citizens and tourists to face difficult facts. For those who would rather not revisit those days, the city's ghost lore makes it easy, turning our attention to murdered gunsmiths and fabled prostitutes. But that's not to say that these other ghosts are not omnipresent. "I started weeping and couldn't stop," recalled Delores McQuinn, chairwoman of Richmond's Slave Trail Commission, when those bits of china and porcelain doll were discovered. "There was a presence here. I felt a bond. It's a heaviness that I've felt over and over again."

Nor was she the only one to feel the ghosts of those who passed through Shockoe. When Lupita Nyong'o won an Academy Award for Best Supporting Actress for her role as Patsey in *Twelve Years a Slave*, she opened her acceptance speech by invoking ghosts. "It doesn't escape me for one moment that so much joy in my life is thanks to so much pain in someone else's," she told the Los Angeles audience. "And so I want to salute the spirit of Patsey for her guidance." Then, as she thanked the film's director, Steve McQueen, she told him, "I'm certain that the dead are standing about you and watching and they are grateful and so am I."

The dead are watching, whether or not we choose to listen to their stories.

CHAPTER SEVEN

BABY

Reno, NV

Among the great tall tales of the Wild American West is that of Bella Rawhide and Timber Kate, two prostitutes who worked the brothels of Reno, Nevada, in the late nineteenth century, when money and lives ran fast and dried up quickly. Bella was blond-haired and blue-eyed, buxom and sweet, known for a routine she performed called "Eve's Leaves": she would appear onstage wearing nothing but gilt fig leaves; a patron could remove a leaf for a pinch of gold dust, and the man who removed the last leaf could take her off to bed. Timber was tall, muscular, brusque, known as much for her wild haymakers that could knock a man flat as for her talents in bed. The two were always together and claimed to be sisters, though this was a cover for their romantic relationship. In advance of their shows, Timber would plaster the town with posters advertising their act, and in the boom-and-bust towns of the West, both women got rich.

Then a deadbeat grifter named Tug Daniels came to town. Daniels had heard of Bella and Timber's success and set out to use them for all he could get. He seduced Bella first, but soon both women had fallen madly in love with him, and in jealousy they turned on each other. Rather than deal with Timber, Daniels ran away with Bella to nearby Carson City, where he pimped her out in a brothel on North Quincy Street called the Beehive. While Bella continued to rake it in, Timber fell into a depression and hard times. She tried dressing as a man and performing as a weight lifter, but this routine flopped.

After a few years Daniels stole everything Bella had saved and skipped town. Bella was heartbroken and despondent—until, that is, Timber showed up in Carson City and the two reconciled. They continued working the Beehive, and though they were back together again, Timber became increasingly worried that Bella might leave her once more. Then Tug Daniels reappeared.

Seeing the man who'd humiliated her and absconded with her love, Timber set out for revenge. The two squared off in the Beehive's parlor. Timber let loose with one of her trademark haymakers, only to have Daniels sidestep it neatly, produce a knife, and gut her savagely. As Timber Kate lay dying, Daniels fled out a back window. Not long after, Bella Rawhide killed herself by drinking a dose of cleaning fluid.

None of this story is rooted in any real fact, and even the carefully placed details that seem so specific lead only to dead ends; for one, there is no North Quincy Street in Carson City. And yet for much of the early twentieth century, people in northern Nevada claimed to see mysterious posters still advertising Timber Kate and Bella Rawhide. Those who tried to remove the posters would be met by a ghostly haymaker from the spirit of Timber Kate. Others claimed to see Timber's dying, ragged form straggling down moonlit streets, clawing at her stomach where Daniels had fatally cut her open. Bella, for her part, still haunts the building of her once-famous brothel, the Beehive—even if no one knows where it actually stood.

Kate and Bella are far from the only brothel workers who've entered the annals of hauntings in this country. The Red Onion Saloon of Skagway, Alaska, is haunted by a woman from its heyday in the late 1800s, a Lydia, about whom nothing is known but who announces her presence through the scent of strong perfume. The Dumas Brothel of Butte, Montana, claims similar spirits; reports include mirrors falling from the wall, beds that shake by themselves, and visitors touched by ghostly fingers. The Hotel Lincoln in Manns Choice, Pennsylvania, now stands as an antiques store, but ghosts of ill repute still wander its halls, disturbing tchotchkes and trinkets. And of course there is New Orleans, home to so many reputedly haunted brothels that one company gives a tour specifically devoted to them.

Why do brothels and their employees loom so large in collections of ghost stories? Perhaps it has something to do with the fact that a brothel is a secret place: mostly illegal and under the radar, its goings-on are, for the most part, hidden, and often even its location is a mystery, passed through word of mouths that have long since quieted. Any old grand house, any long-standing bar in a former boomtown, seems a likely candidate as a onetime brothel; they seem to hide in plain sight, no different from any standard hotel, bar, or mansion. The haunted building in Richmond on East Cary Street is assumed to be a brothel, but ghost hunters attribute this to rumor rather than any kind of established record. Brothels—despite being real, functioning businesses—belong to a special subterranean oral tradition, one that's highly ephemeral.

The picture of the Wild West whorehouse is one associated not just with illicit sex but also with violence: saloon brawls, depravity and revenge, disfiguring attacks (such as the one that drives the plot of Clint Eastwood's *Unforgiven*), rape and murder. Outside the reach of polite society, the brothel would seem to be a magnet for the kind of intense, violent human experience that often becomes the fodder for ghost stories and hauntings.

The Lincoln House in Manns Choice is reported to be haunted by a woman who worked there, whose enraged husband shot her one night when he discovered that she wasn't bringing in enough money. Then there is what came to be known as the Murder Bordello of Galena,

Kansas, which in the 1890s was operated by a woman known both as Nancy Wilson and as Ma Staffleback, who was convicted, along with her husband and two sons, of murdering a miner named Frank Galbraith and were ultimately implicated in the murders of upward of thirty other men.

Brothels are *liminal* (from the Latin *limins*, "threshold") places, borderland places where the traditional rules of a society are momentarily suspended. Both for good and for ill, the world of the brothel seems a world in extremis. And so perhaps no other business venture is so primed for ghost stories. The brothel, with its mix of tragedy and hiddenness, rowdy violence and erotic allure, seems the perfect place for spirits to take up residence.

In late November 2014 I was sent by a magazine to Reno to interview Lance Gilman, the owner of the most famous legal brothel in the country, the Mustang Ranch. I was there to profile him because of his role in securing a half-billion-dollar deal with the car company Tesla, which had just agreed to build a massive factory to make electric car batteries on Gilman's industrial park outside Reno. For two days I spent time with Gilman and his employees, including several working girls and the Mustang's madam, Tara Atkins. The photographer on assignment with me brought an SUV's worth of equipment, and while he was setting up an elaborate shot featuring a number of the women, I stood idly chatting with Atkins, killing time. It was then that she mentioned that the Mustang Ranch was haunted.

Not just haunted but extremely haunted.

Brothels in rural Nevada have always been tolerated, and while not explicitly illegal, they sometimes ran the risk of being shut down as "public nuisances." Joe Conforte, often described as the godfather of legalized prostitution in Nevada, bought the Mustang Ranch in 1967 from a

competitor, and in 1971, after extensive lobbying and legal battles, he finally wrangled from Storey County the first legal brothel ordinance.
From the beginning the allure of brothels for most counties was the licens-
ing fees, but there were always the citizens who saw prostitution as a blight
on the county. Alexa Albert, who lived at the Mustang Ranch for a
month as a researcher and observer in 1993 (and who later wrote a book
about her experiences), described the original brothel as "a seedy biker
bar, minus only a pool table and a pinball machine."

Just as with those Wild West saloons, trouble was at home in the
Mustang Ranch. In 1976 professional heavyweight boxer Oscar Bonavena
was killed in the parking lot. He had been brought in by Conforte to help
publicize the ranch, but in short order he began an affair with Conforte's
wife, Sally. After being banished from the Mustang, he returned on May 22
and demanded to speak to Conforte. While arguing with the guards in
the parking lot, Bonavena was shot in the heart; Conforte's bodyguard,
Willard Ross Brymer, later pled guilty to voluntary manslaughter and
spent fifteen months in prison.

Conforte managed to avoid any implication in Bonavena's death, but
he eventually ran afoul of the federal government, which charged him in
1980 with tax evasion. He fled to Brazil to escape extradition, and the
Feds subsequently seized the ranch.

By that point Lance Gilman had purchased a monstrous business park
on the edge of Reno, the Tahoe Reno Industrial Center. Storey County
desperately needed the tax revenue that brothels brought in, and announced a plan to issue new brothel licenses. Realizing that another seedy,
lawless brothel could damage the area's reputation and his plan for attract-
ing modern technology firms, Gilman went ahead and bought a license
himself and opened the Wild Horse Ranch in 2002. A few years later the
federal government auctioned off the Mustang Ranch—its name and
copyright, its assets, and the building itself—on eBay. Again seeking
to forestall unsavory competition, Gilman bought the Mustang with a

winning bid of $145,100, eventually consolidating the two brothels under one name.

Moving the Mustang Ranch required more than just cutting it up and putting it on trucks; structured as a massive octagon, its frame was too wide and unwieldy to be moved into the narrow canyon where the Wild Horse was built, so Gilman's team ultimately had to bring in much of the building via helicopter. It was reconstructed across the parking lot from the Wild Horse, and today the two buildings have an uneasy relationship.

The layout of the Wild Horse is straightforward. One walks in first to a bar (technically, it's an entirely separate business that has nothing to do with the brothel, since one can't sell liquor on the premises of a brothel in Nevada). Walking through a back door reveals a plush room made up to look like a high-end hunting lodge, with a perpetually roaring fire, overstuffed leather couches, (barely) tasteful nude paintings, and a wall of taxidermy. Under the watchful eye of a moose, a bison, and a bevy of elk are a high-tech security operation, a clinic, and a well-stocked kitchen. The only element not in keeping with this hunting lodge aesthetic is the mirrored wall, used for "lineups," in which all the women working at the moment are summoned to line up so the customer can select a favorite.

The lighting throughout is subdued but clear; there are no dingy corners, no dark passageways. There are smells of recirculated air and baby oil, which no doubt mask a number of other odors, and while it may be a stretch to call the place "cozy," it's certainly pleasant enough. It's laid out symmetrically: from the lodgelike parlor, two wings, which hold the individual bedrooms, extend out to either side; in the back is the pool, flanked by two smaller wings with "party rooms."

The original Mustang Ranch building, set at a slightly lower grade, has none of this openness. One enters into a dark, neon-lit bar, with jarring neoclassical columns wound with fake ivy. From there, hallways branch off in different directions, leading down corridors that fade into darkness.

From the outside you can guess at a vaguely octagonal shape, but what's not evident (the entire building is ringed with hedges) is that from this central octagon radiate five hallways of uneven length. "It's an octopus of a building," Gilman told me, and an aerial view confirms this, with its tentacles spreading out in all directions into the Nevada scrub.

If anything, the Mustang is slightly smaller than the Wild Horse, but it feels like it goes on forever. As with the Winchester Mystery House, the building distorts one's sense of space, inviting mystery and ambiguity. It's not intentional that the overall shape is masked, but the resulting effect is the same: entering the building, one more or less succumbs to it.

Atkins has been the Mustang Ranch's madam for a few years; its ghosts have been around much longer. In 2013 investigators from the reality show *Ghost Adventures* came to the Mustang to check out these spirits, bringing with them a bevy of equipment and machismo. During the show, Atkins took them to the original Mustang building and told them that many women refused to go down "B" hall in particular, where they reported being held down by an unseen force, after which they occasionally discovered bruises they could not explain. Women who spent time in Room B1, she said, were prone to wild mood swings. Nor was this restricted to the working girls; housekeepers reported having their hair pulled by invisible hands. At one point the ranch called in a shaman of some kind to purge the building of evil spirits.

The ghost of Oscar Bonavena, naturally, roams the premises, too, though he was shot in the parking lot at the Mustang's original location. One housekeeper told the *Ghost Adventures* crew of a man she'd seen standing outside the building in a white shirt; when she was shown a picture of Bonavena, she affirmed that it was him.

I tend not to put too much stock in reality shows like this. Any paranormal activity on *Ghost Adventures*, or any of the many similar shows, inevitably is presented via highly selective and suggestive editing; re-creations tend toward melodrama and often are presented to the viewer as fact. As most viewers know by now, reality television is anything but real, and this is no less true of supposed paranormal encounters.

But that afternoon, standing with Atkins while we waited for the photo shoot to finish, I heard the story of one girl we'll call Jean, to whom a spirit seemed to have attached itself. Not malevolent but certainly omnipresent, the ghost knocked over trinkets on a dresser and moved objects around. When the ranch brought out a psychic as part of the *Ghost Adventures* shoot, Jean asked about her personal spirit and was told that it had a name: Baby.

"Baby apparently likes water," Atkins relayed to me, and so at some point Jean placed a small fountain in her room, which appears to have quieted the ghost. We talked about other hauntings, and I suggested that usually hauntings were tied to the land as much as the building, and that one would assume that once the Mustang was transplanted from its earlier location, the reports of ghosts might have subsided. But Atkins says that the paranormal activity has, if anything, increased since the ranch was moved to its new site. Whatever is causing the paranormal activity here, it's in the bones of the house.

I listened politely until, almost as if on cue, Jean walked by. Atkins grabbed her by what little clothing she was wearing and said, "Hey, go get your videos—the ones with the ghost." Caught a little off guard, Jean nonetheless complied, returned a few minutes later with her phone, and proceeded to show me two videos.

The first video she shot for her husband; when she's at the Mustang, she's separated from him for weeks, and so she sends him videos from time to time. In this one she dances seductively, apparently unaware of the small ball of light—maybe an inch in diameter—that seems to be floating behind her head. The orb dances throughout the frame, out of sync with her, sometimes flitting across her face, while she carries on. At one point it disappears, then, a few seconds later, it rushes back into the frame, seems to career straight for her head, and, at the moment it makes "contact," she topples over rather comically.

The second video is shot from her bed, as though she's just woken up. A slightly shaky hand holds the camera toward the window, where Venetian blinds half block the morning sun. Then the camera pans upward, and emblazoned on the ceiling appears to be the number 13. On the video it's clear as day: a white-blue light projected on the ceiling of the room. When she first showed the video to her coworkers, they all tried to figure out what the "13" could possibly mean and what its significance was, until Atkins noticed how close together the 1 and 3 were and suggested that instead of a "13," perhaps it was a "B."

"B" as in "Baby."

The Mustang doesn't hide from its heritage, but neither does it revel in the lawless days of Joe Conforte. There is a suite named after him (including framed newspaper clippings of the murder trial), but the overall vibe is one of a high-end (if sometimes gaudy) hotel with unusually high security.

When Gilman got into the brothel business, together with his partner, Susan Austin, their goal was to remake legal prostitution as a luxury commodity. No more trailers, no underhanded financial deals—everything strictly by the book. Here the women are classed as independent contractors and paid by check, and there are extensive and constant health checks, redundant security features, and personal security.

They may be selling liminality, but it feels very much like business as usual. No sense of tragedy clings to the women who work here; the Mustang has an extensive waiting list of women looking for work, and Gilman and Atkins say they turn away nine out of ten applicants. It's a good, high-paying job, and the women are treated well; a fair number of the Mustang's independent contractors started at other legal brothels in Nevada but quickly applied at the Mustang because its reputation is so much better.

This doesn't mean the work itself is, by any stretch of the imagination, easy. After I'd spent two days talking to the women at the Mustang Ranch, it became abundantly clear to me how psychologically demanding the work was. In addition to the sex itself, the role of the sex worker has a complicated emotional and intellectual component. To the extent that these women are selling sex as a luxury product, their job involves not just creating a fantasy but being able to read their client: his needs, fears, desires, things he's ashamed of, things he's unable to say, the parts of himself he hasn't worked through. At one point, musing on the emotional labor involved in working at a brothel, I suggested that perhaps 90 percent of the job was psychological.

"No," Gilman corrected me, "more like 100 percent." The women I interviewed agreed completely. "This is the epitome of caregiving," Gilman said.

At one point in our conversation about hauntings, Atkins mentioned to me that the women who are most likely to see ghosts at the Mustang are the most psychologically taxed and worn out, her most nervous and high-strung girls. I thought of the complaints surrounding Room B1, and in particular reports of wild mood swings from women who'd spent too much time there. But when I pointed out that there might be an obvious corollary here, that the sightings may be more a manifestation of burnout and emotional exhaustion, Atkins immediately rejected the idea. After all, she told me, she sees them, too.

In the architecture of the traditional brothel, form will mirror function. In a place designed to be liminal, outside the law, where power relationships are upturned, the building itself will be secretive, strange, distorted. A nameless mansion, a secluded château, an unmarked basement entrance, a distant shack at the edge of civilization—such places play to our sense of mystery, of the wonders of the invisible world, which include not only sex but ghosts, too. The ghosts at the Mustang Ranch may have less to do with the things we traditionally associate with brothels—lawlessness, violence, secrecy—and more to do with the fact that, as a place of business, it's simply a highly stressful place to work.

I still can't shake those two videos. Assuming, of course, that they weren't digital manipulations (and why would they be?), my best guess is that the "B" shining on the ceiling was somehow reflected off the Venetian blinds—a piece of shiny metal hardware that somehow caught the light in a strange way. The orb knocking her over I assume to be just some kind of visual noise in the recording, which happened to coincidentally line up with her losing her balance. But I'll be the first to admit that there are days I don't feel particularly confident about these rationalizations. Of all the places I have visited in search of spirits, the place where a psychological explanation seemed most likely also happened to be the place where I found the strongest evidence of the paranormal.

CHAPTER EIGHT

PASSING THROUGH

Los Angeles, CA

Why does Elizabeth Short—the Black Dahlia—haunt the Biltmore Hotel in downtown Los Angeles? True, it was the last place she was seen alive, but why doesn't she haunt the sad stretch of sidewalk in South Los Angeles where her body was found? Why doesn't she haunt wherever she was actually murdered?

The Biltmore is old Hollywood, classic Hollywood. Opened in 1923, at the time the largest hotel west of Chicago, it displaced the nearby, equally opulent Alexandria as the epicenter of LA glamour. It was here, in the grand Crystal Ballroom, that the Academy of Motion Picture Arts and Sciences was founded, in 1927, and where eight early Academy Awards ceremonies were held, in the hotel's underground banquet room, the Biltmore Bowl.

I understand why people feel the Biltmore is haunted. I've stayed there, heard the heating pipes creak and tick in unpleasant, unfamiliar ways, as though the whole building were alive, breathing. I've stared down the desolate hallways, half assuming that some vague butchery was taking place behind one of those doors, something to be hushed up and forgotten, something whose trace would come to inhabit the walls like a stain—even as its grand ballrooms still speak to the glory and allure of

Hollywood. In October of 2010 a woman named Laura Finley fell six flights down the stairwell to her death; a few hours after her half-naked body was found, her husband auditioned in the lobby in front of Piers Morgan, Sharon Osbourne, and Howie Mandel for the next season of *America's Got Talent*.

As though these things happen all the time. One former employee later claimed, "There are many stories about ghostly presence on the 10th and 11th floor. I know when I used to work there lots of employees, even security, didn't like working the graveyard shift there due to a lot of ghostly presence. My sister used to work the 10th floor VIP lounge . . . , and there have been ghosts touching and moving stuff around there. People might say ghosts don't exist. Try staying there. I know—I have experienced it myself."

Los Angeles has its haunted houses, its haunted bars and haunted restaurants, but its best-known ghost stories involve hotels. Not just the Biltmore: nearby, the Alexandria Hotel, now apartments, supposedly hosts Rudolph Valentino, still dancing under its oval skylight. Valentino also haunts the retirement home that was once the Hotel Knickerbocker, along with the ghosts of Elvis Presley (haunting the perennially cold Room 1016) and William Frawley (who played Fred Mertz on *I Love Lucy* and dropped dead in the Knickerbocker's foyer). Frances Farmer was dragged from the Knickerbocker to be institutionalized against her will, and the Hollywood costume designer Irene Lentz jumped from its roof in 1962, distraught over the death of Gary Cooper. Marilyn Monroe, too, haunts the Knickerbocker, but she also haunts cabana room 246 of the Roosevelt Hotel on Hollywood Boulevard, where she shares duties with the malicious spirit of Montgomery Clift, who plays his trombone all hours of the night. Carole Lombard, Clark Gable, and Harry Lee all have been seen at the Roosevelt. The Culver Hotel hosts the ghostly traces of the dwarf actors who played the Munchkins in *The Wizard of Oz*, filmed across the street at Sony Studios; none of them died here, but it's their voices you hear conspiratorially whisper as you move through its halls. And finally there's the Hollywood Tower, a hotel so famous for its ghosts that Disney built a ride (the Twilight Zone Tower of Terror) based on its haunting.

But, then, all hotels are haunted. You're kidding yourself if you don't see this, if you don't recognize that you sleep with ghosts. Every hotel staff has its stories; any cleaning person or bellhop knows the score. In Wilkie Collins's 1878 gothic novel *The Haunted Hotel*, an Italian villa is converted to a hotel shortly after hosting an unexplained, horrific tragedy. On opening night a guest ("not a superstitious man") takes Suite 14 and leaves hurriedly the following morning. The next night a couple takes the suite; throughout the night the woman has horrifying dreams; awake, "afraid to trust herself again in bed," she, too, makes excuses and leaves.

Assume, then, that every nightmare you've ever had in a hotel was a cry for help, some violence from the past reaching out to you.

You can go searching for Marilyn and Valentino, but, truth be told, these are among the least interesting ghost stories that Hollywood has to offer. The postmortem celebrity sightings have their tragic elements, to be sure, but after a while they feel banal. You can't hope to understand Hollywood, its glory and debauchery, if all you care about is the marquee names. You have to seek out the forgotten stories.

"How many times do you need to hear what's-his-name playing the trombone in the Roosevelt Hotel?" Lisa Strouss asked me. It was August 2012, and we were sitting at an outdoor café in the Hollywood Hills, talking about ghosts. "Why are ghosts only famous people? It's so stupid."

Strouss is a co-founder of the Ghost Hunters of Urban Los Angeles (GHOULA for short), which she and Richard Carradine started in the summer of 2008. She has believed in the paranormal in one form or another since she was a teenager. Carradine, on the other hand, is a skeptic, though by his own account he's had multiple experiences with full manifestations (when a ghost appears not just as an orb or a voice but as a visible, full-bodied translucent specter)—the gold standard of paranormal sightings. For several years GHOULA has been holding monthly meetups, called "Spirits with Spirits," each at a different haunted location in Southern California, always on the thirteenth of the month.

"There are people who came to GHOULA in the early days," Strouss told me, "who I had known for years, never heard a peep from them about ghost stories, and then they come to a meeting and just barf up this story. It's always preempted by 'I totally don't believe in ghosts, I'm totally logical, I'm a scientist, whatever . . . but there was this one time.' That's always the kicker." From there, a story spills forth, one that's been bottled up for who knows how long. "They almost get weepy," Strouss said, and then as soon as it's over, they go back to their shell of logic. "But they feel relieved to get it out there. It gives them reassurance somehow, hope," she added, looking away. "It's a comfort to hear this story, even if it scares you."

It was at a GHOULA meeting in 2009, at the Eden Bar and Grill in Pasadena (a building that had formerly operated as a morgue), that Craig Owens met Bobby Garcia. Owens was working as a still photographer in the film industry when he started carrying around ghost-hunting equipment. He'd been spooked once while working at the Warner Bros. lot, and what started out as a side hobby has gradually taken up more and more of his life. Garcia had been seriously exploring the paranormal for about five years; he'd started out on Yahoo! chat groups, trying to find people in the San Gabriel Valley who might be interested in going on investigations with him. The two hit it off, making for an almost perfectly paired odd couple. Garcia is a large guy, soft-spoken, a stark contrast to Owens's wiry frame and loquaciousness. "We're two different people," Garcia told me, "but our fascination with history and LA history is what we talk about a lot. . . . My connection with Owens is that we both love the history of LA and read into it."

Unlike Owens, Garcia sees the paranormal in terms of science. "It has a lot to do with physics," he explained, "and natural phenomena—as natural as lightning. They have guys that feel that it could be a wormhole, and you have an opening, and it just shuts, and during that moment you have voices or something coming through. And the wormholes open and close all during the day, like right now, they could be doing it right now. It could be something related to the geomagnetic magnetism coming out of our earth or something, I don't know. But it seems like it's more of a science thing than an actual religious or an actual mystical thing."

After that first GHOULA meeting, the two decided to team up, seeking out places in Los Angeles where they could hunt for ghosts. Among the places Garcia suggested as possible venues was the Aztec Hotel.

Far from downtown Los Angeles, in the tiny hamlet of Monrovia, stands the Aztec Hotel. A Mayan revival designed in the 1920s by Frank Lloyd Wright's contemporary Robert Stacy-Judd, the hotel was one of the many roadside attractions that made Route 66 famous. But with the rise of the interstate freeway system, Route 66 became a footnote to history, along with the Aztec. Forgotten in suburban Monrovia, the hotel struggled financially for much of its history, going through a succession of owners.

Owens earned the trust and friendship of the then owner, Kathie Reece McNeil, who allowed him and Garcia to hunt for ghosts in the hotel after hours. "Craig was the one who pretty much set up everything," Garcia recalled. "He talked to the lady and he was able to get it, which a lot of people couldn't, so I give him credit for that. . . . The management didn't seem too friendly with people walking around there, and when you're asking questions, they didn't seem too forthcoming." (Said Owens: "She took a shine to me.")

They'd spend all night in the basement and unoccupied rooms, sometimes three or four nights a week, sometimes with others, sometimes not. Garcia and Owens found the most psychic activity in the basement. Garcia repeatedly heard the same woman's voice, barely a whisper, and later was able to hear it more audibly on his recorder. Another time, just as he was packing up to go, without any recorder, he heard her say his name, loudly, as if to say, "Where are you going?" "I think she became familiar with me," he said. Owens heard a voice on one of his EVP recordings stating, "My name's Quiggle"—a reference to James Quiggle, Monrovia's chief constable, who used to participate in the raids on the basement when it was a speakeasy. "My guess," Owens told me, "is that some really bad, dark stuff happened in that hotel and he's somehow associated with that. . . . I think he's a corrupt cop." Eventually Quiggle was replaced by a guy named Frank Scott, and one night Owens got the other investigators he was with to ask for Scott—only he screwed up the name and told them to ask for "Frank Little" instead. "When I listened to the audio," he told me, "I get this weird voice going, 'Frank *Scott*' . . . so it's like we were corrected. The mistake actually makes the evidence more compelling."

But it's not the basement that the Aztec is most known for; it's Room 120—haunted, most agree, by a ghost named Razzle Dazzle, a name divined by psychics who've visited the room over the years. According to one version of her story, Razzle Dazzle was a prostitute murdered in Room 120 by her john. Another version casts her as an aspiring actress, newly married, who fell on her wedding night, hit her head on the heater, and died instantly.

Her story, told and retold in so many conflicting versions, is never about celebrity; it's about a no one, such a nobody that no one even knows her actual name. Herein lies the darker side to classic Hollywood: its promise lured so many starlets and other hopefuls to LA throughout the past century, but some instead found fame only in death. Virginia Rappe, dead in 1921 from a ruptured bladder after a wild party involving Roscoe "Fatty" Arbuckle, or perhaps dead from a violent rape, or perhaps from complications of a botched abortion. Peg Entwhistle, a failed star whose 1932 leap from the "H" of the HOLLYWOODLAND (later, HOLLYWOOD) sign began a vogue of thematic suicides. Lou Tellegen, stabbing himself repeatedly in the chest with sewing scissors, his former glory as a matinee idol long faded. One could spend all day listing these tragedies, as Kenneth

Anger did with savage detachment in *Hollywood Babylon*, pillorying those who wagered and lost as so much used-up trash.

Strouss spoke of Los Angeles's turbulence, its reputation as "a violent, exploitive place. . . . LA is really effed up, so we technically should have more ghosts." The world Hollywood manufactures is uncanny; it's a world of strange similarities, repeated without end. Freud describes one aspect of the uncanny as involving unusual repetition, or "involuntary repetition"; a random number may not be particularly striking or noteworthy on its own, but if you see it over and over again in a single day, "or if we begin to notice that everything which has a number—addresses, hotel rooms, compartments in railway trains—invariably has the same one," then it does start to feel uncanny. Add to this aspiring actress Elizabeth Short, brutally dismembered and left as a grotesque calling card, famous now not because of what she accomplished in life but because of the barbarity of her unsolved murder. The haunted hotel manages to record both sides of the great narrative of classic Hollywood, its light side and its dark, kept close within tattered walls in buildings that seem to live on beyond death.

Stare down a long hotel corridor and you'll feel something like this: there's something uncanny about the very nature of a hotel, its endless, involuntary repetition of home-seeming spaces, rooms that could almost be home but are always somehow slightly off. Cultural critic Wayne Koestenbaum writes, "The uncanny is home defamiliarized—its rule book torn at the seam. The hotel mutates the unhomelike into industry and canned hospitality." And behind each one of those uncanny doors, perhaps, another uncanny aspiring star, each like the next and yet somehow slightly different.

A short walk from the Biltmore is the Cecil Hotel. Built in 1924 and originally advertised for traveling businessmen, the Cecil fell on hard times immediately. Already by 1935 Raymond Chandler could refer to it as "an old hotel that had once been exclusive and was now steering a shaky course between a receivership and a bad name at Headquarters. It had too much oily dark wood paneling, too many chipped gilt mirrors. Too much smoke hung below its low beamed lobby ceiling and too many grifters bummed around in its worn leather rockers." It's been recently refurbished and renamed Stay on Main, as though a name change might help it escape its past, though its original name is still painted in stories-high letters on the building's side.

After World War II the core of Los Angeles emptied out as people fled to the suburbs that sprawled endlessly in every direction, leaving downtown an increasingly empty space. Smaller hotels were torn down, but the larger hulks, too big to be torn down but not too big to fail, were left behind. The Cecil, with its seven hundred rooms, became a transient hotel, edged against Skid Row. Its reputation took a further nosedive as a result of two particularly notorious guests. Richard Ramirez, a serial killer known as the Night Stalker, lived at the Cecil, as did Jack Unterweger, an Austrian serial killer. Unterweger had been convicted of murdering a prostitute in 1974 and served fifteen years in prison, during which time he established himself as a successful writer. Upon his release in 1990, he came to Los Angeles on a writing assignment, stayed at the Cecil, and killed at least three more prostitutes. While neither man, so far as has been established, committed any murders within the walls of the Cecil, Ramirez and Unterweger nonetheless remain inextricably linked to the hotel as its most famous residents.

Until, that is, the strange death of Elisa Lam captivated the Internet in 2013. A Canadian student vacationing in Los Angeles, Lam had been staying in the Cecil when she disappeared. Her body was found almost three weeks later in the hotel's rooftop water tank, after residents complained about the smell and color of the water coming out of the tap. An elevator security video showed her shortly before her death. She enters the elevator and presses a button, but nothing happens; after a few seconds she goes back into the hall and appears to be engaged in a heated conversation with someone who can't be seen. She returns to the elevator, pressing her body against the wall as if hiding from someone. Even though nothing is obstructing the door, and Lam herself is not pressing any button that could be holding the elevator, the doors never close, not during the entire three-minute video, until the moment she leaves the elevator.

Amateur sleuths became obsessed with the video and Lam's story, convinced that the unknown figure she was talking to was her murderer or that the elevator's odd malfunction was evidence of a malevolent spirit in the hotel. Police later determined that Lam had most likely been experiencing a psychotic episode and at some point had climbed onto the roof and either deliberately or accidentally ended up in the water tank, where she drowned.

What should have been a private tragedy for a family who'd lost their daughter became a circus: an Internet spook story, an urban legend, and the inspiration for the fifth season of the TV series *American Horror Story*. Elisa Lam's story proved irresistible in the modern age: the surveillance video, the inexplicable malfunction of the elevator, her bizarre actions, the hotel's history—it was all too much. This is how ghost stories are born, after all: not from a complete story so much as from bits and pieces that don't quite add up, a kaleidoscope of menace and unease that coalesce in unpredictable ways. And what better breeding ground for such stories than a place like the Cecil?

The Cecil Hotel (or, if you must, Stay on Main) leaves one feeling trapped between spaces, neither here nor there. For years it has operated as an uneasy mix of a residence hotel and a backpacker hostel, and despite being a permanent fixture downtown, it seemed perpetually out of time and out of place.

Almost three years after Lam's death, I spent two nights at the Cecil. Its lobby has rentable computer terminals and pumps techno music at all hours, and every morning the staff rolls out one of the dreariest complimentary hotel breakfasts I've ever had. The furnishings in the room are

IKEA pieces installed on top of a hotel over ninety years old. There's been no visible attempt to scour the rooms of the decades of slow accumulation of grime—though, in full disclosure, it was by no means the worst hotel I've ever stayed at.

But this is what it feels like being in a hotel: attuned to a past that you can't understand and yet can't ignore. Hollywood doesn't do messy, it doesn't do unresolved, and it doesn't do ambiguous. Ghost stories are unresolved, ambiguous. There's a vision, a noise, maybe a voice that speaks a name, offering the tiniest bit of a story. Usually not much else. You have to go digging through the archives; unearth a story of a long-forgotten murder, a jilted lover whose name has been lost to history, local lore that no one bothers with anymore. Even then it's hardly a guarantee you'll be able to put the pieces together.

Many times a ghost story is simply an attempt to account for some scattered tidbits, some disconnected facts, that don't add up. We tell spooky tales and scary stories because the alternative—the open-ended chaos of the unknown—is even more terrifying. That's why ghosts cling to Hollywood, why they whisper underfoot.

It's not the mansion of Norma Desmond from Billy Wilder's *Sunset Boulevard* that best exemplifies old Hollywood's history. It's the Hotel Earle from Joel and Ethan Coen's *Barton Fink*, a building that the directors described as a "ghost ship floating adrift, where you notice signs of the presence of other passengers, without ever laying eyes on any."

One of the strange beauties of *Barton Fink* is how the film eschews standard cinematic practice and avoids establishing shots: we're brought immediately into interior scenes without a sense of what the buildings look like. And so we see the Hotel Earle's lobby, its elevator, its corridors, and its rooms, but never its exterior. We have no sense of its size, its layout, how it appears to the unsuspecting passing by. It could go on forever. If not for the diffused light coming through the windows, the hotel could be miles underground.

When Barton Fink checks in at the Earle, the desk clerk asks him,

"Are you a trans or a res?" meaning transient or resident. Fink doesn't get it, he's confused, as though he's not yet ready to commit to the implications of the question. He stammers out a vague response: "I, uh, I don't know. I mean, I'll be here indefinitely." The clerk finally answers for him.

By the time I started attending GHOULA meetings, they had already exhausted the usual suspects: the Biltmore, the Roosevelt, the Culver, and, of course, the Aztec. Because they try not to repeat a location, after the first few years the meeting spots became more and more unexpected, including Burbank's Pickwick Bowl, the haunted bowling alley, and the haunted *Queen Mary* in Long Beach. Which is how I ended up at a seemingly unlikely candidate for a haunted hotel: the top-floor revolving restaurant at the futuristic Westin Bonaventure in downtown LA.

Designed by architect John Portman in 1976, and still standing as the largest hotel in the city, the Bonaventure's easily recognizable shape of five clustered glass cylinders has made it a landmark of Los Angeles. Inside, a massive atrium dominated by a central concrete pillar is populated with floating plazas, rings, and balconies. A lobby bar circles the central pillar, which in turn is bordered by a gentle moat and escalators and circular staircases lead off in all directions. It has no exterior windows, so you can quickly lose track of what time of day it is. Iconic enough that it's been featured in dozens of films and is visible from two major freeways, it stands out easily against the tepid skyscrapers surrounding it, even those that tower over it.

By the time the Bonaventure was built, much of downtown was a dead zone. Unlike many downtowns, Los Angeles's has had, for much of its history, a curious excess of space. Boosters who tried to sell the city as a tourist destination in the 1920s and '30s built up a massive downtown filled with monstrous hotels like the Biltmore and the Cecil, and much of that real estate was gradually vacated after the war. Unlike in San Francisco or Manhattan, here few geographical barriers stood in the way of suburban sprawl. Many of the old buildings were too big to demolish, so for decades they stood emptied out in an emptied-out city. With little commercial interest to dictate how one experienced the city, downtown Los Angeles became, in its own way, a dream space—free to be colonized by alcoholics and junkies, of course, but also by artists and writers who found cheap living space and no one looking over their shoulders.

The Bonaventure, whose street-level façade is grim and bunkerlike, seemed to want to insulate itself from the dream world around it. Despite (or perhaps because of) its status, the hotel has over the years become almost universally reviled. It was most famously excoriated by literary theorist Frederic Jameson in 1991: "It does not wish to be a part of the city," he wrote, "but rather its equivalent and replacement or substitute." Jameson singled out not just the façade but also the glass cylinders, which achieve "a peculiar and placeless dissociation of the Bonaventure from its neighborhood: it is not even an exterior, inasmuch as when you seek to look at the hotel's outer walls you cannot see the hotel itself but only the distorted images of everything that surrounds it."

Without a doubt, it is a disorienting space. Though it seems symmetrical, not every elevator bank goes to the top floor, and not every stairwell in the atrium leads to every other floor. Though it's wide and airy, sightlines are oddly obscured by the concrete pylons, so it's difficult to see sometimes which stairway will take you to the floor you need to get to. Describing the central core as a "bagel," architect-critic Charles Willard Moore commented, "You are likely to move around and around that bagel with increasing frenzy, since you can't help feeling that you're lost. The place is as frustrating as a Piranesi prison drawing." As open as the atrium is, it feels perpetually claustrophobic.

The Bonaventure's tendency to disorient its visitors, to confound space, and, yes, to turn the simple into the uncanny has no doubt helped attract its fair share of ghosts. There are those of Eli and Esther Ruven, murdered in the Bonaventure in 1979 during a drug deal gone south, their bodies dismembered and carried out in trash bags. In the basement lives another ghost, a young red-haired girl who wanders the tunnels beneath the hotel's parking garage. Those tunnels were once part of LA's original trolley line, the Red Car, already in disuse when they were caved in to form the foundation of the Bonaventure. Even as the hotel looks toward a *Blade Runner*–esque future, in the decades since it first opened, the space has become as haunted as every other hotel in Los Angeles.

Which is to say, even in a place as sprawling as Los Angeles, whose buildings aren't nearly as old as New England's, you can't build anywhere without building on top of some other ruin, on top of some old ghosts. Hawthorne's character Holgrave might be happier here than in Salem, since Southern California has less compunction about demolishing the old to make way for the new, but even here the ghosts remain. The problem with ghosts is that they can never figure out if they're transients or residents—they don't quite stick around, and yet they never really leave.

In Los Angeles, a city of endless dreams and endless dreamers, the old, glamorous buildings—historic yet faded, baroque yet underused—are vulnerable to a different kind of infestation: not ghosts but ghost hunters. At some point a shift happened in the paranormal community in which money and fame began to eclipse earnest, solitary searchers. Around the time GHOULA formed in 2008, more and more shows started appearing on basic cable, shows called *My Ghost Story, Fear, Ghost Hunters, Ghost Hunters International, Ghost Hunters Academy, Most Haunted USA, A Haunting, Paranormal State, The Othersiders, Celebrity Paranormal Project*, and on and on and on. Nearly all these shows follow a basic routine: a "crew," usually in matching T-shirts and usually consisting of three or four guys and one woman, in a default pose of a tough, crossed-arms stance staring straight at the camera, investigating a reputedly haunted locale. They bring with them a variety of devices for locating ghosts:

infrared cameras, audio recorders for EVP sessions, thermometers for lo-cating "cold spots," and the ever-popular KII meter, a handheld device for measuring electromagnetic fields of electrical devices.

Los Angeles's status as the mecca of movies and television has guaran-teed an explosion of near-identical outfits imitating the crews on TV: LA Ghost Patrol, LA Paranormal Association, Ghost Interactive Investiga-tions, Paranormal EXP, Darklands Paranormal, California Society for Paranormal Research and Assistance, and so forth. These groups range from the serious to the absurd—at the more absurd end of the spectrum is perhaps the Paranormal Hot Squad, an all-female group of several models and exotic dancers whose motto is "We'll scare you stiff."

All these ghost-hunting groups sell T-shirts and other merchandise on their Web sites, and each of them, more or less explicitly, is gunning for its own show, trying to build up enough street cred and cult following for producers to notice them. People come to LA to get famous for all sorts of reasons; the ghost hunters are only the latest round of starlets who want to make their names in show business.

"I come from the old school," Craig Owens clarified, "where you don't try to capitalize on this. . . . That used to be completely unethical ten, fifteen years ago. . . . I associate hauntings with pain and suffering of somebody; why capitalize on that to make a buck? Something horrible might have happened."

For GHOULA it was never about getting famous. "They want to capture the ghost," Strouss told me. "We want to capture the ghost story." And yet, she admits, GHOULA, with its clever acronym and its ability to bring together so many lone investigators, might have inadvertently birthed many of these groups. "We triggered that," she said after a pause.

This may seem harmless, but the proliferation of guys in T-shirts and event planners hoping to make a buck off of LA's haunted past has had unforeseen effects on the city's fragile historical buildings, and it was the pursuit of the dual succubi, money and fame, that contributed to the downfall of the Aztec. "Some paranormal groups want to hijack a location," Owens scoffed. "They want to be the house band, and charge money, and commercialize it." The *Queen Mary* is one such location. The Aztec was another: groups began charging money for fans to essentially hang out in the bar, and without giving a cut to the hotel, they quickly alienated the owner, who turned to Craig Owens. "She just appointed me to weed through people to see who was legitimate and who was not," he said, still sounding bitter about the whole affair. "Well, I wasn't getting paid, I wasn't earning a dime." He all but gave up, as did the Aztec, which called off all investigations, and what meager income these groups were contributing to the failing hotel dried up.

As Garcia put it, you try to be respectful, do your research, but most of all you try to distinguish yourself from these types of people. "We were on the *Queen Mary*," he recalled. "We were in one of the ballrooms, and it's quiet, and then all of a sudden you see this group of people running through, and then you see security chasing them." Wanting to be entertained is one thing; the larger problem is guilt by association. "It's the people who're wanting to be scared, waiting for Halloween to come— that's the ones who're kinda ruining it. They're looked at as your peers, and when they're there, they're seen as the same as you."

One of the last GHOULA meetings I attended was in the summer of 2012, in downtown Venice, at the Townhouse Bar, which has been around since 1915 and that operated a speakeasy in its basement during Prohibition. According to stories, the former owner still occupies his booth downstairs in the former speakeasy, a basement that currently features local bands on weekends. We were there on a weeknight, so the basement wasn't open, but one of the bartenders told us she was going off shift soon and if we waited, she'd take us down there for a few minutes. So those of us assembled milled around, waiting for something to happen.

Overall, the evening was, as I had been prepped to expect, mostly devoid of the magic that Strouss and Owens described of the early days.

Neither of them was at the Venice meet-up, and while Garcia showed up late, he didn't say much. The paranormal groups, however, were there, and while they weren't wearing T-shirts, for most of the night, people stayed in their little cliques without interacting. I spoke to one ghost-hunting crew, whose name I've forgotten now: it could have been the LA Paranormal Association or the LA Ghost Hunters, the Ghost Busters of LA—they become a bit interchangeable after a while. The leader could've been any generic guy just out of USC or UCLA: short but muscular, close-cropped hair, answering my questions in as few words as possible. The obligatory girl—his girlfriend, naturally—was the bubbly, outgoing member of the group; the third guy didn't say anything at all.

It will be a shame if groups like this become the face of LA's paranormal community. Asked during a local TV affiliate's Halloween coverage one year why they do what they do, the lead investigator of the LA Ghost Patrol said, "We want proof. We want to be the team that proves that this stuff is real. We want to be the ones that capture it and prove to the world that this stuff does exist." It's the kind of fairly pat, unexamined answer that one finds again and again; it's one of the many reasons why the whole enterprise threatens to teeter into nonsense. Contrast that with the work of someone like Craig Owens, obsessed as he is with the history of a place and how that history may imprint itself on one's psyche. Not just the re-corded history but also a forgotten history, and a history that will never, ever be known.

Take, for example, the mystery of Room 120 in the Aztec, the supposed home of Razzle Dazzle. Searching the Monrovia city archives, Owens found no mention of any prostitute or actress killed at the Aztec. "The room does appear to be haunted, but her name was never Razzle Dazzle, if in fact someone died there."

He did find something else, though. When the hotel opened, the local Elks Lodge operated a monthly gambling and drinking night in the base-ment, something unsanctioned by the cops during Prohibition, except perhaps by the few, like James Quiggle and Frank Scott, who might have been bribed or might have taken a cut of the action. Owens believes that some dark aspects of Monrovia's history might have surfaced in that basement, perhaps a murder or a violent incident during one of those parties that had to be hushed up.

Those monthly parties, Owens learned, had an informal name. They called them Razzle Dazzle Nights.

"No one would know that," he told me, "unless they went through those darn Monrovia papers."

This is perhaps as close to proof as one could possibly hope for: a random name that some psychic had pulled out of thin air during some séance turned out to have a very specific connection to the hotel's history. Maybe this does tell us something about the Aztec, but what? It will never lead to a clear, complete narrative of events, as anyone who might have been able to tell us about what happened during those Razzle Dazzle nights is dead now.

Ghost stories like this will never have a perfect Hollywood resolution. Another LA ghost hunter, Michele Yu, once referred to this as "paranormal archaeology," which is as good an analogy as any: you get fragments that suggest histories, that hint at a purpose, but have nothing definitive to offer, which ultimately stare dumbly back at you.

Unlike those in search of some holy grail of definitive, objective evidence of supernatural life, Lisa Strouss seems interested in the paranormal more as a means of self-reflection. Though an avid believer, she told me that she herself had never seen a ghost. "I would like to have my own ghost story," she said, almost mournfully. "I really want to believe, but I keep discrediting my own stories. I'm my own worst skeptic." Besides, as she'll tell you, even if you have proof, what—really—does that get you? It's not just a question of finding proof of the paranormal, because "even when you get the evidence," she offered, "you're still at the same place you were before the evidence. You can prove all you want. It's like the god question: you come back to the same point."

This existential problem of proof is the thing that all ghost hunters have to wrestle with, something each person seems to face in a different way. "Say we take [proof] to a scientific board," Garcia surmised, "which is really what it's going to come down to. They're not going to say, 'Yeah, that's a voice from the dead.'" He's given this enough thought to know it'll never come down to a single sighting, a single EVP, a single video. "You gotta have so much, an overabundance of each event, and then you have a whole bunch of those events, and *then* you might have something." He stops for a second, perhaps taking in the quixotic nature of the quest he's set before himself, the enormity and the impossibility of a quest that's taken up the last seven years of his life, most of it in solitary pursuit. "It's going to take a lot more than what we're doing now, and a collective thought of everyone on the same page . . . and that's not going to happen."

If there are thirteen ways of looking at a blackbird, there are as many ways of looking at a ghost. For Bobby Garcia, it's a means of understanding science. For people like Richard Carradine and Craig Owens, ghost hunting is a way of unearthing history, of figuring out the past. For Lisa Strouss, who's left the LA ghost-hunting community, it's a means of understanding something about herself. But none of these kinds of discussions took place the night of the GHOULA event in Venice, and I couldn't help but feel that I was years late to a party long over—like showing up at Haight Ashbury after the '60s or CBGB's after the '70s. There was a brief moment in time, it seems, when a remarkable—remarkably weird and remarkably thoughtful—collection of passionate oddballs came together and found one another. Almost as soon as it had begun, the scene was co-opted, standardized, and commodified, and the thoughtful ones all scattered to the winds.

I was about to leave the Townhouse when, as promised, the bartender got off shift and offered to take us downstairs to the former speakeasy. We all trudged down to the event space, which, unsurprisingly, looked like an LA venue on an off night: stage at one end, bar along one wall, a smattering of velvet curtains and leather booths—including the one supposedly still inhabited by the former owner. As I watched these milquetoast ghost hunters mill about the room, furtively taking EVP recordings on their phones, asking one another if they saw anything, felt anything, I could've been in any bar in Los Angeles—heck, it *was* any bar in Los Angeles.

And then an old man rose up out of the crowd—a guy in his eighties at least, shock of white hair, baggy in his skin, someone who wasn't a ghost hunter but who'd heard about the GHOULA event, heard about Richard Carradine's fascination with LA history, and had come out for a drink, some son of a former mayor or councilman from decades ago, from some other time. He stood on the lowest step of the basement stairs, floating just above the rest of us, and he started to speak about old Venice, about the trolley line that used to run from Venice to Santa Monica, about the time when Orson Welles filmed *Touch of Evil* across the street, strange memories and stories of local corruption and gossip. He didn't really have any point, and he meandered, getting confused, trailing off, repeating himself, but none of this mattered. There—among the ghost hunters scurrying around, amid enthusiasm both naïve and cynical—there, for the briefest of moments, this ghost-made-flesh appeared above us, speaking of the forgotten and the fragmentary stories that make up a city, stories told barely above a whisper in basements such as this.

III

CIVIC-MINDED SPIRITS

prisons and asylums, graveyards and
cemeteries, a park

F rank Wattron wasn't sure what to do. He'd been elected to the position of Navajo County sheriff three years earlier, in 1896, and in that time he had become known throughout the county and its county seat, Holbrook, as fair and tough-minded. With his black handlebar mustache and the sawed-off shotgun he kept under his black trench coat, Wattron looked ever the part of an Arizona lawman. Newspapers described him as "a generous, whole-souled man whom no one can charge with any dishonesty," though his capacity for boundless charity was matched by his mercurial temper and his reputation for being a "gruff, hard-boiled joker." He had a mild opium addiction, to which some attributed his mood swings, but he'd been liked well enough to get reelected. As the Holbrook *Argus* put it, "Hundreds of persons who read this article can no doubt recollect instances in which they have received personal favors from Mr. Wattron."

Now he had to figure out what do to about George Smiley. Smiley had been working for the Atchison, Topeka & Santa Fe Railway in 1899 as a trackwalker when he confronted a previous foreman over a missing paycheck. An argument broke out between the two men that quickly escalated, and before it was over Smiley had shot his former foreman in the back. Smiley was caught, convicted of murder, and sentenced to death, and his execution was set for December 8, 1899.

Wattron had no problem with seeing this murderer off to his reward: the case was clear-cut, the conviction straightforward, the punishment just. But it was Wattron's first execution, and he was obligated by Arizona statute to notify the public prior to the execution to ensure that witnesses would be present. Without any sense of how such notifications were supposed to look, Wattron composed an invitation that reflected his dark sense of humor:

> You are hereby cordially invited to attend the hanging of one George Smiley, murderer. His soul will be swung into eternity on December 8, 1899, at 3 o'clock p.m., sharp.
>
> Latest improved methods in the art of scientific strangulation will be employed and everything possible will be done to make the surroundings cheerful and the execution a success.
>
> F. J. Wattron, Sheriff of Navajo County.

Smiley's was the first major trial held in the brand-new county courthouse. Simple, elegant, defined by the bell tower rising up from its peaked roof and by its generous arched entryway, the courthouse was built to signify order and law in a lawless land, its tower looming over the small frontier town as though a beacon or some searching eye. And it was here that Smiley was to meet his end.

Wattron's tongue-in-cheek announcement of Smiley's impending execution soon hit the newswires and spread across the country. His gallows humor was met with a mixture of chagrin and outrage, bringing notoriety to the tiny county. Ultimately President William McKinley got word of it and, since Arizona Territory was under federal control, issued word to its governor to address the situation. Governor Nathan Oakes Murphy mandated a thirty-day stay of execution to give Wattron time to reissue the notification with a more funereal tone.

Wattron hated nothing as much as sham and hypocrisy, and no doubt saw this unwanted federal intrusion as more of the same. Perturbed, he issued a second execution announcement, this one in the style of a Victorian mourning card.

Framed in a black border, it read:

Revised Statutes of Arizona, Penal Code, Title X,
Section 1849, Page 807, makes it obligatory on sheriff
to issue invitations to executions,
form (unfortunately) not prescribed.

Holbrook, Arizona

Jan. 7, 1900.

With feelings of profound sorrow and regret, I hereby invite you to attend and witness the private, decent and humane execution of a human being; name, George Smiley, crime, murder.

The said George Smiley will be executed on Jan. 8, 1900, at 2 o'clock p.m.

You are expected to deport yourself in a respectful manner, and any "flippant" or "unseemly" language or conduct on your part will not be allowed. Conduct, on anyone's part, bordering on ribaldry and tending to mar the solemnity of the occasion will not be tolerated.

F. J. Wattron, Sheriff of Navajo County.

I would suggest that a committee, consisting of Governor Murphy, Editors Dunbar, Randolph and Hull, wait on our next legislature and have a form of invitation to executions embodied in our laws.

This time, to prevent any further interference, Wattron sent the invitation out a day before the execution. And on January 8, 1900, George Smiley, age thirty-seven, was hanged from the scaffolding of the courthouse—not only the first person executed on the courthouse grounds but the only legally executed criminal in the history of Navajo County.

The *Argus* noted in its January 13 edition that Smiley had converted to Catholicism shortly before his execution and received baptism and confession before going to his death. "Smiley exhibited great coolness and composure until the last," the paper reported. "He ascended the scaffold unassisted; he spoke clearly and without a tremor in his voice and showed not the slightest sign of nervousness." With his final words Smiley thanked Wattron and his deputies for their kindness.*

Such a report implies a sense of finality and closure and that Smiley went to his death calm and at peace. But according to Marita R. Keams, who worked in the courthouse building after it was converted into a museum in 1981, Smiley has since grown restive. Teenagers using a Ouija board one Halloween, she reports, claimed to have contacted a ghost who told them his name was George. Keams says she and other employees have felt and heard Smiley, that he has turned on the faucets in the men's restroom, and that she's felt him playing with her hair when no one is around. The prevailing feeling among those who work in the building is that Smiley haunts the place of his execution, awaiting a second reprieve from the president that has yet to come.

Whether you believe that Smiley haunts the courthouse may have

---

*Wattron's own death was considerably less serene: five years after the execution he over-dosed on laudanum, and when friends came to aid him, he reportedly told them, "I have a ticket punched straight through to Hell with no stopovers" (*Crooked Trail to Holbrook*, 218).

something to do with your attitude toward capital punishment. Cultur-
ally, after all, attitudes on the subject vary widely and fluctuate over time,
and it's likely not a coincidence that the stories of Smiley's restless soul
have gained ground as the mode of his original punishment has lost popularity. The story recorded by the *Argus* suggests that Smiley's death
sentence was instrumental in his reform: only when faced with his imminent execution did this wayward murderer find his way, facing death with
peace and dignity. The ghost stories, on the other hand, suggest that
Smiley's ghost haunts the courthouse grounds, still hoping for a reprieve.

Navajo County's Superior Court is now housed in a larger complex that
includes not only an enlarged county jail but also the board of supervisors
and other essential government services. Its architecture suggests a changing face of government: low-slung and economical, lacking ornament or
ostentation, it projects frugality, a reluctance to spend taxpayer money.
Arizona is no longer a Wild West frontier, so the power of government
need not be telegraphed to the citizenry anymore. The new building is
boring, but that is its point.

More so than houses, civic structures—not just courthouses but prisons, asylums, and other government buildings—are purpose-built. They
are rarely constructed for convenience's sake; they are built to send a message. They may incorporate Greek or Roman colonnades and rotundas to
suggest that their lineage stretches back millennia, as though to grant
further legitimacy. They may—as is common with libraries of a certain
era—have the names of famous philosophers, statesmen, artists, and writers
carved into the exterior stone. When they are built simply or modestly,
that is part of their message, too.

A common feature of many of these buildings is the idea of permanence:
they're meant to last forever. And yet many of the ideas and philosophies
that drive these constructions change over the course of time. Demographics
shift, political affiliations change, new administrations are voted in,

aesthetics evolve—but the buildings often are left behind, bearing traces of whatever impetus drove their construction.

How a public building—or, as we'll see, a cemetery or even a park—can come to be haunted has a lot to do with the evolution of our cultural ideas, which change faster than our landscape can keep up with, rendering these places obsolete, archaic, and anachronistic.

Unlike businesses or private residences, these civic-minded places have less control over their haunted reputations and less power to keep out the spirits and the spirit seekers. Partly this is out of necessity: places like the West Virginia State Penitentiary in Moundsville don't receive enough public funding to cover operating expenses and need the revenue from dark tourism to avoid the wrecking ball. Ghost stories have become an important tool for preservationists, as a means to keep alive buildings that have civic and cultural value, buildings that might otherwise get plowed under. But as inherently public places, they belong to the public imagination. You cannot keep a paranormal researcher out of a public park, after all. Hauntings keep alive neglected spaces and make them relevant to their communities once again.

CHAPTER NINE

MELANCHOLY
CONTEMPLATION

Moundsville, WV

In the wilds of Greenbrier County, West Virginia, along Route 60, stands a particularly odd national landmark sign. Erected in 1979, in sixty-four words it tells the strange tale of the Greenbrier Ghost.

INTERRED IN NEARBY CEMETERY IS ZONA HEASTER SHUE. HER DEATH IN 1897 WAS PRESUMED NATURAL UNTIL HER SPIRIT APPEARED TO HER MOTHER TO DESCRIBE HOW SHE WAS KILLED BY HER HUSBAND EDWARD. AUTOPSY ON THE EXHUMED BODY VERIFIED THE APPARITION'S ACCOUNT. EDWARD, FOUND GUILTY OF MURDER, WAS SENTENCED TO THE STATE PRISON. ONLY KNOWN CASE IN WHICH TESTIMONY FROM GHOST HELPED CONVICT A MURDERER.

The husband's name was Erasmus Stribbling Trout Shue, not Edward, though he was known by most as Trout. When he arrived at the West Virginia State Penitentiary at Moundsville in 1897 as inmate number 3255, it was not his first time. A competent blacksmith, he'd been convicted of horse thievery and had spent twenty months in prison for it. His first marriage had been in 1885, and he'd divorced four years later under clouded circumstances (some would later claim that his wife had feared that he would kill her). In 1894 he married again, a woman named Lucy A. Tritt, who died less than a year into their marriage in February of the following year. Little is known about her death: the newspaper recorded only that she "died very suddenly at her home" and apparently never followed up on the cause of death. When Shue met Zona Heaster, she had several suitors, but she chose this newly arrived blacksmith, and in October 1896 they were married.

Once again it took less than a year before Shue's marriage ended in death. On the morning of January 22, 1897, he had been out running errands and had sent a young boy, Anderson Jones, to stop by his house and see if his wife needed anything. Jones found Zona's body on the floor, "stretched out perfectly straight with feet together, one hand lying by the side and the other lying across the body." Her head, according to news reports, "was slightly inclined to one side."

By the time the coroner, George Knapp, arrived, Shue had laid out his wife's body and was cradling her head and sobbing uncontrollably. Knapp, attempting to determine the cause of death, noticed some "slight discolorations on the right side of the neck and right cheek," but when he went to investigate further, Shue "protested so vigorously" that Knapp gave up and left the house, having made only a cursory investigation. He later reported that the woman had died from "an everlasting faint."

Zona Heaster Shue was taken to her mother's house and laid out for viewing, but during the wake her husband's behavior, according to eyewitness accounts, became increasingly erratic. He claimed to have dressed her body himself and seemed agitated whenever anyone came too close to it. He had placed a pillow at one side of her head so she should could "rest easier," he said. Even in such a state, people noticed an odd looseness to her head whenever the corpse was moved. She was buried the next day, Monday, January 25.

The ghost came shortly thereafter.

Shue's mother-in-law, Mary Jane Heaster, had always disapproved of the marriage. The news of her only daughter's death left her inconsolable, but in the days afterward she would claim that she began receiving regular visits from Zona's ghost. As she later would testify under oath, "It was no dream—she came back and told me that he was mad that she didn't have no meat cooked for supper." The ghost told Heaster that Shue had killed her, driven to rage by such petty things as a lack of meat. The ghost then told her that if she "could look down back of Aunt Martha Jones', in the meadow, in a rocky place; that I could look in a cellar behind some loose plank and see" some traces of blood where he had done it. Heaster did exactly as she was told and, sure enough, saw blood exactly where it had been indicated. Then, most significant, was this revelation: "She cames [sic] four times, and four nights; but the second night she told me that her neck was squeezed off at the first joint."

After several nights of this, Heaster could stand it no more and went to the county prosecutor, John Preston, telling him she believed that Zona's death was no accident and that Zona's ghost would haunt her until justice was done. Nearly a month after Zona's death, her body was disinterred and an inquest was convened. The body had kept well through the West Virginia winter; little decomposition had taken place. Though Mary Jane Heaster had claimed that the ghost had told her that her neck had been broken, the autopsy started with a search for signs of poison. Only after that came back negative did they investigate her neck, determining that Zona Heaster Shue had indeed had her neck broken and that without other bruises on her body that might indicate a fall or other accident, it was a strong likelihood that she had been murdered.

Shue was tried and convicted of his wife's murder that summer but, unusual in the case of murder, was not given the death penalty. Instead, he was sentenced to life imprisonment at the West Virginia Penitentiary in Moundsville. He never left there, dying behind bars on March 13, 1900.

In the decades following Shue's death, the penitentiary gradually developed a reputation for its poor treatment of inmates—so much so that in

1981 a prisoner named Robert Crain sued the state, claiming cruel and unusual punishment and initiating a lengthy legal battle. In a 1986 opinion the West Virginia Supreme Court found a list of deplorable conditions so voluminous that they had difficulty accurately summarizing them. Back-flowing toilets leaking sewage onto the floor were common, as were bird droppings from the pigeons roosting in the eaves. The lack of temperature control meant freezing in winter and scorching heat in summer. "Because of lack of ventilation and cleanliness and sewage spills," the justices reported, "much of the living facility is permeated with a stench. Fire and safety hazards abound and are compounded by numerous health hazards in the food service area. Food is contaminated with hair, insects, and other foreign substances." The state's failure to remedy these problems in the ensuing years led finally to the facility's closure almost ten years later, in 1995.

The prison's ghosts moved in around the same time as the inmates were cleared out. One former inmate, William "Red" Snyder, who was murdered in his cell in 1992, has been heard calling out to tour guides and has occasionally shown up on EVP recordings. Shadowy figures have been seen in the hallways, and near the North Gate roams the indignant ghost of Arvil Adkins. Adkins had been one of three men condemned to death in 1938 for a botched kidnapping that had led to their victim's death. Adkins's hanging did not go smoothly; the trap door beneath him was sprung prematurely, and he plummeted twenty feet onto the concrete below. Still alive, the bloodied and injured Adkins was carried back upstairs on a stretcher to be hanged properly.

After 1995, the state turned the operation of the penitentiary over to the Moundsville Economic Development Council but provided no additional funds for its upkeep or restoration. So the council turned to the haunted reputation of the prison to keep it open to the public, running a staged haunted attraction each fall, the Dungeon of Horrors, and regular ghost-hunting sessions throughout the year.

The Dungeon of Horrors tour, according to one employee I spoke to who worked there for a season, didn't have to rely on ginned-up shocks. Even without any canned effects, strange sounds could be heard: dripping water from an unknown source and unidentified clanging sounds cutting through the eerie silence. As part of the tour, guides would recount real stories of murder, torture, and abuse that had taken place in the prison. Its reputation was such that a haunted tour could rely heavily on well-established facts.

Attractions like these have become enormously popular. Sociologist Margee Kerr explains that they are "frightening yet intriguing—creating a kind of attraction/repulsion dynamic." Though they're places we hope never to find ourselves confined in, we nonetheless are attracted to them because of what they stand for. In Kerr's words, "In the public act of confining the criminal, or the 'abnormal' other, societies reaffirm their shared values, the differences between 'us' and 'them' become visible, and the dividing lines are fortified." If you are terrified by the thought of one day finding yourself behind bars in a place like Moundsville, Kerr suggests you're also relieved by the recognition, at the tour's end, that you are not one of the "bad guys," and once past the gift shop you're allowed to go free back into civilization. The good attractions, she notes, push your boundaries while leaving you safe and inspired; the less reputable ones, on the other hand, "leave you there or drop you."

But perhaps we *should* be left slightly disturbed by a place like Moundsville. The employee I spoke to recalled how, after a month at that prison, the place began to work on him. There was little after-hours bonding among the staff; no sharing of beers or stories after a job well done. "No one wanted to stick around," he said.

Prison architecture evolved, after all, to elicit extremely specific emotional and physical reactions. While the idea of solitary confinement and cellular prisons grew out of the monastic tradition, in a punitive context isolation rarely produces rehabilitation. Repeated studies have, in fact, shown the opposite: that solitary confinement acts as a barrier to mental and physical health, creating increasing psychological instability and antisocial behavior among those subjected to it.

When prisons like Moundsville were being planned and built, little of this was known. Prior to the nineteenth century, prisons were temporary spaces. You were imprisoned while you were awaiting trial, and in some cases, after you'd been sentenced and were waiting for the sentence to be carried out. The punishments themselves were almost uniformly physical: beatings or death. The notion that imprisonment itself could be a punishment, that one could be made to pay for crimes by the loss of time, is a relatively recent phenomenon.

So at the time Moundsville was built, treatments like solitary confinement seemed novel, even humane. The commissioners appointed with the design and construction of Philadelphia's Eastern State Penitentiary wrote, "Its good design is to produce, by means of sufferings principally acting on the mind and accompanied with moral and religious instruction, a disposition to virtuous conduct, the only sure preventive of crime." Alone with only one's thoughts and a Bible, one could focus on penance and self-correction, unencumbered by the distractions of one's surroundings and any further temptation to sin once more.

But this wouldn't work with all criminals, of course, hence the other factor of Eastern State's design: its imposing façade, its castlelike exterior, which exudes a gothic dread to all passing by. This malevolent exterior was intentional, meant "to impress so great a dread and terror, as to deter the offender from the commission of crime in the state where the system of solitary confinement exists."

Moundsville, like Eastern State, was designed explicitly to spread this sense of gloom and melancholy, a means of further inspiring penance upon those trapped in its walls or those on the outside who might contemplate a life of crime. An 1826 encyclopedia noted, "The style of architecture of a prison, is a matter of no slight importance. It offers an effectual method of exciting the imagination to a most desirable point of abhorrence." Continuing, it recommended that "the exterior of a prison should, therefore, be formed in the heavy and sombre style, which most forcibly impresses the spectator with gloom and terror. Massive cornices, the absence of windows or other ornaments, small low doors, and the whole structure comparatively low, seem to include nearly all the points necessary to produce the desired effect."

The architects who designed institutions like Eastern State and Moundsville, then, attempted to inspire the same sense of foreboding that London's Newgate Prison had long been famous for, inciting in their inmates (in the words of one commentator) a sense of awe and "melancholy contemplation." Eastern State, though far more expensive than other prisons of the day, continually succeeded in creating this impression, at least among the law-abiding. "The design and execution impart a grave, severe, and awful character to the external aspect of this building," George Washington Smith noted in 1830. "The effect which it produces on the imagination of every passing spectator, is particularly impressive, solemn, and instructive."

Even today the prison feels deeply unsettling, and walking through its halls leaves you with a pervasive sense of unease. It feels both claustrophobic and endless, forlorn and merciless. The cool stone sucks out all the available heat in the room; no doubt the place gets unbearable in summer, but even when I visited in late April, it felt unnaturally chilled, as though the whole building were a cold spot. The walls ricochet sound in unexpected ways, making for strange echoes. Moundsville *works* on you, even as a tourist.

The prison also speaks to you, giving the history of its former occupants through the paintings and words that decorate the walls. Somewhat anomalously, the wardens at Moundsville began allowing prisoners to paint murals on the walls, starting in the 1960s until the prison's closure in 1995. The insides of Moundsville are covered with cryptic imagery, traces of the lives lived inside these walls—everything from the Teenage Mutant Ninja Turtles to lyrics by Guns N' Roses and Hank Williams. For the most part there is a mixture of fantasy and nature imagery (mountain waterfalls, medieval knights, dinosaurs), gang signs, Confederate flags, skulls and demons, along with cartoon characters. The prison failed to keep records of the artists, and aside from what's passed down in oral history, the purpose and meaning of the images have become ambiguous. Once a series of faceless cells and corridors, Moundsville today, through these murals, preserves strange, elliptical stories of the people who were once imprisoned here.

Many buildings—most notably the houses we live in, but, really, any building in which we spend a great deal of time—establish a kind of feedback loop with their inhabitants. Through the placement of furniture and decoration, patterns of wear and habit, even the unpacking of luggage in a hotel room, we arrange and order the spaces we move through to suit our needs. But this doesn't happen in a prison. The effect here is entirely one-way; the prison molds the inmate and gives the inmate no quarter to be himself or herself, to step out of line, to change the circumstances of the prison to suit personal needs. The caged-in hallways, the towering rows of identical cells, the naked toilets in plain sight—everything is designed to remind you that no human could live here, despite the reality that thousands do.

Eastern State Penitentiary gets more press than Moundsville—it's bigger, more famous, and more likely to show up in online roundups as the "most haunted" prison. But it's also right in the middle of Philadelphia, hemmed in by restaurants and cafés and upscale salons and nice houses, and despite the gothic ambiance of its façade, it is integrated into the city. Moundsville is itself remote, and the prison rises out of the ground as an anomaly, forlorn and distant.

And then there's the mound across the street.

Nearly seventy feet tall and nine hundred feet in circumference, consisting of some fifty-five thousand cubic yards of dirt, the Grave Creek Mound is the largest extant burial mound in the country. It was constructed some two thousand years ago by the Adena, a culture that had mostly died out by the year 200. The Adena remain a mystery to anthropologists, and the very existence of the startling-looking mound has belied attempts to definitively explain its purpose or its creators.

Joseph Tomlinson discovered it in 1770. After a day on his land, south of Wheeling, he climbed a small knoll less than a quarter mile from his cabin, only to realize that he was standing not on a hill but on an enormous mound of excavated dirt that had been more or less hiding in plain sight. Gradually, it began to draw curiosity seekers, and theories abounded as to what might be inside the massive mound, with people speculating that it held the keys to ancient civilizations long gone. By 1838, the Tomlinsons had raised enough money to fund an excavation of the site.

The mound, as it happened, contained not mysteries to vast civilizations but only the remains of two individuals. A museum of sorts was created in the middle of the mound, where a visitor could pay a quarter to see the mound's contents. Upon entering the mound, one found a central room supported by a brick column. "Around the base of this column there is a circular shelf provided with wire cases," recorded one visitor in 1842, "in which the bones, head ornaments, and other objects of interest, found in the vaults are arranged. The place was dark, or but dimly lighted with a few tallow candles, which cast around a sepulchral glare on the wired skeleton and other bones spread around." But without a railroad or other easy access to Moundsville, the mound couldn't attract widespread excitement.

As a tourist attraction the Grave Creek Mound had failed by 1846, but over the years other attempts were made to wring some value from this inexplicable earthwork: a saloon was built on top of it at one point, and during the Civil War artillery cannons were stationed there. In 1874 a former warden of the penitentiary bought it; he first installed a dance platform on it but was hoping to use it to support a water tank to supply the prison and the town. This plan, too, failed, and the state finally purchased the site in 1909.

The mound was in serious disrepair by then. The state used prison labor to refill the holes in the mound and repair other damage. A cultural center was added, but while it does an admirable job of reconstructing early Adena culture, there's so much that simply isn't known. The mound stands as a monument to the gaps in our history, the things in the past that we can no longer access.

Numerous blogs have connected the haunted prison with the Grave Creek Mound via a variety of bizarre speculations involving aliens, buried giants, and more. The two structures are a study in contrasts: one ephemeral, composed of dirt, perpetually threatening to return to the land; the other cut from solid rock, utterly impregnable, not likely to ever come down except by the most strenuous effort. The mound has stubbornly resisted attempts by the local white population to monetize it, whereas the prison has been relatively successful in turning its legacy into much-needed funds that keep it alive. And while the Grave Creek Mound remains unknowable, the prison lends itself remarkably well to a narrative of crime and punishment, of good and evil.

No matter your crime, once you were in Moundsville, your life was pretty much forfeit. The place was underfunded and understaffed, and there was no room for pity. The world of the penitentiary is one of lawlessness, of anarchy, which is in part why it's so frightening. By one estimate, at any given time in Moundsville's operating history, inmates outnumbered guards by at least 20 to 1. Designed to hold 650 inmates but often holding in excess of 2,000, it was staffed with fewer than 50 guards on shift at any given time during the day.

This chronic lack of guards and resources led, as one might expect, to a level of violence among the inmates that approached pure anarchy. In November 1992, a leader of the Aryan Brotherhood, "Red" Snyder, was stabbed repeatedly by his neighbor Rusty Lassiter. The two had been good friends, but a price on Snyder's head by a rival proved too enticing for Lassiter.

This betrayal perhaps accounts for why Snyder's restless ghost continues to haunt his cell, calling out to the former guards who now give tours of the prison. But his murder is only one of many instances of horrific brutality that have transpired behind the prison's walls. Its history is filled with savage violence by inmates—prominently involving rival gangs making examples of each other. Moundsville is perhaps most notorious for the underground recreation room—the Sugar Shack, as it was known—which was unsupervised and played host to countless beatings, rapes, and murders.

The desire for a quick and ready dispatch of justice underlies so many of our ghost tales. Part of our belief in ghosts, you could say, comes from our belief in perfect and unambiguous justice. As opposed to tales of, say, a poltergeist, a spirit that is mischievous without direction, or a demon or other actively malevolent spirit, ghost stories often revolve around crime and punishment. The story of Zona Heaster Shue's murder is a perfect example: a murderer nearly gets away with a crime, but the ghost returns to see justice done. The mother avenges the daughter, an inverted *Hamlet*, where the ghost will not rest until its relatives stand up for it. Indeed, the story of the Greenbrier Ghost is so perfectly literary that it almost seems like something out of a book.

But did a ghost actually help convict Trout Shue?

In the early 1980s author Katie Letcher Lyle, having heard the story of the Greenbrier Ghost from one of Trout Shue's descendants, set out to discover what was fact and what was fiction. She interviewed living descendants, scoured news stories and trial records, and while she found that the main elements of the story are by and large true, there are odd discrepancies between how Zona's story is usually told and the actual history.

For one, while Zona's mother did testify to having seen a ghost during Shue's murder trial, she did so at the behest of the defense, not the prosecution. John Preston, the prosecuting attorney, apparently thought the ghost story too fantastic to be of any actual help and did not call Mary

Jane Heaster as a witness for fear of sabotaging his case. It was the defense who summoned her to the stand, hoping to discredit the whole proceedings by implying it had been initiated by a hysterical mother.

Aside from her testimony in court, there is no other record of the ghost visiting Heaster until after the conviction, and the supposedly telling detail—that the ghost had told her mother about the broken veterbrae—doesn't explain why the autopsy (if done at the ghost's urging) would have started by searching for signs of poisoning.

Lyle came up with her own theory as to what really happened: In the January 28, 1897, edition of the *Greenbrier Independent*, news of Zona Heaster Shue's death was covered on page three, but on page one was a curious story out of Australia. "One of the most famous murder cases in Australia," it read, "was discovered by the ghost of the murdered man sitting on the rail of a dam (Australian for horse pond) into which his body had been thrown. Numberless people saw it, and the crime was duly brought home." The item continues:

> Years after, a dying man making his confession said that he invented the ghost. He witnessed the crime, but was threatened with death if he divulged it as he wished to, and the only way he saw out of the impasse was to affect to see the ghost where the body would be found. As soon as he started the story, such is the power of nervousness that numerous other people began to see it, until its fame reached such dimensions that a search was made and the body found, and the murderers brought to justice.

Mary Jane Heaster was no idiot, nor was she hysterical. She had strong suspicions that Shue had killed her daughter and that the local officials, whatever their own beliefs might have been, weren't doing anything about it. The Australian ghost story inspired her, according to Lyle, to concoct her own vision of justice, which she then used as leverage to spur the authorities back into action.

Lyle admits that, as Mary Jane Heaster is long dead and left no confession, this hypothesis is circumstantial. And yet so, too, was Shue's conviction. Though the autopsy proved that Zona was murdered, during the trial the prosecution provided no physical evidence that Trout was the culprit. He was convicted based entirely on his suspicious actions after her death.

The case of Trout Shue is unsettling, I think, not because of its supernatural element but because of the obviously roughshod manner in which justice was carried out. Shue might very well have been guilty; the people of Greenbrier certainly thought so. If so, why couldn't they convict him through more substantial means? What is more troublesome about Zona Heaster's story: that a possibly innocent man was convicted of her death based on nothing but circumstantial evidence? Or that a guilty man could not have been convicted through the accepted legal framework on which we usually rely?

The ghost story does away with this unsettling quandary. In the years since the verdict and Shue's death, the Greenbrier Ghost has come to stand for a kind of certainty, the same certainty we seek in the thick walls of an old prison. Offering a vision of pure justice, the unavenged ghost wipes away all the legal ambiguities of the case with a brush of a spectral hand, leaving only the pure truth.

CHAPTER TEN

THE STAIN

Danvers, MA, and Athens, OH

Towering above the local landscape on a hill in northeastern Massachusetts are the remains of the Danvers State Hospital, its imposing clock tower still looming over the traffic on nearby I-95. Here, it is said, John Hathorne—one of the head judges of the Salem witch trials, known for his harsh interrogations, his presumption of the guilt of the accused—built his home. In the curious way that America sometimes piles one tragedy upon another, as if to quarantine the evil, the land that had been Hathorne's became the site of the Danvers State Hospital, a place built with the best of all possible intentions that would, in time, be known as the worst of all possible worlds.

The hospital was made famous by H. P. Lovecraft, who used it as a model for his fictional Arkham Sanitarium. The real-life hospital was built in 1874 and has long had a host of legends attached to it. Even after the hospital was closed in 1992, its legacy as a haunted asylum remains.

If you call to mind a haunted mental asylum, you are undoubtedly thinking of Danvers: an ornate but sinister Victorian façade, long wings, and, in the center of the building, a glowering clock tower. This is no accident; Danvers is one of many asylums based on a similar model, a design by architect Thomas Kirkbride that was first implemented in 1848, at the

New Jersey State Lunatic Asylum in Trenton. By the end of the nine-teenth century, Kirkbrides dotted the country, from Salem, Massachu-setts, to Salem, Oregon—home of the Oregon State Insane Asylum (where Ken Kesey's novel *One Flew Over the Cuckoo's Nest* was set). But within the past few decades, most of these buildings have been aban-doned, demolished, or repurposed—few still operate as mental health institutions.

Danvers began shuttering its facilities in the late 1960s and shut down entirely in 1992. In 2006, after a lengthy process, a developer bought the property and set about renovating what was left of the asylum into luxury condos; the hospital's massive wings were demolished, but the central ad-ministration building with its clock tower was preserved. Inside it smells of new carpet and fresh paint. If it feels eerie now, it's perhaps not because of its provenance as a haunted asylum but because of its utter generic feel-ing: once you step inside its doors, you could be in any modest hotel chain in the country.

Unlike Moundsville and Eastern State, which were meant to exude a melancholy terror, their architecture part of the punishment, Danvers and its many sisters were designed to be welcoming, to reassure both patients and their families that they were in good, safe hands.

For centuries the mad belonged to the same group of society as the blind, the poor, the sick, and the elderly; all who could not work or other-wise easily contribute to society were more or less treated equally, regardless of the specificity of their situations. Prior to the rise of asylums, the mad were often sequestered in off-limits parts of their house. (Most famously, of course, in *Jane Eyre*, when Jane confronts the "madwoman in the attic," Bertha.) But gradually, in the seventeenth and eighteenth centuries, the first madhouses began offering a place where wealthy families could seques-ter relatives. The madhouse, in this light, was simply the attic, or the base-ment, of the house, made external and moved elsewhere.

Early madhouses were often revealed to be nightmares of abuse and neglect. Reports of incontinent patients hosed down with icy water, naked women chained haphazardly to the walls, fleas and rats rampant, and other horrors gradually prompted a desire for something more sanitary and humane. In England, Bethlehem Royal Hospital—more often known as Bedlam—became so associated with chaos, horror, and depravity that its name has entered the dictionary as a catchall for chaos and lunacy.

In 1843 Dorothea Dix emerged as a powerful voice calling for social reform. In a memorandum sent to the legislators of her home state of Massachusetts, she railed against "the present state of insane persons confined within this Commonwealth, in cages, closets, stalls, pens! Chained, naked, beaten with rods, and lashed into obedience!" She found instances of inmates padlocked in cellars, left in the dark to wail in torment for years without aid or treatment. Something had to give.

The "moral treatment," as it came to be known, became the solution: rather than chained and forgotten, patients would be unshackled and allowed to move about the asylum at will. Instead of being tortured and imprisoned, patients would work and play. Through labor and sports, hobbies and other recreations, the moral treatment promised rehabilitation and freedom from insanity. The moral model was held out as a means of actually curing patients, rather than simply bundling them out of sight. "All experience," Dix claimed, "showed that insanity reasonably treated is as curable as a cold or a fever."

The Kirkbride asylum came to be the architectural style most thoroughly associated in the United States with the moral treatment. Rather than terrifying, the new asylum would be inviting, surrounded by lawns and gardens that patients could tend themselves. The defining features of the Kirkbride asylum include the central administration building, stately and elegant, with a central tower and elongated wings, forming a shallow V that extends back farther and farther. Part of the beauty of this architectural model was that wings could always be added farther out indefinitely. As a result, they were often massive, growing to hundreds of thousands of square feet.

There was another reason for the ostentation in the Kirkbride design: while insanity, in its various forms, has accompanied humankind forever, the discipline of psychiatry was still nascent, and the idea of "treating" mental patients was not yet fully accepted. Kirkbride believed that, unlike other diseases, mental illness could not be treated at home, and required an institutional setting, but at the same time treated their asylums as home: doctors referred to themselves as "fathers," the asylum as "the house," the patients as "the family." The asylum provided a large and visible monument to psychiatry. Built with sturdy stone, designed with grace and care, it made real the role of the psychiatrist; like a badge or a uniform, the building itself established authority and legitimized the discipline. People could see and point to it as a place of healing; it allowed people to see insanity as a disease that could be cured, and a psychiatrist as the doctor to cure it. It also became a clearinghouse for all the various maladies that could now be grouped under the notion of mental health. The asylum, in its own way, created both the doctor and the patient.

Dozens of Kirkbride asylums were built throughout the country during the second half of the nineteenth century. They became a way for middle- and upper-class families to transfer care of sick relatives to private facilities where professionals could assume the burden of care. They were inseparable from the burgeoning industrialization of the day; academic Benjamin Reiss refers to the asylum as a "laboratory for the purification of culture and the production of useful citizens."

The Kirkbride asylum was meant to be the antidote to the kinds of horrific treatments at places like Bedlam. Why are we so afraid of them today?

Kirkbride asylums are, by design, huge. Danvers was originally 70,000 square feet, but this is modest compared with some of her sisters. The

Trans-Allegheny Lunatic Asylum of West Virginia was 242,000 square feet; the Northern Michigan Asylum in Traverse City was, when completed, more than 380,000 square feet; Greystone in New Jersey and the Ridges in Athens, Ohio, were both more than 660,000 square feet.

Originally the asylums' size and amenities were subsidized by the affluent families who wanted the best for their relatives. But in the wake of the Civil War, veterans began to crowd the only federal Kirkbride asylum in Washington, D.C. (the Government Hospital for the Insane, since renamed St. Elizabeths Hospital), and it became clear that insanity was not simply a problem for those with money.

By the second half of the nineteenth century, psychiatric care fell more and more under state control. Private Kirkbride asylums were turned over to the states, and many states built their own in imitation of the same model. For the first time size and cost began to be an issue.

Public officials balked at lavishing taxpayer resources on so few inmates. One opponent, Hervey B. Wilbur, tallied up the cost of various asylums alongside their relative capacities: Danvers, built at a cost of $1.6 million, was designed to house only 450 patients; the Ridges, built for $950,000 for just 600 beds; Worcester State Hospital in Massachusetts, built for $1.25 million for only 450 beds; Greystone, built at a cost of $2.5 million for just 800 beds; and so on. Wilbur ultimately estimated that the Kirkbride asylums were costing around $2,600 per bed—and that excluded the site's land value and its furniture, to say nothing of its staff and upkeep.

The solution seemed to be to take these great buildings and cram into them as many humans as possible. Buildings that were meant to be expansive and give patients a great amount of freedom were now stuffed with bodies, creating a downward spiral of deplorable conditions, understaffing, overtaxed resources, and inhumane treatment.

Whatever the Kirkbride model promised by way of rehabilitation rates was effectively destroyed by this civic disengagement. The asylums became host to the worst kind of neglect and abuse that had typified their precursors—precisely what they had been designed to address.

By the end of the nineteenth century, the Kirkbride plan was being abandoned in favor of another form of architecture: the so-called cottage plan, which focused on campuses of smaller, freestanding buildings instead of giant, imposing façades. The Kirkbrides seemed anachronistic, reflective of an earlier age in which tax money was wasted on frivolous architectural details and massive floorplans.

In a short time the Kirkbride ideal went from being seen as progressive to being a symbol of neglect. And so the clock tower of the administration building became menacing and the loving touches meant to look like home became grotesque parodies.

Through it all the stately façade of the Kirkbride asylums remained stately, even if now the boastful architecture projected not sanity and sanitary conditions but a living nightmare. Stories of deaths inside the walls, bodies forgotten, "treatment" that resembled sadistic torture, gradually gave way to stories of ghosts, poisoned land, and haunted buildings.

The ghost stories surrounding the haunting of Kirkbride asylums, like the Danvers Hospital, often originate in a very real, very troubled past. Danvers quickly became notorious for its overcrowding, with almost four times as many patients as the hospital was designed to house. Patients sometimes died out of sight of the staff and their bodies decomposed for days before they were noticed. A report from 1939 noted that more than 10 percent of the asylum's population had died within its walls. Add to the hospital's grisly reputation the ignoble distinction of being the place where the prefrontal lobotomy was refined and widely implemented. It's precisely this accumulation of horrors behind its walls that has led to the prevalence of spirits at Danvers and made it a mecca for paranormal enthusiasts. Thrill seekers trying to get access to the hospital even after it closed its doors led to heightened security on the property; more than 120 would-be ghost hunters have been arrested for trespassing since 2000.

Among those who claim to have seen things there is Jeralyn

Levasseur, who grew up on the grounds (her father, Gerald Richards, was a hospital administrator). Levasseur recalls apparitions angrily scowling at her and her sister when she was a child, and once in high school her bed-covers were yanked off in the middle of the night without warning. Levasseur explained her experiences as a function of the changing nature of psychiatric health: "If you think back to the beginnings of medical science and the things done to people," she told a local newspaper in 2003, "not because they thought they were doing bad, but because they were trying to do right, you have to wonder, did people think they were being tortured?"

The history of the asylum, as with the hospital, is the history of practices that once seemed necessary and now strike us as bizarre and troubling. Dr. Henry Cotton, who from 1907 to 1930 was the superintendent at the Trenton State Hospital (the former New Jersey State Lunatic Asylum, first of the Kirkbrides), performed savage surgeries on his patients for decades, extracting everything from teeth to stomachs in the belief that infections were contributing to his patients' psychological instability.

Haunted by such legacies, the ruins of the Kirkbride asylums—and their attendant lore—reveal how uncomfortable we've become with anti-quated methods of "healing the sick." Whatever the intentions behind them, lobotomies, straitjackets, and aggressive shock therapy now strike us as barbaric and unnecessary and hover in the back of our collective consciousness. As a culture we still struggle with unresolvable questions that were once wrongly answered in places like these: Who is crazy? Are we crazy? And what can we do to assure ourselves that we aren't?

The stories of ghosts in the asylums are mostly driven by this anxiety, and for the most part they are the standard, vague stories without much substantiation. But if there is a particularly haunting symbol of the fall of the Kirkbrides—one that is verifiably real—it can be found in Athens, Ohio, in what's left of the Ridges.

The Ridges first opened in 1868 as the Athens Lunatic Asylum—a monstrous campus stretching more than eight hundred feet long. Rather than the single central tower of Danvers, the Ridges is marked by the dual towers of the main administration building, giving its profile vague echoes of Notre Dame.

The plan included not just decorative lakes and fields meant to soothe wandering intellects but also gardens, orchards, and eventually a dairy barn, all tended by the inmates, in an effort to make the facility entirely self-sufficient. For a time it even played host to an alligator, which lived in its fountain during the summer months.

The asylum was built to house just over five hundred patients, but the population quickly grew to double that; like other Kirkbrides, the site soon faced overcrowding. By the 1970s it was underfunded and ill managed, with inmates poorly accounted for and large portions of the complex boarded up or otherwise not in use. In such a setting emerged a ghost story so compelling it ended up in the *Journal of Forensic Sciences*—that of the ghost of Margaret Schilling.

A patient of the Ridges' Continued Care Unit, Schilling, then fifty-three years old, had general freedom of movement and no serious behavioral problems—she was a model patient, her behavior unremarkable in every way. But on December 1, 1978, she failed to show up for dinner, having disappeared without any sign. Within a few hours an extensive search was launched, with staff crisscrossing the wards in search of her. They didn't find her that night—a worrying sign, given the brutally cold winter that had set in.

It wasn't until January 11, 1979, more than a month later, that workers found Schilling's body in the attic of an abandoned wing. There was no sign of foul play. Schilling appeared to have taken off her clothes and folded them neatly before lying down to die on the cold floor. No one could say how long she'd been dead, but despite the cold winter, the room had been warm enough to allow for significant decay.

She left behind no clues as to how she'd ended up there or what had led to her death, but she did leave behind a gruesome mystery: when workers removed her decomposing corpse from the concrete floor, they found a stain in the shape of Schilling's body: a ghostly outline in chalky white, ringed by a fainter, darker outline. And despite how hard workers tried to clean the floor, the stain would not come off.

The stain of Margaret Schilling still remains. Over the years it's been the source of numerous ghost tales and rumors about the hospital, but Schilling's manifestation is not paranormal. A forensic team that investigated the stain in 2007 determined that the image was likely a result of a process called adipocere: the breakdown during decomposition of the body's fat into soap. The investigators found a waxy residue on the floor that had significantly altered the chemistry of the concrete itself, leaving it lighter than the surrounding area. While usually adipocere requires moist, enclosed conditions (say, those of a coffin buried in the right kind of soil), the forensic team's best guess was that Schilling's corpse had undergone some similar process despite the less-than-ideal conditions of the attic.

This strikes me as far more terrifying than an actual ghost. That this woman, placed in the asylum's care, was left to rot on this floor, her body imprinting itself on the cold, unforgiving concrete, seems more disturbing than any tale of an apparition or unidentified noise. Herself unable to tell her tale, Margaret Schilling nonetheless managed to leave an indictment of her caretakers, a savage rebuke of the years of psychiatry that has left a deep stain on our history.

This regime of horrors wasn't always evident. Family members and officials who came to tour these asylums often failed to see anything amiss. One of the benefits of the Kirkbride layout, with its gently flanking wings moving farther and farther away from the main administration building, was that it allowed the facility to segregate patients based on the severity of their condition. Traditionally the more difficult patients—the violent, the noisy, the untreatable—were housed in the wings farthest out, while the more sedate and promising patients were kept closer to the main building.

Visiting relatives, shown the main building and the adjacent wings, left convinced that their relatives were in a stately, dignified place, not a madhouse. This was important, after all, so long as these institutions were private and depended on paying customers in the form of satisfied families. What went on behind closed doors would always remain a mystery.

Stories began to emerge of horrors inside via the reports of those who'd escaped. Some of the more sensational of these came from a man named Ebenezer Haskell. Haskell was involuntarily committed to the Pennsylvania Hospital for the Insane in 1866 and escaped twice, the second time breaking his leg in the process. After a jury deemed him sane, Haskell wrote a book about his incarceration and trial in which he cited a number of horrific examples of patient mistreatment, including what he claimed was called the "Spread Eagle Cure," a treatment that bore eerie similarities to the torture young Armstead Mason Newman endured in Lumpkin's Jail:

> A disorderly patient is stripped naked and thrown on his back, four men take hold of the limbs and stretch them out at right angles, then the doctor or some one of the attendants stands up on a chair or table and pours a number of buckets full of cold water on his face until life is nearly extinct, then the patient is removed to his dungeon cured of all diseases; the shock is so great it frequently produces *death*.

It's hard to say for sure how accurate Haskell's report was, particularly given his obvious ax to grind. But the lack of any clear information of what was going on, mixed with rumors and horror stories, only added to the picture the public began to form about the state of psychiatric care in general and at the asylum in particular.

The asylum in the nineteenth century embodies a tension between the visible and invisible—that is its most disturbing aspect. There is the highly visible and pronounced architecture, which projects one story, and there are the mostly invisible rooms on the edges, in the wings farthest out, hidden from public view.

Poe tapped into this tension in his short story "The System of Doctor Tarr and Professor Fether." A visitor to an unidentified asylum in France ("a fantastic château, much dilapidated, and indeed scarcely tenantable through age and neglect," one whose façade inspires the narrator with "absolute dread") is shown a model of humane treatment, though gradually it becomes apparent that something is off. Only in the climax of the story is it revealed that the patients have overtaken the asylum; they've taken to impersonating the doctors, while the doctors themselves, along with the staff, have been locked up as patients. In the story's final pages the doctors escape and riot; having been tarred and feathered, they unleash a terrifying fury on their captors, "fighting, stamping, scratching, and howling," having been rendered less than human by their captivity. It's a scene that speaks to the fine line between sanity and insanity. Once the doctors escape, they are as dangerous and as frightening as we've suspected the patients to be. Which is to say, once you're inside the walls of the asylum, objective sanity is all but impossible.

Asylums became haunted by what happened inside their walls and also by the walls themselves: an architecture that was purposely boastful but which spoke of a previous generation with different ideals, economic motives, and attitudes toward the sick. The moment when we were most optimistic about our ability to cure the mind is when we built our most ostentatious palaces to psychiatry. There is a danger, then, in telegraphing too prominently one's utopian ideals via architecture.

We design buildings not only for their utilitarian values but to project specific ideals and reflect our shared values. But these ideals and values are prone to change faster than the buildings. Shifting political fortunes, vacillating periods of excess and austerity, evolving attitudes about how the government should best serve its population—these all tend to move much faster than the time it takes for a building to outlive its usefulness.

"These are America's castles," Robert Kirkbride told me, speaking of the hospitals built on the plan of his ancestor Thomas Kirkbride. An architect and architectural historian himself, Robert was involved with the effort to save one building in particular: Greystone Park Psychiatric Hospital, in Morristown, New Jersey. Less than a year after it was closed, in 2008, a scheme to demolish the massive building and replace it with town houses was put forward by the city, only to be defeated by concerned citizens who argued that the hospital deserved saving: even as a gargantuan gothic ruin, Greystone was an important part of New Jersey's history as well as a significant architectural landmark.

Cities have struggled to deal with these albatrosses—massive, unloved, associated with ghosts and an age gone by—as they've been decommissioned and treatment has moved elsewhere. Not only do they haunt our dreams; they haunt our local governments, who must figure out what to do with them. Many are on highly prized land that has developers salivating; even those that aren't are massive buildings that require resources to keep them from falling into disrepair. They are filled with asbestos and lead paint—toxic materials that are another kind of civic ghost, a remnant of a former idea now discarded.

Danvers's Kirkbride is a typical compromise, in which the most striking feature—the administration building's façade—was preserved, while the surrounding structures were demolished. Others have been made into malls, universities, and other structures. The Northern Michigan Asylum, in Traverse City, was reopened in 2005 as the Village, a complex of shops, restaurants, and residences. The Hudson River Psychiatric Hospital, in Poughkeepsie, New York, after sustaining damage from a lightning strike and two subsequent fires, is likewise being reborn as a mixed-use commercial site. Also in New York, the Buffalo State Asylum for the Insane is in the process of being transformed into a hotel and conference center.

Other buildings have not fared as well. The city of Morristown solicited redevelopment bids for Greystone, but despite receiving six serious proposals from developers, it finally opted to spend up to $50 million to tear down the structure. Greystone, like a ghost, did not go quietly. Built with solid concrete, it cost the state more than $30 million to knock it down.

Robert Kirkbride himself is haunted by a different aspect of these asylums: the very materials in their construction. The Northern Michigan Asylum, he points out, is a massive structure built entirely with a form of Michigan pine that has now vanished. Which is to say, these buildings carry another kind of history, another kind of legacy: the raw materials of our changing landscape, an archaeology of our past.

The problem of the haunted Kirkbride asylums—behemoth structures that reflect a failed utopian plan, that have lingered long after they fell from vogue—is representative of many civic structures that we've come to see as haunted. Victims of changing fortunes, they've accrued stories of death, despair, and haunting in part because of their misuse or because the government and the people who built them were attempting to make a statement that no longer resonates in the same way. If the Kirkbride asylums are haunted, they are haunted, you could say, by the difference between how history is conceived and how it plays out.

CHAPTER ELEVEN

AWAITING THE DEVIL'S COMING

Charleston, SC, and Douglas County, KS

T he churchyard of the Unitarian Church in Charleston, South
Carolina, is great with ghosts. Overgrown and rapturously baroque, the graveyard is evocative of the kind of Southern gothic
that seems ripe for spirits and phantoms of all manner. A sign meets you
at the entrance, proclaiming that the paths are uneven and the grave
markers may be unstable. Grass pokes through the disintegrating brick
walkways, tombstones tilt amid the foliage, moss-laden trees drape over
paths. Individual plots are contained by elegant, lacy metalwork, and inside these quadrangles stately obelisks and humble crosses call out, asking
you to keep the memory of the dead alive. The weeds and other flora are
eager to reclaim the markers of the dead. In the years since a man named
Ephraim Seabrook Mikell died, in 1836, the roots of a giant neighboring
tree have begun to consume his tombstone, granite and wood fusing together. The legend across the tombstone now reads ACRED TO HIS MEMORY,
the "S" now buried inside the tree itself.

"The Souls of the Dead appear frequently" in cemeteries, Joseph Addison wrote in 1711, attributing the thought to Plato, "and hover about the
Places where their Bodies are buried, as still hankering after their old
brutal Pleasures, and desiring again to enter the Body that gave them an

Opportunity of fulfilling them." Here in this churchyard is the Ravenel family plot, where one might look—in vain—for the marker of Annabel Ravenel. According to sources, Annabel haunts this cemetery, hankering after an old pleasure, waiting for her beloved soldier to return.

Her father, Dr. Edmund Ravenel, divided his time between Charleston and nearby Sullivan's Island and was famous as a conchologist (several species of mollusk are named for him, including Ravenel's scallop) when in 1824 he was appointed the first chair in chemistry and pharmacology of the brand-new South Carolina Medical College. In time he would be appointed its dean.

In 1827 Ravenel befriended a young soldier by the name of Edgar A. Perry, who was stationed at Fort Moultrie, on the tip of Sullivan's Island. Ravenel apparently functioned as something of a father figure to the young Perry, whose own parents had disinherited him. Eventually Perry met Ravenel's fourteen-year-old daughter, Annabel, and the two fell madly in love.

When Ravenel discovered his daughter was in love with Perry, he closed his house on Sullivan's Island and returned to Charleston. If he'd hoped that that was the end, it wasn't; Perry followed Annabel to Charleston, where they would meet in secret under the weeping willows of the Unitarian Church Cemetery. When these trysts were discovered, Ravenel locked his daughter in her room. Within a few months she had died of yellow fever.

In order to keep Perry from haunting Annabel's grave, as it were, Ravenel disguised her tombstone. Perry soon was mustered out of service and returned to his life. But Annabel still waits for him at their secret meeting place.

Annabel Ravenel's story seems somewhat archetypal of the ghost stories of the old South: a delicate Southern belle, ruled by her passions but trapped within a strict patriarchal system. With a love unrequited, a cruel father, and a tragic outcome, the tale has all the elements of a gothic romance; it is also a universal fairy tale inflected with the genteel manners and diseased miasmas of South Carolina.

The story is particularly endearing to the citizens of Charleston, though, because of the revelation, in 1885, that Edgar A. Perry was not this soldier's real name. "Perry" was a pseudonym of the man who'd go on to (mostly posthumous) fame as the author of "The Raven" and the "Tell-Tale Heart." Annabel's beloved was none other than Edgar Allan Poe.

Poe biographer Arthur Hobson Quinn believes it probable that Poe knew Ravenel while stationed at Sullivan's Island, and there is some likelihood that the conchologist was the basis for the character William Legrand in Poe's "The Gold Bug"—a man "well educated, with unusual powers of mind, but infected with misanthropy, and subject to perverse moods of alternate enthusiasm and melancholy. . . . His chief amusements were gunning and fishing, or sauntering along the beach and through the myrtles, in quest of shells or entomological specimens." Annabel Ravenel, many now believe, would later serve as the basis for Poe's famous poem "Annabel Lee," with Sullivan's Island as the "kingdom by the sea":

> It was many and many a year ago,
> In a kingdom by the sea,
> That a maiden there lived whom you may know
> By the name of Annabel Lee;
> And this maiden she lived with no other thought
> Than to love and be loved by me.

Having fallen in love with his beautiful maiden, the narrator of Poe's poem laments:

> So that her highborn kinsmen came
> And bore her away from me,
> To shut her up in a sepulchre
> In this kingdom by the sea.

All of which, it would seem, tracks with the details of the love affair of Annabel Ravenel and Edgar A. Perry. Theirs is a beautiful story, full of gothic longing, a wasting beauty (so typical of Poe's writing), an elegy for the dead, all spun around an overgrown, haunted cemetery. We should not be dissuaded by the fact that Edmund Ravenel had no daughter named Annabel. "*I* was a child and *she* was a child," Poe's narrator waxes, but if this is truly about a daughter of Edmund Ravenel, then they were children of different magnitudes, for when Poe was stationed at Sullivan's Island, Ravenel's eldest daughter, Mary Louisa, would have been a mere eighteen months old.

The Unitarian Church no longer accepts new burials; the last remaining plots have been filled. Most burials in Charleston happen in much larger places, like Magnolia Cemetery and the more modern Live Oak Memorial Gardens. Magnolia Cemetery was dedicated in 1850, laid out on what was then the outskirts of the city. Unlike the Unitarian Church's cemetery, Magnolia is sprawling, open, and airy, dotted with pleasant lakesand generous views. Dubbed the "City of the Silent," it quickly became a prime tourist attraction for the city. "If you would see Charleston's greatest attraction drive to Magnolia Cemetery," *Appleton's Hand-Book of American Travel* advised in 1866. "This is indeed a lovely retreat; a scene of tangled woods and silvery waters, looking out upon the broad surface of the Cooper River, whose waters find their way into its pretty lake-lets, over which the majestic live-oaks hang their Druid mosses."

Large, rolling cemeteries like Magnolia, with their contemplative waters and acres of green, came about as a solution to a very pressing modern problem. Since the early Middle Ages, towns in Christian Europe (and later in North America) were laid out around a central church, and adjacent to that church would be the town's graveyard. It was necessary to be buried in consecrated ground so that one could await the Second Coming, and so graveyards were as centrally located as the churches they bordered.

This layout, with a churchyard at the center of town, worked fine in small towns, but with the rise of cities, it became untenable. For one thing, there were simply too many bodies to cram into a small plot of consecrated ground. As churches ran out of space, they would re-trench their graveyards and remove the bones to charnel houses or, in some cases, simply pile new corpses on top of the old. Churchgoers complained of the overwhelming foul odor of decaying bodies, with one critic suggesting the real reason behind burning incense during services was to mask the smell of decomposition. And while germ theory wouldn't be fully understood until the late nineteenth century, by the 1700s people already understood that dead bodies could breed disease. In 1744 a story circulated of a funeral procession in Montpellier, France: when workers opened a vault to inter a newly deceased body, a cloud of poisonous gas spewed forth, knocking the priest unconscious and killing three mourners.

The solution, city planners understood, was to move the bodies away from the church and outside of town—far, far outside of town. In 1804 Paris opened Père-Lachaise, a lush necropolis of 118 acres on the outskirts of the city. Green, rolling hills with widely spaced, stately monuments replaced the crammed, gloomy rows of decrepit tombstones, and mourners and picnickers alike were invited to spend their afternoons in Elysian idyll and quiet contemplation.

The so-called garden cemetery concept caught on quickly, and large cities everywhere began exchanging their cramped churchyards for pastoral campuses far removed from the urban metropolis. In the United States the first of these was Mount Auburn, outside Boston, opened in 1831, followed by New York's Green-Wood, in the faraway suburb of Brooklyn, in 1838. The most comprehensive plan was adopted by San Francisco when, in 1900, the city moved all its remaining remains to the tiny suburb of Colma. Fully 73 percent of Colma's land today is occupied by one of its seventeen cemeteries. "Colma," reads the town's motto, "where it's great to be alive!"

Keeping the living from encroaching on such places has proved difficult over time. Chicago's main cemetery, City Cemetery, was laid out in 1842, situated well beyond the city's northern limits, north of North Avenue and east of Clark Street. Subsequent cholera outbreaks strained its capacity, though, and the site itself was far from ideal for the long-term storage of bodies. Because of its low elevation, the cemetery was regularly flooded, and the waters had the undesirable effect of occasionally forcing coffins to the surface.

By 1858 the city was pressing up against the boundaries of the cemetery, and physician John H. Rauch spearheaded a movement to relocate the dead. Rauch, in line with prevailing medical understanding, argued that "the emanations of the dead are injurious to health and destructive to life"; he wanted to move the dead out of their swampy resting places and away from the city's population to a drier, forested location where trees could absorb the noxious gases of decomposition.

The city acted fast. In November Chicago's aldermen acquiesced to Rauch's pleas, agreeing to investigate the possibility of moving the cemetery to new grounds, and within months they had chartered a new corporation, the Rosehill Cemetery Company, to open up a new burial ground on the North Side. Rosehill Cemetery was inaugurated on July 28, 1859, and was followed that November by the founding of the rural Catholic cemetery Calvary, and finally Graceland, in 1860.

As with Rosehill, Graceland was built and operated by a private company chartered by the city. The cemetery's founder, lawyer, and land speculator Thomas Bryan, was intimately aware of the shortcomings of the old City Cemetery. When he had searched for a plot for his infant son, who'd died in 1855, he'd found City Cemetery "neglected" and in an "actually repulsive condition," which had induced him to search for land "for a rural burying ground, more remote from and more worthy of the city." Contrasted to the low-lying, marshy terrain of City Cemetery, Graceland would be on high ground, wooded with old-growth trees. It would be a place of rolling acres, graves ornate and stately, clean fresh air—an idyllic final resting spot. Landscaped with native trees and flowers, it would in time be described as the "most perfect expression" of the "modern, park-like cemetery."

The plan to build these cemeteries well outside city limits was never truly successful, since inevitably cities spread. Brooklyn is of course now incorporated into New York City, and the real estate surrounding Green-Wood is among the most expensive in the nation; one doesn't have to wonder how many salivating contractors would plow those bodies under in a heartbeat if given the chance to build high-rises. Likewise, Colma, California, is today surrounded on all sides by high-priced suburbs. Graceland was a victim of its own success; it was so popular as a destination for day trips that it heightened the value of the surrounding real estate: originally known as the township Lake View, the community adjacent to Graceland grew quickly after the cemetery was founded, first becoming its own city and then, in 1889, merging with Chicago itself.

The shift wasn't just about urban space; it also had ramifications both religious and linguistic. For much of English history, a place where dead bodies were buried was known exclusively as a churchyard; this was true even if the land itself was not adjacent to a church (such as the mass burial pits dug in London during the Black Death). The word "cemetery," whichcomes from the Greek *koimētērion* and originally meant simply a dormitory or a place to sleep, had been adopted first by early Christians, who saw sleep as temporary and used the Latin *coemeterium* to refer to the tombs of martyrs, who were simply sleeping and would soon arise once more. By the fifteenth century "cemetery" had entered the English lexicon as an acceptable synonym for "churchyard," and it is not until the 1750s that "cemetery" had its own distinct definition: "a place where the dead are reposited," according to Samuel Johnson's 1755 dictionary. "Churchyard" still meant consecrated ground, but "cemetery" did not; any place that received remains could be a cemetery.

If "graveyard" and "cemetery" had once been more or less synonymous terms, now they represented two very distinct concepts: one tiny, central, and consecrated; the other expansive, distant, and civic in function. By moving the dead out of the grounds of the church, the garden cemetery could also become a place of national significance. At the dedication of Mount Auburn Cemetery, Supreme Court Justice Joseph Story spoke of transforming it into a "more efficient instrument to elevate Ambition, to stimulate Genius, and to dignify Learning." The grave, he argued, has "a voice of eloquence, nay, of super human eloquence," one that, among other things, "awakens a new enthusiasm for virtue," "calls up the images of the illustrious dead," and "demands of us, as men, as patriots, as Christians, as immortals, that the powers given by God should be devoted to his service, and the minds created by his love, should return to him with larger capacities for virtuous enjoyment, and with more spiritual and intellectual brightness." The eloquent voice of the dead, then, could and should be marshaled to enrich the living, to urge us to a higher calling and civic virtues.

Many small towns, of course, continue to use their churchyards. When I was in college in Oregon in the 1990s, I regularly drove past the Old Scotch Church, just off Highway 27 on unincorporated land near Hillsboro. The church itself is a historic monument, with a striking eight-sided steeple, and its churchyard contains the graves of several early Oregon settlers. It also contains fresh graves, including one for a young child, whose unique and singularly disquieting headstone was visible from the road as you drove by: a two-foot-tall Nerf basketball hoop.

Most of these smaller graveyards have stopped taking new occupants, and some cities, like San Francisco, have paved over their old churchyards for new real estate projects. (Only two cemeteries remain within San Francisco's city limits: one at the Mission Dolores Church, the other at the Presidio.) Others have simply fallen into disrepair. Without an influx of new bodies, these places gradually lost their mourners as well, which is to say that there are fewer and fewer people with a vested interest in maintaining them, and so many churchyards in America have become overgrown and melancholy.

And with the weeds come the ghosts.

Churchyards make for good hauntings, not only because they are places of the dead but because they are anachronistic. As garden cemeteries became the norm, with their emphasis on spiritual uplift, old churchyards, almost out of necessity, came to be seen as their opposite: gloomy and forlorn, dire and dreary. While guidebooks were urging tourists to visit Mount Auburn, Magnolia Cemetery, and Arlington, folklorists were recording stories of supernatural disturbances at old graveyards. Ghosts emerge from places of neglect, and churchyards are the homes of the neglected dead.

The graveyard of St. Paul's Chapel, in lower Manhattan, is home to one such strange ghost: the Shakespearean actor George Frederick Cooke, who was buried there in 1812—most of him, at least. Cooke had been a tremendous success on the American stage when he came over from England in 1810, but he died just two short years later from alcoholism. He had a modest plot at St. Paul's until a fellow actor, Edmund Kean, paid to have his remains reinterred beneath a grander monument. The process was not without incident; Kean removed one of Cooke's toes as a keepsake ("it was a little black relic," recalled one observer, "and might have passed for a tobacco-stopper"). Additionally, Cooke's skull was stolen; no one knows who took it, but the doctor John W. Francis later had it in his possession and years later loaned it out for a performance of *Hamlet*, the deceased Shakespearean appearing in the role of Yorick. Cooke's skull now resides in the Scott Library of Thomas Jefferson University, but his headless ghost still haunts the churchyard of St. Paul's Chapel, looking for what's been stolen.

St. Paul's churchyard, at least, is still in good shape, well tended and surrounded by the bustling metropolis of New York City. Far from the madding crowds you'll find the Stull Cemetery, in Douglas County, Kansas, all the more legendary for its remoteness. Getting there isn't easy: after you leave the freeway near Lawrence, you take a series of back roads that even Google Maps doesn't fully understand. It takes perseverance, more than a little backtracking, and faith. You feel yourself leaving civilization behind as the gas stations and supermarkets fall away and you're drawn farther out into the untrammeled wilds of the country, dead lands not yet explored, or places that have deliberately been left and allowed to go to seed.

Stull is no longer a town; it's unincorporated land, and there are only a few buildings near the graveyard, including a church across the road and a shuttered bait-and-tackle shop. The graveyard itself rises up from the road, occupying the side of Emmanuel Hill and bordered by a chain-link fence. The tombstones these days are mostly in good condition, evenly spaced, with plenty of green grass and small clumps of brush between them. The Evangelical church across the street is new; the one originally attached to Stull's graveyard no longer stands.

The first haunting stories came from an item in the University of Kansas's student newspaper, the *University Daily Kansan*, in November 1974, which reported that the graveyard and its ruined church had been "haunted by legends of diabolical, supernatural happenings" for well over a century. One student recalled how, driving toward the cemetery, she'd seen a house glowing bright red, as if on fire, but as she got closer it returned to normal. An assistant instructor was quoted as saying that he'd heard people who'd gone ghost hunting at Stull would later have three- or four-hour memory lapses they could not explain. A student told the *Daily Kansan* that he and two friends had journeyed to Stull one night. "All of a sudden I heard a noise behind me and felt someone grab my arm," he said. "I'll never forget how cold the fingers felt." Assuming that it was one of his friends, he turned, only to find them both some twenty-five yards away.

Through the 1970s and '80s the *Daily Kansan* continued to report various stories from students—usually anonymous or identified only by their first names—of second- and thirdhand stories about Stull. Two men who'd been wandering in the cemetery felt a strong gust of wind, and when they returned to where they'd left their car in the road, they discovered it had mysteriously been moved to the other side of the highway and was facing the opposite direction. One woman claimed that as she and her friends drove up to the church, they saw before them a giant burning cross. A sophomore told the paper she'd been nine times to the cemetery and on one trip she'd left two of her friends in the abandoned church; she returned to find them lying "in awkward positions on the floor," a wooden cross lying beside them, and when she approached, one began to convulse about on the floor.

Eventually legends coalesced around a specific narrative of a deformed child who'd lived only a few days beyond birth and was buried at the cemetery in 1850. The child's deformity was attributed to a union between Satan and the child's mother, a witch. The ruins of Stull's former church supposedly contained a set of limestone steps that descended into the bowels of Hell; twice a year Satan himself would climb the steps to pay respects to his dead child. Some creative soul at some point suggested that a grave marked "Wittich" had something to do with this consort of the devil, or that the town was not named after its first postmaster, Sylvester Stull, but was in fact a corruption of the word "skull." A pine tree in the cemetery was identified as a preferred gallows for Kansas's witch population, as well as a few errant suicides. Both the Cure's Robert Smith and Pope John Paul II are said to have avoided Kansas because of Stull (the Cure's longtime keyboard player, Roger O'Donnell, denies this; the Vatican did not respond to requests for comments).

The Stull churchyard became the unhappy host to kids from the university, who would show up twice a year—on the spring equinox and at Halloween—in increasingly large numbers, drunk and rowdy and awaiting the devil's coming. In 1978, 150 people were reported to have shown up; by 1999 there were closer to 500. As the devil was a perpetual no-show, in his absence students hid behind trees or set off fireworks to scare their friends, tipped over tombstones or stole them for their dorm rooms, and generally made merry in the land of the dead. In 1985 *University Daily Kansan* reporter Michelle Worrall concluded that, based on the remains of six-packs scattered about the graveyard, "whatever lurks in the church satisfies its thirst with beer—not blood."

The legends of Stull appear to have been fabricated from whole cloth by the staff of the *University Daily Kansan*. Written by and for college students, articles by the paper amped up the folklore surrounding the cemetery further each year, relying on hearsay and rumor. Having unleashed this unholy monster, the paper in subsequent years tried to keep the beast at bay, as its reporting shifted not to ghosts but to the inevitable trespassing fines awaiting any student who came seeking Satan. "The real evil," the paper proclaimed in 1990, "has not been Satan but the vandalism that occurs on the church's grounds."

Increasingly attention turned to the graveyard's ruined church. A few local preservationists tried to save it and restore it to some semblance of its former state, even as it became a safety hazard. In the absence of any movement in either direction, the church was left untended and foreboding. This is what happens when you leave something vaguely gothic looking, something associated with death, to be reclaimed by nature—it gets claimed by thrill seekers, too.

The college kids were harder to exorcise than ghosts would have been, but the community has worked hard to drive them off. Preserving the graveyard was particularly important because, desolate as it may seem, the Stull Cemetery was and is still in use, and families do come to visit their loved ones. A chain-link fence went up to keep people out, and the Douglas County Sheriff's Department began patrolling the site. "When I used to patrol out there," Lieutenant Steve Lewis told the *University Daily Kansan* in 2013, "I would stop people and they would tell me that they were just trying to see something scary, and I told them they were looking at the scariest thing they were going to see all night, and I charged them with a misdemeanor."

The ruined church was finally torn down in 2002, after one of its few remaining walls fell in a storm, leaving an even more dangerous hazard. John Solbach, one of the local citizens who'd worked to save it, lamented its loss to local news site Lawrence.com: "A lot of history fell with that building. Those who wanted to see it preserved were heartsick that it was destroyed."

The demolition of the old church and the removal of the supposed hanging tree have (alongside efforts from law enforcement) helped to cut down on trespassers. A woman who declined to give her name to the paper decried the glut of drunk kids for abusing the cemetery where her ancestors were buried: "One man wrote and said a relative of mine was a werewolf, and that really made me mad." Solbach himself reported that he knew a man whose son was buried in the cemetery. "Some people came out there to have Halloween fun and they tipped over his son's tombstone. He found that out and he broke down and just cried like a baby."

These residents see nothing titillating, or eerie, or good-natured about the legends surrounding Stull's graveyard. "This story about it being haunted just tears the guts out of people," Solbach said. You could almost say that the people of Stull had been presented with something of a devil's bargain: the destruction of the church might have been the price that had to be paid to save the rest of the graveyard.

Whereas some places—historic houses, hotels, prisons, and asylums— have found that there's good money to be had in ghost tours and catering to paranormal enthusiasts, cemeteries have had less success, and less interest, in going down that road. Unlike forlorn churchyards, modern cemeteries don't attract—and certainly don't encourage—the same kind of folklore and ghost stories. As still-functioning businesses, cemeteries like Graceland in Chicago and Forest Lawn in Los Angeles have little interest in being overrun by thrill seekers or conveying the image to potential clients that their loved ones' tombstones might be vandalized.

But that's not to say that ghosts haven't also found their way to the nation's modern cemeteries. Though they're not nearly as numerous as the stories that surround the older churchyards, such as Stull or Charleston's Unitarian graveyard, you can find them if you go looking. Find yourself in Chicago's Graceland and you may hear the crying of a young girl named Inez Clarke, who's buried on the cemetery's grounds.

Inez was only six years old when, in 1880, she was fatally struck by lightning. Her grave is marked by a beautiful stone statue of a young girl. Legs crossed, she sits atop a stone tree branch, her summer hat askew, an umbrella dangling in front of her legs. The entire statue, which reads only "Inez," is itself encased in glass atop the monument for John and Mary Clarke, and for years legends have maintained that Inez's ghost is still scared of lightning; during thunderstorms, people claim, her statue disappears entirely, returning only after the threat has passed.

Inez Clarke was actually Inez Briggs, who died on August 1, 1880, not of lightning but of diphtheria. Her mother had recently remarried, changing her name to Clarke, when her daughter died, and later she denied the existence of the children from the earlier marriage. Compounding the confusion, in Graceland's burial records "Inez Briggs" was mistakenly entered as "Amos Briggs." The story of the lightning strike was perhaps conjured from clues from the statue—the hat and umbrella—though most agree that the statue was made not for Inez but as a sample of the carver's work to drum up business.

The slight confusion surrounding the child's identity and the lack of a readily available explanation of the statue's meaning have contributed to the legend that has swirled up around her, and surely ghosts will follow wherever there is bad record keeping. Is the ghost of Inez Clarke an outlier in a cemetery mostly devoid of phantoms or a harbinger of more spirits to come? Just as we moved away from churchyard burials to cemeteries almost two hundred years ago, we are now, slowly, moving away from the garden cemeteries. Cremation is on the rise, as is green burial and other alternative forms. The era of the lavish, expensive funeral in the rolling hills of the garden cemetery may gradually be coming to an end. If our children or grandchildren have less and less cause to visit these places, they, too, may begin to suffer from neglect.

And if that happens, expect more ghosts to come keep Inez Clarke company.

CHAPTER TWELVE

OUR ILLUSTRIOUS DEAD

Shiloh, TN

In Cold Harbor, Virginia, the battle commences again promptly at I a.m.—soldiers materialize from the earthworks amid the fields, engaging once more in a battle that seems to play on an endless loop. An hour to the south, at Fredericksburg, scene of one of the Civil War's bloodiest battles, ghost sentries stand guard, march in formation, and tend to their wounds. Ghosts of all manner roam the battlefield at Gettysburg: Shouted commands have been heard at Reynolds Woods, shadows roam Little Round Top, and a ragged Texas infantryman known as "the hippie" has appeared to some at Devil's Den. At Manassas, where the first and second battles of Bull Run were fought, a charred smell hangs in the air, which writer Mark Nesbitt has surmised may be a remnant of Sullivan Ballou, the Union major who was killed at the First Battle of Bull Run and whose body was desecrated and burned by Confederate soldiers after the battle.

At Shiloh a visitor reported seeing a young Confederate soldier sleeping against a wall. "He was lying down on the moss with his knees up," she later recalled. "He had one arm lying on his cheek, and one arm at his side with his hat over his face. I said, 'Is he sleeping it off from last night? Is he OK? He appears to be OK' We stood there watching the kid. It was sort of a strange thing to find in the woods. And then he wasn't there. He just dissolved in the air."

Many tourists at Shiloh have seen the nameless Union drummer boy. The story, as it's often passed down, is that as a Union offensive began to turn bad, the commanding officer called out a retreat, but the drummer boy instead gave the call once again to attack. Furious, the commanding officer asked him why, and the boy replied that he only knew one signal: attack. But by then, due to the boy's error, the Union forces had rallied and had taken the hill they'd been fighting for. The commanding officer later sought out the young boy to thank him, only to find he'd fallen in the fighting.

Civil War cemeteries loom large in the American consciousness. After all, the most famous piece of American oration, the Gettysburg Address, was delivered at the dedication of one such cemetery. Lincoln's speech, brief and iconic, makes a simple and elegant point: it is beyond the power of any great speaker—including the president—to consecrate this, since only the bodies of the dead soldiers can do this, and it is they on whom the foundation of the United States rests. At the heart of Lincoln's speech is this solemn belief that the greatness of the country lies in its ghosts, to whom we are constantly indebted.

The creation of the Civil War battlefield cemeteries began in 1867, with the wounds of the war still fresh. The conflict was so savage in its destruction of human life that many men were simply unaccounted for; by the end the lists of casualties included only a third of the total number of men estimated to be missing or killed. By early 1866 journalists, politicians, and humanitarians began clamoring for a system of national cemeteries to honor the fallen. James Fowler Russling, in *Harper's New Monthly Magazine*, asked:

> Shall we permit their honored graves, holding the best ashes
> of the land and proudest of the century, to be left liable to

desecration by hostile hands, or to be obliterated quickly by time and nature, as among other nations and in other ages? Or rather shall we not at once gather their remains tenderly together into great national cemeteries, few in number but centrally located; beautify and adorn these in a moderate but just way, and solemnly commit them to posterity as a part of the precious price our generation paid for the Union, to be the republic's legacy and the nation's inheritance for evermore?

Spurred by these calls to action, the North began to gather its dead, to build monuments not just to individual sufferers but also to the country as a whole. What started at Gettysburg and at a former POW camp at Andersonville was quickly incorporated into a national program, one that ultimately led to seventy-four national cemeteries holding a collective 303,536 dead, at a cost of $4 million—what historian Drew Gilpin Faust has called "arguably the most elaborate federal program undertaken in nearly a century of American nationhood."

Throughout, the goal, explicit and implicit, was not just to provide proper burial for those who'd died in war and been left on the battlefield but also to build on a narrative of the United States in the wake of the war that had almost destroyed it. A nation that had won a battle fought partly over states' rights could not now allow its obligation to the dead to fall to the states; the cemeteries of the Civil War must be overseen by the federal government while uniting the states under this larger sovereignty.

The creation of the Civil War battlefield cemeteries also coincided neatly with the transition from churchyards to garden cemeteries. Coming at the end of that major evolution, in which burial grounds shifted from a religious setting to a civic institution, the battlefield cemeteries became a symbol of how Americans strove to make meaning from dead bodies. These men would never rest in family plots and the cemeteries of their hometowns. Instead, their bodies would consecrate the fields of battle, imbuing these lands with an extra symbolic weight. Thomas W. Laqueur notes that "the body, by the fact of its physical location, infuses its meaning into the land where it rests and decomposes"—what mattered was that these men be buried where they fell. The battlefield cemeteries and the preservation of the battlefields themselves were means of creating a more perfect union, of commemorating a loss that couldn't be fully reckoned with.

The ghosts that have more or less always existed on these fields—ghosts without name or identification, often even without allegiance to the North or the South—would seem to further help unite us. Rooted to these resonant places, they keep alive acts of heroism, relive moments of courage, and remind us of their sacrifice.

But this wasn't always the case. While the federal government was burying the Union dead, the economically destroyed South saw its own dead lying fallow and untended. The work of burying Confederate soldiers fell to civilians and became a grassroots movement that gave a purpose of sorts to defeated Southern culture. Southern whites undertook ad hoc attempts to bury their dead, often raising money through the community to cover burial costs and tombstones. This work was largely the provenance of women—grieving mothers and widows who would honor fallen Confederates one last time. Mourning the Southern dead became a way to subtly repudiate the Union and reject the war's outcome. At a consecration in Savannah, Georgia, of the Confederate dead who'd fallen at Gettysburg, Father Abram Ryan, the so-called poet laureate of the Confederacy, recited an elegy for the dead who'd fallen in a cause "though lost, still just."

The reincorporation of the Confederate dead into the fold took time. In 1900 Congress appropriated funds for a dedicated Confederate section within Arlington Cemetery, and in 1906 the federal government established the Commission for Marking Graves of Confederate Dead, which incorporated earlier ad hoc Confederate cemeteries into the national park system. Finally, the dead of the Confederacy had a permanent home alongside the dead of the Union. The sleeping Southern boy at Shiloh now could haunt alongside the famous Union drummer, the two boys united in the afterlife.

But this left close to four decades in which the Confederate dead had no home to haunt, and in those years, particularly in the immediate wake of the Civil War, it would appear that they roamed free.

"Sometimes we would meet one or two people and they'd ride right on by," a former slave would later say about the years following the Civil War, "and nobody would speak or say nothing, but just keep straight forward; just the foremost ones that would see them would say, 'Shiloh,' and then they'd all hang their heads, or turn their heads, and nobody would say anything." Stories circulated of an incident in Attakapas Parish, Louisiana: A freedman was awakened one night by a night traveler, who asked for some water. The man filled a bucket with water and gave it to the stranger, who proceeded to drink the entire bucket, then demanded another. After he had drunk the bucket dry a second time and then a third, he thanked the man, telling him how thirsty he'd been, that he had traveled more than a thousand miles in the last twenty-four hours, and that that was the best drink of water he'd had since he'd been killed at Shiloh.

The ghosts rose from Shiloh, from Vicksburg, from Cold Harbor and Antietam. In southeastern Tennessee, travelers noticed a strange, foreboding sentinel keeping watch in front of a dilapidated house on a hill. Occasionally someone asked him who he was; and the reply, in low, sepulchral tones, returned: "A spirit from the other world. I was killed at Chickamauga." Ghosts stood guard over dilapidated plantations and, like the man in Attakapas, they rode through the night, demanding water to quench an unquenchable thirst, hanging their heads low, speaking in guttural voices, telling all who asked of their deaths on the field of battle.

One former slave would remember, decades later, ghosts who approached him one night and told him "they had come from Manassas Gap to see that the poor widows are not imposed upon. They also said that the rebels were not going to let the taxes be paid. From the two things you would infer that they were rebels killed at Manassas. They said they were risen from the dead, and that they were rebels, too." A man in South Carolina was awakened one night by a hammering at his door and voices demanding he come outside. Shadowy figures came forth, wanting to know how he'd voted in recent elections—whether for the radical Republicans or for the Democrats—and when he told them he'd voted Republican, one ghost stuck the barrel of a pistol under his chin and dragged him into the woods. There they demanded that he remove his shirt. "What do you all want to whip me for," he pleaded; "what have I done?" The figures replied, "Off with your shirt; if you don't you shall go dead. We come from Manassas graveyard; and by Christ we want to get back to our graveyard and cover up before day, by Christ." These ghosts then whipped him ten to fifteen times, by his recollection, before releasing him, telling him, "You must promise to vote the democratic ticket, or you go dead before we leave you."

What began in Pulaski, Tennessee, as a series of pranks—born when a few bored Confederate veterans formed a club whose only mandate was that its members "have fun, make mischief, and play pranks on the public"—grew quickly into the nation's first major terrorist organization, focused chiefly on harassing recently freed slaves and the Northerners who'd come to empower them. The six founders took their name from a gibberish distortion of the Greek for "circle," *kuklos*, adding the word "Klan" at the end to emphasis their Scottish heritage: the Ku Klux Klan, a name instantly mysterious, terrifying, what one founder described as the sound of "bones rattling together."

In its first incarnation the Klan led a regime of terror throughout the South, harassing, beating, torturing, and killing hundreds and thousands in their quest to maintain white supremacy. With an economy built on the exploitation of free labor, the South in the years following the Civil War was left not only with a ravaged and defeated landscape but with its most fundamental economic structure invalidated by the Emancipation Proclamation and the Thirteenth Amendment. The sharecropping system, and eventually Jim Crow laws, would become proxies for slavery in the sense that, for all Southern whites' racism toward the black community, these freed slaves were still vital to the economy and could not be allowed to migrate to the North. Just as slave owners had prevented blacks from escaping prior to the Civil War, it now became equally imperative to discourage this movement among liberated slaves, a job taken up by the Klan.

It was an enforcement that relied heavily on the presence of ghosts. The man who woke in the middle of the night to find a ghost from Shiloh demanding water was later identified only as a "radical negro," as were most of the victims of the Klan. Members would arrive at the home of a black family in the dead of night, dressed in sheets or other makeshift costumes (the formal robes associated with the Klan would come much later), claiming to be the ghosts of Confederate soldiers killed at various battles. Often stories of these visits would involve some sort of simple stage magic trickery: a skeletal hand would be inserted in a robe so that when a Klansman offered to shake someone's hand, they would get instead a disembodied hand. Another common ruse involved rigging an oilskin bag beneath the robe with a hose going to the mouth so the Klansman could appear to drink voluminous amounts of water.

Whether or not these stage tricks were actually employed or just folktales told by the Klan is a matter of much debate. Even if the stories were real, it's doubtful that such rudimentary jokes were believable. As Wyn Craig Wade notes in his history of the Klan, despite the stereotype of black people being more susceptible to superstition than whites, "the Klan legends of terrified 'darkies' scurrying from ghosts of the Confederate dead probably say more about the aggrandizement of the white ego than about black gullibility." Put another way, it's probable that a freedman awakened in the middle of the night by a (likely) drunk Confederate veteran pretending to be a ghost had plenty to be frightened of that was not supernatural. Wade notes that "it has been suggested that blacks might have played into the Klansmen's hands, hoping that their feigned fright would avert a more violent form of intimidation. It then becomes a question of who was controlling whom."

How often these implausible-sounding pranks were actually employed, and what psychological effect they had on their victims, might never be fully known. But the spectral aspect of the Klan was one of its defining features in its early years. Central goals were to keep liberated slaves in the South to prop up the economy and to keep out white "carpetbaggers" who'd come to provide education and resources to newly liberated slaves. As Gladys-Marie Fry notes in her book *Night Riders in Black Folk History*, "The concept of returning Confederate dead was meant to suggest that the slave regime had not ended, though the South was subdued, and that former controls were still being perpetrated." If anything, the goal was to prove that these ghosts were even more powerful, having returned from the grave and been elevated to a new supernatural status. Southern whites tried—usually unsuccessfully—to convince freedmen and -women that moving north was futile, since spirits of the Confederate dead could follow them anywhere, no longer limited by their physical bodies. In Edward H. Dixon's fantastical novel *The Terrible Mysteries of the Ku-Klux-Klan*, a Klan leader proudly proclaims, "The Klux is the living dead, and it is the strength of weakness. Bound hand and foot with cords that gall and eat into running sores the dead flesh, the living Klux riseth and walketh abroad in the black night."

The use of ghosts as a means of social control predated the Klan. Slave owners employed so-called patterollers, usually poor whites, who would patrol the countryside at night; such patrols would regularly use spook stories, among other tactics, to help keep enslaved people from escaping. "The fraudulent ghost," Fry writes, "was the first in a gradually developed system of night-riding creatures, the fear of which was fostered by whites for the purpose of slave control." A man in a white sheet on horseback riding ominously through a forest could help substantiate rumors that the forest was haunted and that those who valued their lives best avoid it. By spreading ghost stories, Southern whites hoped to limit the unauthorized movement of black people. If cemeteries, crossroads, and forests came to be known particularly as haunted, it's because they presented the easiest means of escape and had to be patrolled.

Now it's common to think of such places as the provenance of spirits. We have stories for such places: a tragic death, forlorn lovers, a devil waiting to make a deal—stories that reflect a rich tradition of American folklore. But all this might have come much later, and these places might have first earned their haunted reputation through much more deviant methods. In the ghost-haunted legacies of many of these public spaces lies a hidden history of patrolling and limiting access. These should be places more or less open to all—meeting points, thoroughfares, public property, the sacred resting places of the dead. But in many parts of the country where access to these places have long been restricted, the spirits of the dead have been marshaled as one more weapon to be used by an invisible army.

CHAPTER THIRTEEN

THE WIND THROUGH CATHEDRAL PARK

Portland, OR

In the video there is first the image of kids, their flashlights to their chins, then giggling in the darkness. One is named Isaiah, another Vinnie, the third Jamison—beyond that there's not much more information about them. They could be in their early twenties, but they continue to giggle like schoolchildren. The camera drops, there's fumbling. They could be drunk, high. They're clearly enjoying themselves, barely keeping it together.

They are beneath the St. Johns Bridge in Portland, Oregon. Portland's bridges are so spectacular that one of the city's many nicknames is "Bridge City," but St. Johns is perhaps its most beautiful. A dual suspension bridge patinaed in copper green, it rises above the Willamette River like a smaller, more refined Golden Gate Bridge. On the west side it crosses over NW St. Helens Road before meeting NW Bridge Avenue; on the east side of the river the bridge towers above a gentle slope, descending gracefully into Portland's St. Johns district.

The land under the bridge on the east side is now called Cathedral Park, named for the sweeping gothic arches that form the supports for the bridge above it. It captures a great deal of the city's scenic beauty: the gently flowing river, the hints of industrialization dwarfed by the mountains and the evergreens all around. It is, though, surprisingly noisy: the cars rushing by a hundred feet above your head and the wind coursing through the gothic arches all around you combine to create a sense of voices and howlings that accompany you throughout the park. On the bridge's supports signs blare out warnings: DANGER: FALLING OBJECTS, PARK AT YOUR OWN RISK.

The kids who have made this YouTube video are there for the ghost of Thelma Taylor. In 1949 Taylor, then fifteen years old, was abducted from under the bridge. At the time there was no park, just dirt, junk, and bushes spilling out in all directions. Taylor was hitching a ride to a summer job when she was picked up by Morris Leland, a twenty-two-year-old drifter.

A week after Taylor's disappearance, police pulled Leland over for stealing a car and took him down to the police station, where, without prompting, he asked to talk to a homicide detective. He proceeded to make a full confession, describing in detail how he'd murdered Taylor, covered her body in driftwood, and wiped his prints off her lunch pail before leaving the scene. He offered to take the police to the place where he'd left her remains. Until that moment he was just a petty criminal who'd stolen a few cars. The murder of Thelma Taylor was something else entirely, and it was weighing on him when he blurted out his confession to the detective. He was tried in 1951, quickly found guilty, and sentenced to death. After several unsuccessful appeals, Leland went to Oregon's gas chamber in 1953.

The stories told about Taylor are predictably gruesome: she was raped and tortured for seven days, they say, before she was finally killed. "Oh yeah," one diner owner told the local news in a 2013 special about the murdered girl, "I've been down there at night and heard her scream, 'Help me, help me—somebody help me!'" This is why people come to find Taylor: they want the chills that go with a brush with death, the intoxication that comes with being close to mortality. Writer Andy Weeks, in his guide *Haunted Oregon*, advises that you "visit the area and see if you can hear the unearthly screams of now-deceased Thelma. They won't be pretty sounds if you hear them, but ones that will make your skin crawl." What better way to spend a chilly evening than trying to scare yourself into feeling alive?

The screams you may hear at Cathedral Park, screams that twine themselves with the wind as it whips up from the water and through the arches of the St Johns Bridge, come, so they say, from the bridge itself, from the massive stone pylons anchoring the span looming above you. When Thelma Taylor was murdered, the theory goes, the bridge itself "recorded" the event and now plays back the horror it once witnessed.

As the guidebook *Ghosthunting Oregon* claims, paranormal researchers say Cathedral Park is an area "primed for a haunting": the water from the river and the limestone blocks used to build St. Johns Bridge are associated with a phenomenon called residual haunting. Also sometimes called the stone tape theory, the belief is that certain inanimate objects are primed to record imprints of certain action that they then play back later. As *Ghosthunting Oregon* puts it, "Inanimate materials, such as stone, can absorb energy from the living, much as a tape recorder absorbs the voice of the living, especially during episodes of high tension, anxiety, and fear. Once this energy is stored, it can also be released, resulting in the display, or replay, of the recorded events."

The residual haunting theory was first popularized by an anthropologist named T. C. Lethbridge, whose career began to decline as he became more and more obsessed with ghosts and spirits. His 1961 book *Ghost and Ghoul* offered no room for skeptics ("The question is not whether people see ghosts or not. There is ample evidence that they do so") and turned instead to a mechanism that could explain spirits, a mechanism that relied less on the afterlife and more on the psychic abilities of the living. Rather than see spirits as distinct entities, capable of agency and will after death, he argued that we the living act as spiritual television projectors, capable of sending ideas mentally that are then picked up by others and interpreted as ghosts. The majority of ghosts, Lethbridge concluded, "are no

more than mental pictures produced by living people," and in the burgeoning technology of television he found a perfect metaphor. Ghosts, he
concluded, "appear to be no more and no less than television pictures. The
television picture is a man-made ghost."

Lethbridge wasn't the first to propose such an idea. Sir Oliver Lodge,
in his 1908 book *Man and the Universe*, speaks of how a haunted house has
"photographed" a past tragedy. But Lethbridge's ideas caught fire in
England, perhaps because of the strong association with television, and in
1972 BBC Two broadcast a made-for-TV film, *The Stone Tape*, inspired by
Lethbridge's idea of television ghosts. A team of scientists who've relocated to new headquarters in a Victorian mansion with a reputation of
being haunted discover that the ghosts they're seeing are a sort of playback loop of an earlier tragedy. The stone tape's playback abilities depend
greatly on the individual acting as the receiver—haunting here, in its
simplest form, is a psychic interplay between place and person, between
a past tragedy and a present witness's ability to attune herself to that
tragedy.

In this version of haunting, ghosts are not able to harm or otherwise
disturb the living, even though the images called forth may be traumatic
or terrifying. With many of the ghost hunters I've talked to, from California to Louisiana, residual haunting is put forth as the most popular
explanation for hauntings, even if its mechanism is as implausible as the
Spiritualist version of ghosts. It holds out the promise that no matter
how creepy the environment, the ghost hunter won't be harmed, and
yet still manages to give people the thrill they want to feel that much
more alive.

The kind of ghost that haunts Cathedral Park, local ghost researcher
Jefferson Davis told me, is an important question. "Is it a remnant spirit,
is it a self-aware spirit, or is it something else?" Davis was born in the
Pacific Northwest, and he has been fascinated with ghosts from an early
age. He describes himself as a "comfortable skeptic": "I believe in the

possibility," he said, but he hasn't seen or heard anything that he believes beyond a shadow of a doubt to be confirmation of the paranormal. "I'm just waiting for something to happen."

Davis's background is in anthropology, so he's trained to see ghost stories as expressions of larger cultural trends and indicative of communal beliefs. If the traditional ghost story formula involves a restless ghost, a task left undone, an injustice not yet addressed, the residual haunting formula doesn't require this—Thelma Taylor's killer, after all, was brought to justice, and so her spirit need not call out to the living to aid her.

The Cathedral Park ghost instead seems to exist as a cautionary tale. Local historian Jim Speirs, who grew up in North Portland, didn't remember much about the murder when he first began writing about Thelma Taylor for the *St. Johns Review* in 2009. "What I do recall is a vague, scary story that circulated around Roosevelt when I attended school there in the 60's," he later wrote. "That tale was of a ghost that haunted the bowels of the St. Johns Bridge . . . and that the place was to be avoided." This, of course, was easy enough to do, since at the time there was no park; "the area," Speirs remembered, "was acres of tangled wild blackberries, stunted trees, abandoned cars, piles of garbage, menacing underbrush, and passing hobo derelicts."

Taylor's story is important for someone like Davis precisely because it's a true story that nonetheless has all the hallmarks of a fictitious urban legend. "A lot of hauntings are not symbolic, a lot of hauntings really happened, and that's what makes it interesting," Davis told me, speaking specifically to how a story like this blurs drama and melodrama, making the archetypal aspects of Thelma's story so closely intertwined with facts that it becomes hard to separate the two.

Erik Meharry isn't sure exactly when he became interested in Thelma Taylor. He'd grown up just outside Portland, and like most kids in the area, he knew the story as just something to scare kids from hitchhiking, nothing specific. Now he works as an investigator for the public defender's office, but at the time he began delving into the life of Thelma Taylor, he was working at a mortuary. ("I got in the funeral business by accident," he told me; "they needed someone to pick up the bodies.") On-call for twenty-four hours at a time, he was living in the funeral home, and at some point—though he says it was unrelated to his job—he became deeply interested in Taylor's life. He doesn't remember exactly what it was that caught his attention. "Mostly," he said, "I just felt *bad* for her."

He started researching—collecting news clippings and trial records, stuff that went beyond the urban legends and ghost stories. For all the belief that Taylor haunts Cathedral Park, Meharry learned that she was killed eight blocks away from the bridge. She wasn't raped, and though it was a week before Leland was caught and confessed, the murder itself happened the morning after the kidnapping; there was no prolonged imprisonment.

In 2012 Meharry put up a Facebook page about Taylor, mainly to keep her memory alive but also to sort out the truth from the lore. On September 25, 2012, about eight months after he'd launched the page, he received a message from a woman named Paulette Jarrett. It was brief and to the point: "Thelma Taylor is my sister—who are you?"

In an oft-quoted passage from his book *Lies Across America*, James W. Loewen writes of a distinction between the dead made by Kiswahili speakers in east and central Africa:

> According to John Mbiti, Kiswahili speakers divide the deceased into two categories: sasha and zamani. The recently departed whose time on earth overlapped with people still here are the sasha, the living-dead. They are not wholly dead, for

they still live in the memories of the living, who can call them to mind, create their likeness in art, and bring them to life in anecdote. When the last person to know an ancestor dies, that ancestor leaves the sasha for the zamani, the dead. As generalized ancestors, the zamani are not forgotten but revered. . . . But they are not living-dead. There is a difference.

Loewen uses this distinction to critique the historical problems in many of the monuments and markers that dot the country. While history is most accurately documented while it is in living memory—the sasha—civic monuments are often products of zamani, and they are, for Loewen, ideologically loaded: "Not primarily motivated by loss or grief, zamani monuments and markers usually go up to serve the political exigencies of the time of their erection." Memorials honoring Confederate war heroes, or the victims of 9/11—hashed out and argued over, long delayed and deployed by politicians for any number of personal ends—typify the kind of zamani monument that has little connection to the actual dead or loss that a sasha monument, like a temporary roadside memorial or a simple gravestone, might honor.

While Loewen is primarily concerned with public monuments, his distinction gives us another lens for understanding ghost stories and how those stories evolve over time. As I've gathered ghost stories over the past decade, I've seen historical specificity reduced to the same clichés and melodrama over and over again. Ghost stories become, in this light, a kind of fetishization of the past, detached from the actual history—a kind of frozen moment in which all of the past mirrors itself. The French philosopher Jean Baudrillard once wrote, "It is not the passion (whether of objects or subjects) for substances that speaks in fetishism, it is the *passion for the code*," and in the melodramatic ghosts we find a passion not for individual stories or histories so much as for a certain set of clichés repeated over and over again. This is the effect of zamani memory: without first-person accounts, without personal memories, the stories become monuments that must serve larger purposes.

Case in point: Cathedral Park itself. One obviously false aspect of the story of Thelma Taylor is where she died: not in the park but some eight blocks away. And yet, despite being easily disproven, the incorrect location has become an integral part of the legend. Why in particular does this fallacy persevere?

The bridge was opened in 1931. But despite such fanfare, the park itself was not built until the 1970s and not dedicated until May 1980. The decision to turn this land into a park was an attempt to capitalize on the dead space under the bridge's long span and to eradicate the kind of forces that might otherwise gather in such dead spaces.

Parks like Cathedral Park are part of a general movement in urban planning under the rubric of what's called adaptive reuse: otherwise-dead zones in the city that have been repurposed. Perhaps the most famous and successful example is the High Line in New York City, an elevated railway trestle that's been converted into a linear park. The idea here is to convert eyesores into habitable spaces.

Adaptive reuse projects have of course also included former Kirkbride asylums, and as with those asylums, it should come as little surprise that many projects bear haunted legacies. A local tour company offers a haunted tour of the High Line, with stories of ghosts like a mysterious figure who lived below the tracks, a "West Side Cowboy" who fell to his death, and various children who died and now haunt the park. Another adaptive reuse project in New York, lower Manhattan's Battery Park, is also haunted, this one by vice president Aaron Burr and his daughter, Theodosia. These buildings and parks attract ghosts because they *are* ghosts: once abandoned, they've been reconstituted, given a new life after death. It shouldn't be surprising that stories of the past cling to them, manifesting themselves in ghost stories and unexplained occurrences.

Cathedral Park, a place that feels new and refurbished but can't entirely cover up the scar of what it was before, was always destined to be haunted. It can't escape the monstrous bridge looming above it, the incongruity of the bustle of traffic and the park environs. It can't escape the wind that tears through it at all hours, the wail and moan that rushes through it. Even had Thelma Taylor never come here at all, one way or another Cathedral Park would've found its ghost.

Kevin Brockmeier's 2006 *The Brief History of the Dead* literalizes the difference between sasha and zamani; it takes place in the city of the sasha dead. In the novel it's the place where those newly deceased go while someone alive still remembers them, a place they leave only once there is no one left alive to keep them in living memory. Thelma Taylor belongs here, in a very different city of the dead than where most ghosts roam. Victorian ladies, Confederate soldiers, silent film starlets—they may have descendants, but they aren't kept alive in living memory. Thelma Taylor's story is unlike many I've come across, simply because there are still so many who remember her.

After Jim Speirs first wrote about Taylor in the *St. Johns Review*, he received several e-mails from people who remembered her in life. Having awakened memories decades old, he collected various e-mails he'd received in a blog post; one woman remembered Taylor from grade school and attending her funeral; "even though Morris had been caught," she wrote, "we were still scared stiff." The murder changed the landscape, turning the world from a place of wonder to one of deep suspicion. While North Portland high schoolers once went to the bridge for expansive views of the Willamette as it flowed into the city, they stopped going near the bridge altogether after the murder. "My friend Thelma is still down there, and I don't care how good the music becomes, or how pretty the park is, I will NEVER step on that land again!" George Parrish remembered Taylor as well: "She was skinny and underdeveloped, but that's just the odd age she was when I knew her. We were classmates . . . but I don't remember much about her, and doubt if I'd remember her at all if she hadn't been killed."

Another man e-mailed Speirs about the killer himself. "It's been a long time," Bill Grubb told Speirs, "but we knew Leland was weird, he didn't have any friends that I can recall, and he was always doing something stupid. . . . He always had a knife, and that made us weary [sic] of him . . . he was always playing with a knife."

Paulette Jarrett was only three years old when her sister was murdered, but she still has two clear memories: one of Thelma sitting outside with her friends, and another of finding her in the living room chewing gum and asking for a piece. "So she pulls it out of her mouth and hands it to me," she told me. "Well, I had a screaming fit, I did not want something out of her mouth—I wanted my own piece! And of course Mom comes around the corner, asking what the heck's going on, and Thelma said, 'Well, she asked for gum, so I gave it to her and she refused it.'" As a memory on its own, it's not much, but it's a snippet of a life, of a person who could be more than just the story of her death. Jarrett still has a cache of photos of her sister—dressed in their father's uniform, posing for a school portrait, living the life of a perfectly normal teenager. Jarrett, who spent the rest of her childhood sheltered because her mother wouldn't allow her to go anywhere by herself, told me that mostly she wonders how Thelma would have turned out if she'd lived. "I just wish I'd known her a little better."

The ghost stories that swarm around Thelma Taylor suggest what happens when an actual life maps too closely on an urban legend. Taylor's disappearance and murder became a warning about hitchhiking or loitering in desolate places. The details were never terribly important—the important thing was to scare people into listening. It was an easy conversion from a life to a lesson, from sasha to zamani, from the messy world of a human being's thoughts, desires, and memories to a cautionary tale.

When I asked Davis about whether it was ethical to give tours or tell stories about Taylor's death, he seemed somewhat conflicted by the genuine moral conundrums involved. "None of us wants to set out to ruin the day—or the month or the year—of someone else's life, like the family member of someone who's been killed." Like many ghost hunters I've interviewed, Davis genuinely believes that his work is not exploitive, that he does his best to get out the true story, to report terrible events without sensationalizing them, without trying to make a buck off of someone else's trauma. At the same time, though, he told me, he maintains his right to tell these stories, since no matter what you do, "People will get offended and misunderstand."

Only when I mentioned the video I'd seen, of the kids in the park trying to contact Taylor's ghost, did Davis push back sharply. "The people smiling and laughing," he said, "they're having a quasi-religious experience: they're trying to contact the other side. You can't gauge from a video what's going on in someone else's mind."

"Have fun with it," said Meharry. "Why not? If you want to go have fun, as long as you're not hurting anyone else, knock yourself out." He admitted that Taylor and the bridge is a good story: an archetypal ghost story about a young girl's tragedy. But then he paused and looked off. "But I've spent so much time on Thelma Taylor, and I know her family, so I'm kinda on guard and a little bit defensive.

"Do it with other ghost stories," he said finally, "but leave this one alone."

Myself, I tend to think of ghost stories as a natural way of preserving—or at least attempting to preserve—a history that might otherwise go unnoticed and forgotten. The story of Cathedral Park, like too many ghost stories, blurs the fact in favor of gory inventions and puts a premium on the thrill of the ghost hunt, the brush with death, rather than on the actual life that was lost in 1949.

At the same time that it's a personal story for this family, it's also a civic story, a story about a community, and the ghost of Cathedral Park isn't merely a cheap stunt, a sensationalized grab for cash. As a cautionary tale, it's a legend that encourages teenagers to turn down rides from strangers, and even if we just leave it here, the ghost story of Thelma Taylor isn't a bad thing. If the casual reiteration of that story—handed down from generation to generation, unmoored from specificity and unnaturally gruesome—helps to prevent another death like hers, it's worth it . . . even if there are those who'd wish it would wait at least until she leaves the city of Sasha and enters the land of Zamani.

As I was researching for this book, I was startled to find myself reading about a longtime friend's fiancé. I'd never known him in life, because a few months before their marriage, he'd walked out onto the fourth-floor balcony of his college dorm and then shot himself, falling to the ground below.

More than fifteen years later his life has become a ghost story, his death an explanation for unexplained chills and creepy sensations that students feel in the dorm. As a legend it's so vague that it's hardly worth mentioning, except that behind the banality is a very real story and a man who left behind people who loved him.

I never expected to be this close to an urban legend. I'd certainly never expected that a friend's tragedy would become a ghost story in so few years. What was once a person's unbearable loss is now someone else's "strange noises and voices," a reminder of how quickly a personal tragedy can be molded, in the hands of strangers, into folklore, taking on a life of its own. Maybe the purpose of a story like this, the reason it gets told and retold, is to shine a light on the very real problem of college depression, to let those suffering know that they're not alone, to encourage them to find support.

More likely, it's just something to pass the time.

IV

USELESS MEMORY

cities and towns

In the fall of 2004 I attended a conference in Binghamton, New York, almost two hundred miles from Manhattan along the Pennsylvania border. My flight arrived late at night, and I caught a cab to my hotel—a hotel that, when I had booked it, had been called the Ramada Limited, but by the time I arrived had been sold (Ramada no longer finding much of value in Binghamton) to a private operator. It was late but I was on West Coast time and still very much alert, and as we drove to the hotel the chatty cabdriver unfurled an endlessly depressing history of Binghamton.

Driving down Front Street toward my hotel, the cabdriver let me know, "This street used to be in the Guinness Book of Records for the most bars on a single street." A dubious claim (and one that several other towns also boast) but still impossible not to hear the pathos in his voice as he listed them as we drove: "That used to be a bar"—he gestured to an empty lot— "and that used to be a bar"—now a Laundromat—"and there, and there, and there, too. All gone now." He continued this the length of the empty, lifeless street. And then he told me about the curse.

No white person from Binghamton, he said, is ever able to leave. Even if you move away, sooner or later you'll be drawn back in. It's the curse on the city, he said, laid on it by the Native Americans who once lived here—revenge for the violence inflicted on them centuries ago, a revenge that is only now coming to fruition.

Binghamton is built on land once occupied by the Onondaga and Oneida people, who, along with the Mohawk, Cayuga, Seneca, and Tuscarora, once made up the Iroquois Confederacy. Most of these tribes sided with the British during the Revolutionary War, and in 1779 Major General John Sullivan led a contingent of American troops through the heart of New York in a scorched-earth campaign, laying waste to at least forty Iroquois villages throughout the state, including the Onondaga and Oneida land that is now Binghamton.

The curse, supposedly, is in the water itself, which saps the drinker of any desire to leave town. Binghamton doesn't have anything close to the reputation of other haunted cities, but mentions of the curse surface occasionally, often in the form of a joke: a lame excuse offered for those townies without the motivation to leave, a dumb anecdote to entertain friends. But the night I heard of it from the cabdriver who bore me into the town's heart, there was no mistaking the sadness in his words, the ache in his voice, as he tried to make sense of his town and what had happened to it.

Binghamton might have lost its bars and its jobs, but what it does have is carousel horses. The benevolent owner of the massive Endicott Johnson shoe factory had given back to the town generously, from building cinemas for his workers to donating six antique carousels for free public use in local parks; stand-alone horses also dot the downtown streets. Once meant to look jolly and inviting, they've taken on a different pallor amid the vacant storefronts. With their mouths open and their ears flared back, the horses could be screaming, or running from a fire—or trying to escape Binghamton itself.

Which is not to say that Binghamton doesn't have dreams of recovering. An investment in Binghamton University, part of the State University of New York system, has helped revitalize the local economy, and the population has stabilized. But the city sustained massive damage during floods in recent years and in 2009 was the site of a mass shooting, when a man named Jiverly Wong killed thirteen people and wounded four before turning his gun on himself. Wong, a Vietnamese immigrant who'd lived in the United States since the early '80s and had become a naturalized citizen, had been taking English classes at the American Civic Association, and on April 3, 2009, he returned to his former classroom and began killing his classmates, along with a substitute teacher. In a letter he'd mailed to a local news station shortly before the killings, Wong hinted that his deepening psychosis was at least in part due to low job prospects.

So Binghamton has experienced its share of hardships and tragedies, and a curse—stretching back as it does to the earliest confrontations between whites and Iroquois—encompasses all of them. Binghamton's troubles were due not to outsourcing or demographic shifts but to an age-old conflict, an act of revenge for violence committed more than two hundred years ago.

And what's more, the specific aspect of the haunting is unusual: rather than whites being driven from the land they wrongfully seized, they're not able to leave. The city in decline is a trap, a dead-end street. The curse on Binghamton renders the city a spectral penal colony, one whose borders are nebulous but still mystically enforced.

How does an entire city come to see itself as haunted? At what point does a city cease to simply have a few haunted buildings and instead begin to define itself as a haunted city?

Most cities commemorate their pasts, often with statues, plaques, renamed streets, or even parades. But cities that are haunted don't just try to keep the past alive; they seem to straddle past and present, as though two versions of the same city are overlaid on top of each other. To paraphrase Hamlet, hounded by the ghost of his father: time in these places is "out of joint." The past seethes in the streets, always on people's lips, always at the edge of one's vision. In such places the past may be dead but it isn't past.

Disjointed history can be a great way to raise money through tourism, as places like Salem, New Orleans, and Savannah have found, but only if that history can be packaged in a way that doesn't offend anyone. Savannah, for example, is famous for its ghosts and its glamorous, dark past, and many tour operators there do a brisk business in ghost tours—but, as former tour guide Elena Gormley later wrote of her experience, the ghost stories she recited would turn the city's turbulent past into a pleasant night's outing. "A few stories came across as fairly light," she wrote, "but most repackaged the rape, abuse, and lynching of vulnerable women into family friendly entertainment."

There are, for example, the stories surrounding the beautiful Sorrel-Weed House, an elegant Greek Revival mansion built in 1841 for Francis Sorrel, a prosperous plantation owner. Though married, Sorrel was secretly having an affair with one of his slaves, a Haitian woman named Molly. In 1860 his wife, Matilda, discovered the affair and threw herself out a third-story window, smashing her head on the paving stones below. Shortly thereafter, Molly was found hanging from a noose in the carriage house, another supposed suicide.

Not unlike the story of Chloe at the Myrtles Plantation, the tour script presents a well-worn version of the Jezebel narrative: a sexually aggressive black woman destabilizing a white man's marriage. Gormley offers another, far more plausible version of events: Francis's wife "may have committed suicide after she discovered her husband had raped his slave, and in the story, Molly's suffering didn't end there. At the tale's conclusion, a group of men, who some locals allege may have been Francis and his sons, lynched her."

As part of the tour script, Gormley would play an EVP recording provided for her that supposedly documented the paranormal screams of Molly from beyond the grave. "Help! Get out! Oh my God!" a disembodied voice on the tape would cry out, and whenever she would ask the guests what they'd heard, Gormley notes, the "white tourists always made smart comments. Once, on a charter tour for auto parts managers, a man yelled, 'Sounds like my regional manager!' His buddies all laughed."

Savannah, like a number of historic cities (New Orleans and Washington, D.C., among them), requires that anyone who gives a tour (ghost or otherwise) pass a test of the city's history. ("Where did Savannah's major Revolutionary War battle take place?" "At which cemetery can graves of the victims of the 1820 yellow fever outbreak be found?" "In which square is the Greene Monument located?") A way to ensure a base level of quality and lack of misinformation, it's notoriously difficult—the college professor who wrote it estimates that it would take three months of full-time studying to master.

But the real goal of the test seems to cement certain narratives of the city over others. Gormley believes that the test is ideologically slanted toward minimizing controversial or problematic aspects of the city's history in favor of things that portray it in a neutral or positive light. "The city's very obsessed with its brand," she told me. This may explain why several groups filed suit against the city, alleging that the test infringed on their right to free speech. "By limiting the universe of speakers to those who have memorized and regurgitated the City's official version of Savannah history," attorneys for the plaintiffs argued, "the City plainly hopes to ensure that tour guides draw upon that official narrative in their speech to tourists." In the fall of 2015 the city backed down, dropping the testing requirement and moving instead to restrict the available hours in which tour groups were allowed in primarily residential areas.

Of the Sorrel-Weed House the testing manual mentions only that it is a "distinguished" building built in 1841 on the southwest corner of Harris and Bull streets. There is no mention of Francis Sorrel's relationship with his slave Molly, nor of her death or the death of Sorrel's wife, Matilda. As Tiya Miles discovered when she began researching the house, the story probably is fictionalized. Miles hypothesizes that the Molly legend was concocted by brothers Stephen and Philip Bader sometime after they purchased the house in 1996 and began renovations (Stephen Bader, however, contends that he has documents attesting to the veracity of the story). Not only could they capitalize on Savannah's reputation, established by John Berendt's 1994 book *Midnight in the Garden of Good and Evil*, as a creepy, haunted city; they could also get away with a half-renovated house, she adds, playing up its ruined, gloomy state of disrepair as part of its haunted aura. And so, for all the city's emphasis on its daunting test of factually correct history, licensed tour companies still do a brisk business on fabricated stories and distortions.

Binghamton isn't trading on its curse to sell tickets to walking tours (not yet, at least). For every city basing a tourist industry on its famous hauntings, there are a dozen other cities that have come to be known as haunted in a different way, one devoid of the charm and cheer of a Salem or Savannah. These cities are haunted by what they once were, what they might have been; towns haunted by some series of past failures or tragedies that encompass more than one or two buildings and swept up the whole city.

For better or worse, the language of hauntings and ghosts is a convenient metaphor for a whole host of problems not connected to the supernatural, and the recourse to such vocabulary becomes a means to process or make sense of experiences that can otherwise seem overwhelming and mystifying.

A city obsessed by its ghosts seems to be weighed down by a conflicted view of the past. Something close to melancholy: a weight it can't quite let go of, a lingering sadness. And though we don't often think of the United States in these terms, this melancholy is as much a part of our history as our triumphs.

CHAPTER FOURTEEN

THE WET GRAVE

New Orleans, LA

Walk through the streets of New Orleans, and you're beset on all sides by ghosts. In the French Quarter it's best early in the evening, when the day-trippers have gone home and what's left of the tourists have quarantined themselves on Bourbon Street or in tucked-away white-napkin restaurants. You can slip past these places into the gloom of old New Orleans, in and out of the pools of light from the streetlamps, in and out of the past.

Perhaps, if you are lucky, it'll be raining—the cool, clarifying rain that drives out the humidity and the tourists—and you'll be free to walk the cobblestones alone. Through the soft hum of the rain pelting the streets, you might hear a murmur of a song, something maybe coming from a nearby bar or perhaps somewhere more distant. Not something you'd hear at a bar. What folklorist Jeanne deLavigne described as "a song which rises like slow smoke from the heavy ashes of experience, fanned by the winds of perplexity."

New Orleans, Lafcadio Hearn once wrote, is a place that "actually resembles no other city on the face of the earth, yet it recalls vague memories of a hundred cities." You are at once in the arcades of nineteenth-century Paris or a Spanish port city and yet still in the bowels of a swamp.

The dampness only adds to the mystery, creating halos of mist around the lights, adding a heaviness to the air that you can't shake; it's a dampness that Hearn called "spectral, mysterious, inexplicable."

Soon the nightly ghost tours will be out, traipsing the quarter in clumps of fifteen to twenty people, gathering at corners to hear stories that stretch credulity but that have been honed through years of telling, polished to a high sheen for maximum intensity.

On the 700 block of Royal Street, a naked woman will appear on the roof of one building under the moonlight. Before and after the Civil War, white men sometimes kept octoroon mistresses—women who passed as white but who had an exotic charm about them. Because of the notorious one-drop rule (the notion that a single drop of black blood makes an individual black), such women could be discarded at will by wealthy men shuttling back to their wives or on to the next mistress. In this particular house, though, things turned out differently.

The wealthy Frenchman who lived here kept a mistress, whose name is sometimes given as Julie. He never saw her as anything more than a plaything, but she fell in love with him nonetheless. After repeatedly denying her entreaties to marry her, he devised a cruel prank and told her that if she lasted an entire night on the roof fully naked, he would marry her. Whether or not he thought that would be the end of it, he underestimated her resolve, and she ascended to the roof and disrobed, preparing to spend the night there to prove her love. At some point before dawn, she caught a chill, and she died shortly thereafter. She can still be seen, they say, when the moonlight is right. Not unlike the story of Chloe at the Myrtles Plantation, Julie is a stock character: the tragic mulatto who wants to join white society but is rebuffed by her white lover, with fatal consequences—a reminder that many of New Orleans's ghost stories are more concerned with affirming stereotypes than with offering proof of the paranormal.

Which is not to say that the city doesn't try hard to convince you it's haunted. As deLavigne wrote in the introductory note to her *Ghost Stories of Old New Orleans*, "There is not a corner of the city that does not harbor some unearthly visitor in one guise or another. They hug close as feathers on a bird." New Orleans is very haunted. New Orleans ghost hunter David Laville told me that the three-hundred-yard radius around Jackson Square is the most haunted place in the country. Asked why, he gives four reasons. First, because the city's so old. Second, its long history of tragedies: not just fires and floods but disastrous outbreaks of cholera and yellow fever, among other epidemics. Third, its history of violence: crime, of course, but the city is also known for public executions in the main square and a preponderance of duels to settle disputes. Fourth, all this activity has, for centuries, been packed into the tiny area of the French Quarter. He offers, finally, a fifth reason: "It's just a city that everybody loves, so, naturally, the people who lived and died here—they don't want to leave."

New Orleans's inordinate obsession with death stems in part from the constant dance it's had with the geology of the area; the city may be old, but the ground on which it stands is new. In a place with such a high water table, it's hard to bury corpses six feet under, so New Orleans is unique among American cities for its necropolises filled with elaborate— and aboveground—mausoleums. These cities of death parallel the city of the living: in places like St. Louis Cemetery #1, just across Basin Street from the French Quarter, family crypts have the stately grandeur of the fine villas they neighbor, though some have begun to majestically decay into ruins. Those who can't afford a grand crypt are entombed along the wall, in vaults sometimes referred to as "bake ovens."

New Orleans is particularly cruel to the corpse, whose bacteria thrive in the humid, temperate environment. A body in the Northeast or Midwest will keep longer, if it's winter; a body in the Southwest will dry out; but in the Pelican State the environment is perfect for the work of decay. In New Orleans you cannot avoid the fact of death and decomposition. The living and the dead have always occupied close quarters here, which helps explain why the city, over the years, has become death-haunted.

There are, of course, ghosts in St. Louis #2, as there are in all of New Orleans's graveyards and cemeteries. But you need not leave the French Quarter on a night like this to find ghosts. From Royal Street wend your way to the Hotel Provincial, on Chartres Street, which guides will tell you operated as a hospital during the Civil War. Countless men died within its walls, some from wounds received in battle but many from the barbaric methods of healing employed on them. Guests on the fifth floor claim to see a doctor, still in his bloodied apron, walking the halls. Forget for a moment that the building was operating during the war as a hair salon, according to journalist Paul Oswell. Allow yourself instead to be captivated by the city's spells, its love of the tall tale and legend, and let yourself be carried on past the Hotel Provincial to the corner of Governor Nicholls and Royal.

On the southeastern corner stands a particularly majestic building, the highlight of any ghost tour in the French Quarter, a place of legend: the Lalaurie Mansion.

The Lalaurie Mansion is larger than many of the houses in the French Quarter, its façade stretching down both streets. It's been a part of New Orleans's tourist industry for more than a century; by the 1890s the mansion was already being advertised as a haunted house. An Italian immigrant who bought it in 1893, Fortunato Greco, complained that its "reputation for spooks" had rendered it unsalable. In order to make a profit off his white elephant, he hung signs announcing that it was not haunted and charged people ten cents if they wanted to come in and see for themselves. Within a few years he'd made enough on ghost tours that he opened a thematic bar on the ground floor, the Haunted Exchange. In the early twentieth century the building was cut up into tenement slums and occupied by immigrant Italian and Sicilian families; the tradition continued, children charging five cents for tours of the haunted house while they dragged chains across the attic floor and ran past windows dressed in sheets. In an 1895 guide to New Orleans, Henry C. Castellanos wrote that while "no spirits wander through its wide halls," there was indeed a curse on the house "that follows every one who has ever attempted to make it a permanent habitation . . . every venture has proved a ruinous failure." That curse may help explain why actor Nicolas Cage, who bought the house in 2006, lost it to foreclosure only three years later.

The house was built in 1831 by Delphine and Louis Lalaurie. Louis was her third husband. Delphine's first marriage had been to Ramon López y Ángulo de la Candelaria, when she was fourteen and he was a thirty-five-year-old widower. López y Ángulo died in a shipwreck five years later, while Delphine was pregnant with their child. The day she turned twenty (March 7, 1805), she married again, to another widower more than twice her age. Her second husband, Jean Paul Blanque, died in 1815, leaving her a widow once more. Having inherited considerable real estate holdings upon her mother's death, she was already wealthy when she met Louis Lalaurie, a doctor, with whom she had a child out of wedlock before marrying him in 1828. The marriage, according to friends, was not a happy one. As the young doctor was still establishing his medical practice, their lavish lifestyle was funded by his wife's considerable real estate holdings and other assets. By 1832 their marriage had grown so intolerable that she petitioned a judge to allow the couple to reside separately.

It was during her third marriage that Delphine's reputation for beating slaves emerged. Several times in the late 1820s and early 1830s she was accused of what a neighbor termed "barbarous treatment of her slaves contrary to law": willfully mistreating them, incarcerating them, and depriving them of necessities.* Despite these allegations Lalaurie repeatedly

---

*While it's true that there were laws against the mistreatment of slaves, it would be a stretch to draw from this that New Orleans was a place where enslaved blacks had it good. According to Article 38 of the city's Code Noir, a slave absent without leave for one month would "have his ears cut off and [be] branded on one shoulder with the fleur-de-lys; if he is guilty of a second offense . . . , he shall be hamstrung and also branded with the fleur-de-lys on the other shoulder, and a third time, he will be put to death."

escaped prosecution, since testimony by slaves against whites was inadmissible. Court records don't preserve the specifics of her alleged crimes, but what is clear is that an unusually high number of her slaves died while they were owned by her. Later apologists tried to justify this by asserting that Delphine Lalaurie's mother was killed at the hands of slaves, either in the Saint-Domingue slave rebellion or by family slaves—but neither of these stories bears any ring of truth.

The Lalaurie legend truly begins on the morning of Thursday, April 10, 1834, with a fire. It broke out first in the kitchen, on the first floor of the outbuilding. A crowd quickly gathered, both firefighters and dozens of concerned onlookers, as the flames quickly started to spread to the slave quarters above the kitchen.

A local judge asked Delphine's husband for permission to have the slaves moved to a place of safety and was met with a harsh rebuke. "There are those who would be better employed," Louis spat at him, "if they would attend to their own affairs instead of officiously intermeddling with the concerns of other people." Neighbors already believed that the slave quarters were operated by the Lalauries as something of a prison, and the judge, thankfully, ignored the doctor's insult and had the doors to the slave quarters broken down. Rescuers found a horrible sight: "several wretched negroes," reported the *Louisiana Courier*, "their bodies covered with scars and loaded with chains." The *New Orleans Bee* gave a similar account, of "seven slaves, more or less horribly mutilated . . . suspended by the neck with their limbs stretched and torn from one extremity to the other. . . . They had been confined . . . for several months in the situation from which they had thus been providentially rescued, and had merely been kept in existence to prolong their sufferings and to make them taste all that the most refined cruelty could inflict." An elderly woman claimed to the mayor that she had been the one who'd set the house on fire, "with the intention of terminating the sufferings of herself and her companions, or perishing in the flames."

It was too much for the people of New Orleans to take. Even in a city that was built on slave labor, whose slave markets—the largest in the country—were a symbol of the vile predation on black bodies by speculators and planters, the cruelty found at the Lalaurie Mansion and the desperate act of an old woman struck a deep chord. The *Bee* reported that after Delphine's slaves were removed from the house and taken to the jail for their safety, "at least two thousand persons visited the jail to be convinced . . . of the sufferings experienced by these unhappy ones. Several have also seen the instruments which were used by these villains: pincers that were applied to their victims to make them suffer all manner of tortures, iron collars with sharpened points, and a number of other instruments for punishment impossible to describe." The newspapers did their part to whip the citizens into a frenzy; the *Louisiana Advertiser* editorialized its hope that "justice will be done and the guilty be brought to punishment."

It was too late for justice: the Lalauries had already fled. They left their home the afternoon of the fire, first making their way to New York City, then crossing the Atlantic on their way to France. By the time the mob arrived at the mansion, Delphine and her husband were already gone, so a crowd "composed of all classes and colors" broke in and destroyed everything in sight. According to the *Bee*, the riot "continued unabated for the whole of the evening" and into the next morning. By the time the sheriff dispersed the mob, nearly the entire edifice of the building had been pulled down, and all that was left of the house was its walls.

Delphine Lalaurie died in Paris, in exile, in 1849. Her remains were eventually repatriated to New Orleans. Despite the outrage of the people of New Orleans regarding the treatment of the Lalauries' slaves, the newspapers of the period are entirely silent on what happened to them after they were rescued.

Judging by contemporary news reports, it's clear that the Lalauries' treatment of their slaves was absolutely horrific, without excuse. They displayed an utter savagery and indifference toward their fellow men and women, which they hid behind a veneer of civilized society. But what is also undeniably clear is that in the decades since that 1834 fire, the accounts of the Lalaurie Mansion have been consistently amplified and exaggerated as storytellers and historians have continued to pile atrocity on top of atrocity, blurring the historical record in a way that does no small amount of insult to the actual victims of Delphine and her husband.

As the house has become known as haunted, Delphine Lalaurie has come to be seen as a figure of monstrous duality: both her elegance and her sadism have been exaggerated for effect. Herbert Asbury (author of *Gangs of New York*) wrote of her that "this bewitching and engaging creature, who entertained the great of New Orleans at her sumptuous table and fascinated her guests by the brilliance of her wit, in reality had the heart of a sadistic demon and was unquestionably mad." Jeanne deLavigne, in her inimitable style, writes:

> Madame Lalaurie, under her soft and beautiful exterior, possessed a demon's soul. Laughing and lovely to her friends and family, she would suddenly fly into rages which none but her slaves ever saw. On these occasions (which were by no means rare), her sadistic appetite seemed never appeased until she had inflicted on one or more of her black servitors some hideous form of torture. As her word was law in that house, and as she had the power to punish in ways far more excruciating than mere death, she could command and receive assistance in her diabolical drama.

In deLavigne's telling, the first responders to that fateful fire found naked men chained to the wall, "their eyes gouged out, their fingernails pulled off by the roots"; others "had their joints skinned and festering, great holes in their buttocks where the flesh had been sliced away, their ears hanging by shreds, their tongues drawn out and sewed to their chins, severed hands stitched to bellies," and on and on. Women whose orifices were crammed with ash and chicken offal, or smeared with honey to attract masses of ants. "There were holes in skulls, where a rough stick had been inserted to stir the brains."

This is how Lalaurie's reputation has solidified over the years: as a figure of barbaric cruelty par excellence, a Creole Marquise de Sade. Despite some attempts at rehabilitation by the white community, and by Lalaurie's own descendants, in the first half of the twentieth century, this is the image of her that endures. This is how she is portrayed by Kathy Bates in *American Horror Story*: not just cruel but a sadist beyond compare, one who reduces black bodies into objects.

It's not clear why subsequent accounts of the Lalaurie Mansion have exaggerated this story to such a great degree. The imprisonment and barbaric conditions of those enslaved apparently became, at some point, insufficient to raise the pity and sympathy of visitors. Why were the actual crimes not enough?

Writing of New Orleans's history, the scholar Joseph Roach notes that here "memory operates as both quotation and invention, an improvisation on borrowed themes, with claims on the future as well as the past." Ghosts are part of the city's tourism now, like jazz and voodoo, brothels and booze. If places like Richmond, Virginia, have built a tourist industry by effacing certain aspects of their past, New Orleans has thrived by trumpeting these same aspects, though in the process there are bound to be inventions alongside the quotations, elaborations accompanying the documentation.

The city has always used its black culture as a commodity, taking living culture from the fringes and repackaging it for tourists in the French Quarter. Jazz, pioneered by poor blacks living in brothels, is now an upscale entertainment. The dynamic religious practices of the city, which combine Catholicism, evangelical Protestantism, and voodoo, are flattened out and reduced solely to the exoticism of voodoo, which is further misrepresented. And while Disneyland has borrowed the culture and aesthetics of the French Quarter for its "New Orleans Square," the opposite could also be said: New Orleans has borrowed heavily from Disneyland's tactics and aesthetics, in creating a French Quarter that exudes a mysterious allure while promising safety for tourists.

For those of us who don't live there, the image of New Orleans that comes to mind is that of a bifurcated city. In the French Quarter one finds music, laughter, excess, and fun while beyond its invisible walls lie the specter of poverty and crime. As welcoming as Louisiana's tourist board assures the city is, tour operators and guidebooks also warn about straying too far from the quarter. A recent Fodor's guide to New Orleans, for example, recommends a visit to St. Louis Cemetery #3 for its beautiful sepulchral architecture and its ghost stories but also cautions, "This is a higher crime area, so take a group tour to see it." For all the violence described on a typical New Orleans ghost tour, this violence is contrasted against ominous warnings of a different kind of violent experience. And by telling tales of two cities, New Orleans's tourist industry only further heightens the economic disparity of the city.

Scholar Anna Hartnell refers to the French Quarter as a "site of translation," in which the living, breathing aspects of the city—complicated, ambiguous, sometimes dangerous, but also palpably alive—are translated into a safe commodity to experience in easily digestible packages. Anthropologist Helen A. Regis more bluntly calls this "spatial apartheid." The ghost stories are part of this mythmaking, of packaging the city for consumption, not unlike the branding of Salem. They tread on the city's violent past while sectioning off that violence into a distant, romanticized past, a past that no longer has any connection to the city's actual politics, racial relations, or history.

The Lalaurie Mansion offers a particularly stark example of this. For years it was left as a ruin. When Harriet Martineau, the English sociologist who abhorred slavery and used her travelogues to urge its abolition, visited New Orleans in 1836, she stumbled upon what was left of the house. "The house stands, and is meant to stand, in its ruined state," she later wrote. "It was the strange sight of its gaping windows and empty walls, in the midst of a busy street, which excited my wonder, and was the cause of my being told the story, the first time." Asking around, Martineau gathered eyewitness accounts and other local lore, filling in the gaps of the story of the house, but she was "requested on the spot not to publish it as exhibiting a fair specimen of slave-holding in New Orleans"; Lalaurie's crimes could be held up only as an exception, not the rule. This, Martineau was willing to concede, but she quickly added that "it is a revelation of what, may happen in a slave-holding country, and can happen nowhere else. Even on the mildest supposition that the case admits of,—that Madame Lalaurie was insane, there remains the fact that the insanity could have taken such a direction, and perpetrated such deeds nowhere but in a slave country."

But even left as a ruin, Lalaurie Mansion wasn't considered haunted. It wouldn't acquire that reputation until the publication of a short piece by George Washington Cable, "The 'Haunted House' in Royal Street," which appeared in 1889. In Cable's telling, the house exudes an uneasy aura:

> The house is very still. As you stand a moment in the middle of the drawing-room looking at each other you hear the walls and floors saying those soft nothings to one another that they so often say when left to themselves. While you are looking straight at one of the large doors that lead into the hall its lock gives a whispered click and the door slowly swings open. No cat, no draft, you and ——— exchange a silent smile and rather like the mystery; but do you know? That is an old trick of those doors, and has made many an emotional girl smile less instead of more; although I doubt not any carpenter could explain it.

Cable and his two research assistants unearthed contemporary news-paper accounts and interviewed those present at the riot and their descendants. While he recounts the grotesque stories of the Lalauries, he's far more concerned with a different troubling event that happened within the house's walls. Because for Cable, who was an ardent champion of the rights of the black community in the postwar South, the mistreatment and torture of Delphine's slaves is only the first—and not the most pressing—horror that occurred on that corner of Royale Street.

By 1872 the house had been rebuilt and was operating as a public high school for girls. The Lower Girls' High School, as it was called, had been integrated and had some twenty black students attending. In 1874 a group of young white boys took it upon themselves to purge the school system of black students. They forcibly removed three black women from one school and a few days later the teenagers arrived at the Lower Girls' High School, where they intimidated the black students there and finally drove them out. Neither the school superintendent nor the police intervened, and the local paper, the *Daily Picayune*, congratulated these "young regulators" on their "admirable firmness and propriety."

Whatever the severity of Delphine and Louis Lalaurie's crimes, the mansion's reputation as "haunted" didn't begin until after this second tragedy, as though the first outrage wasn't enough to prove by itself that something sinister inhabited the house's walls. Cable saw Delphine Lalaurie's outrages as part of an endemic, systematic brutality that also included these "young regulators"—the true evil haunting the mansion's walls.

Abolitionists like Harriet Martineau seized on the story of Lalaurie because they saw it as exemplary of a horrific system. If they embellished a little bit, it was only as a means of highlighting what they saw as the intrinsic barbarism of slavery. In the years since slavery ended, as Delphine Lalaurie's crimes have been so exaggerated as to defy all rational conception, she's been transformed from a brutal slave owner to something outright demonic, a sadist without a soul, an emblem of pure evil. Rather than becoming emblematic of slavery, then, she's become its opposite: an outlier, an exception. Apologists can thus seize on the story of the Lalaurie Mansion for completely apposite ends: here is a sole example of cruel barbarism that was completely at odds with the "civilized" institution of slavery, with its fair treatment of slaves.* New Orleans exists on this kind of mythmaking, on turning tragedy into story, on making legends as a means of building and rebuilding.

From the Lalaurie Mansion, head toward Canal Street. If it's still raining, you hear that same strange music when you reach Jackson Square, a humming you can barely make out, a singing without a voice. By now you know it's not coming from any bar or any band in the plaza. It's always close but just out of earshot, and it disappears when the rain stops.

They will tell you it's the voice of Père Dagobert, a Capuchin monk who came to New Orleans in 1722, known for a voice like "liquid honey," a benevolent presence throughout New Orleans in the mid-eighteenth century. In 1745 he was appointed priest of the St. Louis Cathedral, the central church in the French Quarter. Universally beloved, Père Dagobert was a pillar of the community, a man people came to for all manner of problems.

Not much historical data has been preserved of Père Dagobert, but he participated in a strange drama in the annals of New Orleans history. When France announced that it was turning Louisiana over to the Spanish crown in 1768, local Creoles rose up in bloodless rebellion, driving out the newly arrived governor. Spain responded by sending Alexander O'Reilly as his replacement: O'Reilly was an Irish officer who abandoned the English army in favor of Catholic Spain and rose through the ranks of the Spanish army. When he arrived in New Orleans in August

---

*In deLavigne's account of Lalaurie's torture, there's a foul irony in her mention that some slaves were found with their "ears hanging by shreds," considering that cutting off ears was a legal, sanctioned punishment for escaping slaves, which deLavigne repackages as a torture beyond the pale.

1769, he immediately set out to put down the rebellion. Offering friendship, he invited the leaders of the rebellion over for dinner, where he had them arrested. Of the ten men accused of being ringleaders, O'Reilly had five of them—Nicolas Chauvin de Lafrénière, Jean Baptiste Noyan, Pierre Caresse, Pierre Marquis, and Joseph Milhet—executed by firing squad in the Place d'Armes (now Jackson Square), on October 25, 1769. Afterward he commanded that their bodies be left where they fell as a deterrent to any other would-be conspirators.

The slain men's families went to Père Dagobert, believing that, as a priest, he would be allowed to remove the bodies and give them proper burial. The priest had never before run afoul of the law and appeared reticent to violate O'Reilly's orders. In deLavigne's telling, Père Dagobert replied to the women who'd come to him, "Wait here until night. I have a great deal to do. Spain is on us like a wolfpack. Do not venture out, for any reason whatsoever. Tell your prayer beads, and sleep a little if you can." And so, the story goes, they waited for night, to see if Père Dagobert could redeem the fallen bodies of their loved ones.

That night a rain started as the Spanish troops stood guard. And then Père Dagobert emerged, somehow attended by an entire funeral procession of mourners, and without being noticed, they retrieved the bodies of those men, carrying them through the city through the night, singing "Kyrie eleison, kyrie eleison"—"Lord, have mercy"—as they made their way to St. Louis Cemetery, under the oblivious eyes of the Spanish guards. No one knew how Père Dagobert could lead so many people, carrying those five bodies, those long blocks to the graveyard, singing all the while, and never be stopped, but many New Orleanians will tell you that on nights when it rains, you can still hear his voice singing softly, "Kyrie eleison, kyrie eleison . . ."

But by now you're past the square, and the colonial intrigues of centuries ago have likewise faded. Across Canal Street a new kind of ghost begins to appear. A local tour guide told me that several National Guard troops were driving down this street one night in the aftermath of 2005's

Hurricane Katrina when the driver saw in his headlights a group of disheveled pedestrians, who seemed to appear from out of nowhere. Going far too fast to avoid them, he braced for impact, but they disappeared as quickly as they'd appeared.

Other responders who came to New Orleans in the wake of Katrina found ghosts as well. If you keep walking far enough down St. Charles Street, you'll reach the Sophie B. Wright Charter School, on Napoleon Avenue. During Katrina, the California National Guard was stationed here, and several Guardsmen reported strange goings-on. Sergeant Robin Hairston told a local television station, "I was in my sleeping bag and I opened my eyes and in the doorway was a little girl. It wasn't my imagination." Ghost sightings at Sophie B. Wright were confirmed by another member of the Guard: Specialist Rosales Leanor. "I was using the restroom and I just saw a little shadow," Leanor reported, "kind of looming in front of me." A third soldier claimed that when she opened a cleaning supply closet, she saw a little girl laughing.

This is unsurprising. After Katrina, bodies were left unburied for days, and some were never buried at all, washed away into Lake Pontchartrain and the Mississippi River. The disaster, the ineptitude of the response, and the breakdown of civil services created an entirely new relationship between the dead and the living. As Michael Osterholm, a doctor on the scene, later told the *Washington Post*, "One of the many lessons to emerge from Hurricane Katrina is that Americans are not accustomed to seeing unattended bodies on the streets of a major city." As with soldiers in combat, those who survived Katrina have faced a variety of emotional fallout as they attempt to process what happened. As one resident said on the ten-year anniversary of the storm's landfall, "Even cities feel trauma. It's not just people."

For a city that has long translated its tragic past into tourist entertainment, the response to the devastation wrought by Hurricane Katrina has moved along lines both predictable and unexpected. Within months of the event, disaster tourism had already sprung up. Visitors came to New

Orleans now not just for gumbo and beignets but to photograph the ravaged Lower Ninth Ward and get a firsthand glimpse of what the disaster
had wrought. Before long, tour companies had organized this fascination
with poverty and destruction into bus tours that narrate and contextualize
the storm. Too often, critics have suggested, these tours write out of history New Orleans's poor black citizens, focusing instead on ecological
issues and depopulated ruins. But this is what New Orleans has always
done: take culture from its populations at the margins, smooth off the
rough edges, and sell it to tourists around the globe. As with jazz, voodoo,
and ghosts, so, too, with Katrina.

Given the city's history of selling trauma, will those killed in the wake
of Katrina find themselves in the illustrious company of New Orleans's
famous ghosts? Ghost stories, for good or ill, are how cities make sense of
themselves: how they narrate the tragedies of their past, weave cautionary
tales for the future. More than ten years later, the water has receded and
some of the scars have healed, if unevenly. Yet even as the city continues
to rebuild, some spirits remain.

Meanwhile, you've arrived at the corner of Jackson Avenue and Magazine Street, where the high-end burger joint Charcoal's stands, home to
the ghost of Vera Smith.

A squat, two-story brick rectangle, Charcoal's is, as one reviewer dubbed
it, a "mammoth temple of burger worship." Inside are reclaimed-wood
bars, low-wattage vintage lightbulbs dangling from the ceiling, and jars of
pickled vegetables lining the wall. And, of course, burgers. "As Gourmet
as a Burger Gets" is Charcoal's tagline, and this seems fairly accurate: you
can get your choice of not only beef, chicken, and veggie burgers but also
antelope, elk, buffalo, venison, shrimp, and salmon. In short, anything you
could possibly want in a burger.

The restaurant's opening did not go well: a brand-new meat grinder
failed, water lines inexplicably broke, and other strange mishaps troubled

the place. Charcoal's struggled to get a foothold in the community, and business was slow. The idea that the place was haunted started as a joke among employees, a way to explain the problems, but about a year after it opened, the restaurant's owners, Craig Walker, Jr., and Blaine Prestenbach, announced that the problems were in fact due to the ghost of Vera Smith, who'd died on that corner eight years before, at the height of the storm.

No one knows for sure what happened to Vera Smith. The sixty-five-year-old went out on August 29, the night after Katrina made landfall. According to her common-law husband, C. N. "Max" Keene, she went out to find cigarettes and beer; the next morning her body was found at the intersection of Jackson and Magazine. Most likely she was hit by a drunk driver who fled the scene, but what is beyond doubt is that by then Katrina had begun its decimation of the city, and as the crisis escalated and emergency response focused exclusively on the living, Smith's body was left unattended and abandoned. Keene, himself also elderly and not in great health, laid a sheet over Vera's body, unsure of what else to do in those days of nightmare and chaos.

"I saw a bloodied corpse weeping body fluids onto the street," resident John R. Lee later told reporters. Aghast at finding Vera's body in such a horrific state, seemingly ignored even as it started to rot in the heat and humidity, Lee went to the police, begging them to take care of the body. The cops refused, claiming that their priority was the living, and when Lee asked if he could move the body himself, they told him this was illegal. The only thing the cops were prepared to do, they told Lee, was to let Vera Smith's body rot on the street until they got around to dealing with it.

Lee refused to accept this answer, and finally, after enough badgering, the police allowed him to bury her, so long as he didn't move the body. So he set about building a makeshift grave for her, right there on the corner of Jackson and Magazine.

A few other neighbors joined in to help and managed to cover her body with a white tarp, which they then weighted down with bricks.

Another neighbor, artist Maggie McEleney, painted on top of the tarp a cross and a few stark words: HERE LIES VERA. GOD HELP US.

Vera's body was ultimately recovered and cremated; her remains were sent to relatives in Texas, where she was given, finally, a proper burial. She has not been forgotten in New Orleans, though. The neighbors who knew Smith later made a more lasting memorial for her at the site of her death: built by the local artist Simon Hardeveld, the memorial was a simple iron cross at the center of which was a clock face wound in barbed wire. Above the clock were the words VERA, DIED AUG 29, '05.

It might have been then that the stories of Vera's ghost began to appear. At one point the property owner, who'd been having difficulty finding someone to take the lot off his hands, became convinced that Hardeveld's memorial was some kind of voodoo charm preventing him from selling the lot and took a sledgehammer to the memorial, almost completely destroying it.

Vera's spirit would not depart so easily. In a city filled with tragedies, Vera Smith's death became emblematic of the horror of Katrina, what a local shopkeeper referred to as "symbol of the quiet suffering people endured." In part because her death remains a mystery—the official autopsy noted her injuries were not consistent with being hit by a car, and left the cause of her death as undetermined. In part because she was loved.

Many assumed, given the situation and the fact that she'd struggled sometimes with alcohol, that she had been homeless, a drifter, a no one. But she had two daughters in Texas and a network of friends and loved ones in the community. Known for her costume jewelry, her brightly colored wigs, and her elaborate dresses, she lived with two small dogs and her common-law husband. "She was not a sad woman. She had a very good life. In the neighborhood, everyone knew her and loved her," Hardeveld said.

A woman like Vera deserved much more—more assistance during the storm, more dignity in death. The work of Lee and the other neighbors who gathered to help became a defiant gesture in the face of the storm and the ineptitude, poverty, and failures of the city. Even in the depths of such anguish and despair, this much could be done.

When Abraham Lincoln addressed the dead at Gettysburg, he made plain that it was the bodies of the fallen that consecrated the burial ground, not words. So, too, with New Orleans, whose ground was consecrated by the bodies of men and women like Vera Smith. The corner of Jackson and Magazine is a *haunt*, a place we must always come back to. To be haunted by Vera is to return to this place, to remember.

Because of stories like Vera's, the ghost of Père Dagobert has become increasingly important to New Orleans, leading this phantasmal funeral procession through the night rains, singing, "Kyrie eleison, kyrie eleison"— Lord, have mercy, God help us—promising to bury the bodies that have been left to rot, offering rites for all those that have been abandoned. His legacy is a reminder that, no matter what else happens, we must care for our dead.

As for Charcoal's: after a year the owners commissioned Hardeveld— the artist who'd built the original memorial for Vera—to create a second memorial honoring her, this one attached to the restaurant, in hopes that it would quiet her spirit. One neighbor told me there were those who felt that the ghost story was likely fictitious and that Charcoal's used Vera's death as a marketing ploy to raise interest and business. But this is what New Orleans has always done, and this may just be the next stage of mythmaking for a city that manages to remain the same even as it's constantly reborn. When co-owner Walker told reporters, "Our message to Vera is our heart and soul is in this restaurant. We want you to support us," it may not matter whether or not he was speaking to a paranormal entity or simply through Vera to the people who remembered her and wanted her honored.

One way or another, regardless of motives, regardless of what you believe, Vera has returned to her corner. On the side of the building facing Jackson Avenue is a small fountain adorned with a cross and flanked by two wings: one that reads VERA, DIED AUG 29 '05, and the other, a sly play on words, that reads QUI VERA SERA—"Who is Vera, will be."

CHAPTER FIFTEEN

AMONG THE RUINS

Detroit, MI

The ghost of Daniel Scotten didn't wait long to materialize. Prior to his death, in 1899, Scotten had been a titan of Detroit's business community, beloved by everyone who knew him. He'd started the Hiawatha Tobacco Company and turned it into a massive enterprise, complete with a monstrous factory on Fort Street. Woodcuts of the building show a stately rectangular building with arched windows along its first floor and a giant American flag flying from the roof. In an age when factory owners could be less than humane toward their workers, Scotten built a reputation as a philanthropist, funneling his wealth back into the city, even leaving stacks of firewood out for workers or anyone else who needed them to get through the long Michigan winter.

Shortly after Scotten died, his factory was closed and put up for sale. Once a beacon of Detroit's manufacturing success, it now sat dark and empty, an imposing tombstone to Scotten's legacy, a leering monolith with an uncertain future at the dawn of the twentieth century. Two of his former workers were walking past it when they were confronted by what they later described as "the figure of a man, white and terrible," which sent them both screaming in fright. Despite their terror, they recognized the ghost as their former boss, who bellowed at them, "Ever more must I walk until the smoke comes out of the chimneys of the old plant."

By June of the following year, ownership of the factory had transferred to Scotten's nephew Owen Scotten, who reopened the plant. The smoke of industry began once again spewing from its chimneys, and the ghost disappeared. It has not been seen since, not even after the company relocated to Buffalo, New York, in 1969, or after the Detroit factory was demolished in 1971—where it once stood, on the corner of Fort Street and Campau (since renamed Scotten Street), there's now a parking lot.

One wonders if we'll see the ghost of James Ward Packard on the city's east side, roaming the grounds of the massive, forty-acre Packard Automotive Plant. The plant, one of the most modern factories when it opened in 1903, operated until 1958, when the Packard brand died, but continued to be inhabited by various other businesses until the 1990s. Since then it has stood vacant, looming, ghostly—a sprawling ruin, a symbol of devastation stretching twelve city blocks.

A number of investors have tried to purchase the property and revital-ize it, but despite vague plans for the future, it remains a wreckage a half mile long, a playground for vandals and disaster tourists. And if the ghost of Packard is here, no one's yet seen him.

Goethe wrote in 1827,

America, you have it better
Than our old continent,
You have no ruined castles
And no ancient basalt.
Your inner life remains untroubled
By useless memory
And futile strife.

That was then. Now, almost two hundred years later, we've started to catch up to old Europe. We have plenty of ruined castles now, plenty of wasted strife to call our own.

Detroit has its abandoned hotels and office buildings, towering over the skyline but emptied out within. The once-beautiful theaters of a golden age, neo-Renaissance temples that have been left to decay and deteriorate. In these formerly grand palaces, failing plaster now drips from gouged ceilings and the sweeping balconies and cornices lord it over trash and dust. One such place, the Michigan Theatre, was converted into a parking garage; its vaulted ceilings are still visible above the cars and trucks.

These buildings have become the playgrounds of urban explorers, who've taken to breaking in where necessary to see the insides of abandoned hulks and fallen beauties. Before it was boarded up, the Roosevelt Warehouse at the corner of Fourteenth and Marantette was a popular destination. In use as a book depository for the Detroit public schools when it was heavily damaged by fire in 1987, it was subsequently abandoned, the school district leaving behind a surplus of usable supplies, including hundreds of books. In the slow decay of the building, trees have sprouted from the wreckage and books and other supplies left behind, offering a particularly stark image of Detroit's abandonment and, to some extent, its rebirth—or at least its reclamation by nature.

Detroit's downtown is anchored by the mammoth Renaissance Center. It was designed by John Portman, the same architect who designed LA's Westin Bonaventure, and the two properties are markedly similar, except that the seven-tower Renaissance Center is larger and its central core—a Marriott—is much taller. Inside, though, is the same style of confusing atrium, the same sense of a Piranesi prison come to life. But unlike the Bonaventure, the Renaissance Center isn't haunted. Why would it be? There are so, so many other haunted buildings in Detroit.

Ghosts fester in places untended to, where the usual patterns of behavior aren't or can't be enforced. Where once-regular places become strange, where it's no longer clear what a building's function was. Where the shadows multiply and nothing restricts your mind from projecting your thoughts and dreams and nightmares onto the walls and corridors. New Orleans gets its haunted reputation in no small part from carefully scripted stories that have been cultivated over decades, a way of packaging the city's history for tourists. Detroit's haunting feels more organic, sprung from the wreckage like a ghost from the well at the bottom of some forlorn dungeon.

"In the ruin history has physically merged into the setting," the German philosopher Walter Benjamin once commented. The ruin does not give history eternal life, he added; rather, it transforms the past into a thing that offers only "irresistible decay." As moss and foliage reclaim the remains of an old statue or aqueduct, the normally sharp line between the works of humanity and nature blur. A young Gustave Flaubert wrote of the "deep and ample joy" that filled him upon seeing ruins and their "embrace of nature, coming swiftly to bury the work of man the moment his hand is no longer there to defend it." A few decades earlier, the Reverend William Gilpin wrote similarly that "a ruin is a sacred thing. Rooted for ages in the soil; assimilated to it; and become, as it were, a part of it; we consider it as a work of nature, rather than of art." Sacred and enigmatic, for centuries ruins have been seen as appropriate places for philosophical reflection; it's not a coincidence that two of the best-known Romantic poems, Wordsworth's "Lines Composed a Few Miles Above Tintern Abbey" and Shelley's "Ozymandias," are both meditations on ruin.

In the same way that a ghost story told on a dark night might quicken one's pulse, ruins have a strange attraction, an exhilaration that accompanies the melancholy contemplation. Faced with the pitiless passage of time, the reality of one's own insignificance, we are awakened to our own death without actually facing a life-threatening experience. The eighteenth-century French writer and encyclopedist Denis Diderot spoke for many of us when he wrote:

> The ideas that ruins awaken in me are grand. Everything vanishes, everything dies, everything passes, only time endures. How old it is this world! I walk between two eternities. Everywhere I cast my eyes, the objects which surround me announce an end and make me yield to that end which awaits me. What is my ephemeral existence in comparison with that of the rock which is effaced, this valley which is forged, with this forest that trembles, with these masses suspended above my head which rumbles. I see the marble tombs crumble into dust; and I do not want to die!

Detroit is filled with ruins like no other city. And certainly they are beautiful. The buildings that remain are primarily from a single period: the early decades of the twentieth century, when the rise of the automobile catapulted Detroit to the forefront of American consciousness. We may think of the city as a petrified ruin, but for the first century of its history, it focused on new construction instead of preservation. Very little of its architecture from the nineteenth century still stands; much of it was demolished to make way for the great Art Deco and Beaux-Arts landmarks of the early twentieth century, when the city was in its heyday.

So many people fetishize Detroit's ruins in particular, because loving other ruins is often off-limits. "Is it unseemly now or ever to talk about the beauty of the World Trade Center ruins?" Sarah Boxer asked in the *New York Times* in 2002, and while the cultural consensus seems to be yes, Detroit is fair game, or so it would seem. Detroit has become our nation's favorite morality tale: a series of ineffectual mayors, bad public policy, and servitude to unions have all allowed a popular conception that Detroit "deserves" its fate. Just as we once visited circus sideshows, gawking at the

Bearded Lady and the Dog-Faced Boy—freaks whose display not only titillated but reminded customers that they were themselves normal—those of us who don't live in the Motor City peer at its haunted architecture to remind ourselves that our lives are normal. An architectural freak show, these ruins are both cautionary tale and stone and copper mementos mori, reminders that we, too, will all one day age and die. The haunted theaters of Detroit entice outsiders because they suggest decadence, extravagant wasting. The Michigan Theatre that is now a parking garage—what can that mean except a perverse excess, as though Beaux-Art landmarks are so plentiful here that you can throw them away.

In 2009 Detroit-based writer and photographer James D. Griffioen complained to *Vice Magazine* about the prevalence of a certain kind of image of Detroit: one of blight and destruction and little else. Professional photographers from around the world had been contacting him, asking for tours of the city, but he soon sensed a pattern. "At first you're really flattered by it, like 'Whoa, these professional guys are interested in what I have to say and show them.' But you get worn down trying to show them all the different sides of the city, then watching them go back and write the same story as everyone else. The photographers are the worst. Basically the only thing they're interested in shooting is ruin porn." The term Griffioen coined, "ruin porn," caught on and has since become ubiquitous, a phrase describing a certain kind of approach to urban decay, one that for better or worse has become associated with Detroit. In these images the ruins of places like the Roosevelt Warehouse and the Packard Plant are captured in their eerie beauty.

In the past few years the subgenre of ruin porn has exploded; coffee-table books that depict Detroit's abandoned spaces in lush, stunning photography have become a reliable industry. In works like Andrew Moore's *Detroit Disassembled*, Yves Marchand and Romain Meffre's *The Ruins of Detroit*, and the architectural history *Lost Detroit: Stories Behind the Motor City's Majestic Ruins*, by Dan Austin and Sean Doerr, Detroit is captured in its faded glory and displayed, like an anatomized corpse on a dissecting table, for the rest of us to gaze upon with awe and delighted terror.

A mile and a half from the train station is Detroit's Masonic Temple, the largest such building in the country. A sixteen-story gothic behemoth with more than one thousand rooms, it was built by George D. Mason to display the pride of a city that had only recently begun to emerge as the manufacturing hub of an entire nation. As Detroit, and the Masonic lodge, have fallen on hard times in the past few decades, ghost stories have emerged about the lodge, including a popular one about Mason himself. As it's told on one Web site:

> Mr. Mason went slightly overboard when financing the construction of the building, and eventually went bankrupt, whereupon his wife left him. Overwhelmingly depressed about his financial and personal circumstances, Mason jumped to his death from the roof of the temple. Security guards claim to see his ghost to this day, ascending the steps to the roof. The temple, abundant with cold spots, inexplicable shadows, and slamming doors, is known to intimidate visitors with the eerie feeling of being watched.

A popular story, yes, but among the most patently false and easily disproved ghost stories out there. Mason was eighty-eight at the time of his death, from natural causes (as any quick Google search will tell you), which took place more than twenty years after the Masonic Temple was finished. And yet the story has cachet in part because it reflects a narrative that many have about Detroit: one of ostentatious overreach, folly, and death from financial ruin. So even though it's obviously false, it still gets told and retold.

If the legend of Mason's ghost reflects the downfall of the city, other ghosts stand guard trying to ward off further ruin. Such is the strange ghost of Colonel Philetus Norris, who appears at the haunted Two-Way Inn, several miles north of downtown. Even had he not returned as a ghost, his life would have been spectacular enough. Born in 1821 Norris served in the Union Army during the Civil War, rising to the rank of colonel and working as a spy in Confederate territory. After the war he served in the Ohio legislature before moving to Detroit, building the home for himself that is now the Two-Way Inn. He stayed in Detroit until he was hired to become the superintendent of Yellowstone National Park. In his later years he did ethnographic research for the Smithsonian Institution, dying in Kentucky and returning to Detroit only to be buried.

In photographs Norris looks every bit the Wild West mountain man, sporting a full, bushy beard and dressed entirely in buckskin. It's this figure that has been seen repeatedly in the Two-Way Inn: the frontiersman image easily recognizable in the postindustrial landscape, an unlikely candidate for protector of the Motor City.

In most retellings of the story of Norris's ghost, he's credited with protecting the inn from arson, which has long been endemic in Detroit. As with Daniel Scotten, you could say Norris's ghost is looking out for the city, acting as a steward against its decline, militating against its abandonment. It is rare for the supernatural to adopt such a civic responsibility, but here in Detroit it is perhaps essential.

Ghost stories like this reveal an evolving attitude toward buildings after their collapse. The remnants left behind after a ruinous rapture, they've become burdens a city must bear and a constant reminder of a past now faded. The ghost stories of Detroit that focus on its old buildings are of a different caliber from those that center on the gothic high-rises of Manhattan or Chicago, where land is precious and useless buildings don't stick around. The reputation of the Merchant's House in Manhattan comes in no small part from the contrast with the surrounding buildings: an anachronistic anomaly in a bustling, forward-looking metropolis. In Detroit the ghosts stand guard, preserving the past against the decay of the future. They command the living to reclaim the former pride of these factories and mansions, or, like Mason, they lament their own folly and hubris.

And then there is the curious figure of the Nain Rouge, the mysterious Red Dwarf that's haunted Detroit for more than three hundred years. If Daniel Scotten and Philetus Norris are the supernatural defenders of Detroit, the Nain Rouge is the city's assailant. If George Mason laments the end of the city's glory days, the Nain Rouge celebrates it.

Stories of the Nain Rouge begin with the founding of the city. In 1701 Antoine Laumet de La Mothe Cadillac (the French explorer who would found Detroit) had been in attendance at a lavish ball in Quebec when a strange fortune-teller appeared. The author of the 1883 collection *Legends of Le Détroit*, Marie Caroline Watson Hamlin (about whom not much else is known), who tells the story that follows, described her as "a woman of unusual height, a dark, swarthy complexion, restless, glittering eyes, strangely fashioned garments yet in harmony with her face." On her shoulder was perched a small black cat, which would lick her ear occasionally during her sessions, leading some to assume that the devil was whispering instructions through the body of the feline.

Finally she came to Cadillac, who bade her to tell him his fortune as well. "Sieur," she told him, "yours is a strange destiny. A dangerous journey you will soon undertake; you will found a great city which one day will have more inhabitants than New France now possesses; many children will nestle around your fireside." But as with Macbeth's fortune, there was another side to Cadillac's future: "Dark clouds are arising and I see dimly your star," the fortune-teller went on. "The policy you intend pursuing in selling liquor to the savages, contrary to the advice of the Jesuits will cause you much trouble, and be the cause of your ruin. In years to come your colony will be the scene of strife and bloodshed, the Indians will be treacherous, the hated English will struggle for its possession, but under a new flag it will reach a height of prosperity which you never in your wildest dreams pictured."

Confused, Cadillac pressed her for more information, and she ended her tale with this warning: "Your future and theirs lie in your own hands, beware of undue ambition; it will mar all your plans. Appease the Nain Rouge. Beware of offending him. Should you be thus unfortunate not a vestige of your inheritance will be given to your heirs. Your name will be scarcely known in the city you founded."

That same year Cadillac founded the settlement that would in time grow to be Detroit, and as it flourished quickly, he became arrogant and proud, disregarding the soothsayer's warnings. One night when he and his wife were out walking, on the path in front of them jumped "the uncouth figure of a dwarf, very red in the face, with a bright, glistening eye; instead of burning it froze, instead of possessing depth [it] emitted a cold gleam like the reflection from a polished surface, bewildering and dazzling all who came within its focus. A grinning mouth displaying sharp, pointed teeth, completed this strange face." Unwisely, Cadillac struck the dwarf with his cane, shouting, "Get out of my way, you red imp!" The Nain Rouge responded with a fiendish, mocking laugh, then disappeared.

True to the fortune-teller's predictions, Cadillac's own fortunes soon fell precipitously, and in the years since, the Nain Rouge has become not simply a personal antagonist but a villain for the city as a whole. He is seen shortly before every major disaster that's befallen Detroit. Just as Binghamton has its curse, Detroit has its Red Dwarf.

In another collection of folktales, Charles M. Skinner writes that the Nain Rouge was "seen scampering along the shore on the night before the attack on Bloody Run, when the brook that afterward bore this name turned red with the blood of soldiers. People saw it in the smoky streets when the city was burned in 1805, and on the morning of Hull's surrender it was found grinning in the fog."

Little record of the dwarf, a harbinger of tragic romanticism and falls from grace, can be found in the years of the city's great boom. Only starting in the 1960s did the Nain Rouge supposedly return, making an appearance again shortly before the devastating race riots of 1967. In the decades since, he's shown up again before major ice storms and other calamities.

Meanwhile, another class of ghosts has emerged here. Among the most iconic images of contemporary Detroit is Yves Marchand and Romain Meffre's image of Michigan Central Station: their photograph takes the building head-on, cropping it so closely that there's nothing else in the frame: no sky, no land, no other buildings. The building is imposing, and the impression it gives can be quite chilling. But what's not captured in the image is what was happening behind them as they took the photograph. Across the street from Michigan Central Station is a row of shops and restaurants, including a barbershop and a real estate firm, a fancy espresso place, a barbecue joint, and a vodka bar.

The simple fact, after all, is that while ruin porn focuses on abandoned buildings, devoid of any humanity, Detroit is not empty. As historian Thomas J. Sugrue notes, "Detroit might be depopulated, but it's not a blank slate. Over 700,000 people, more than four-fifths of them Black, call the city home. For them, Detroit's ruins are not romantic: they are a taunting reminder of how the city has lost capital and jobs, and how many lives have been ruined in the process." The images of emptied buildings have to efface blue-collar workers who are almost always just out of frame. They have their own stories, of course, these lives that exist just beyond the camera's eye—and they haunt the aesthetic of ruin porn with their refusal to vanish.

Our ruins are not centuries-old testaments to the civilizations long gone; they are not the mysterious ciphers of Stonehenge or ancient Egypt. They have been birthed in modern memory, documented for all to see. And ruin porn photographs offer no way to understand the decline we're witnessing; they're anti-history, even as they embody the past and its decline. A ghost story's reduction of a complex moment or the history of a building into a series of clichés is reproduced in beautifully staged photos that fetishize the past without truly representing it. Ruin porn is the visual analog of the ghost story.

Meanwhile, Detroit is still teeming with people. It's one of the top twenty largest cities in America—more populous than Seattle, Denver, Boston, or Washington, D.C. It's down from its historic highs of two million people, to be sure, and its massive size means a lower population density, but it's by no means empty. On the contrary, on an early spring weekend, Detroit's downtown struck me as a good deal more lively than Chicago's Loop or downtown Los Angeles would have been at the same time. To see Detroit as a ruin—and as nothing but a ruin—is to see it emptied out of people. It is to erase some 713,000 residents from view. It is to transform them, against their will, into ghosts.

Sometimes, though, the ghosts fight back. Since 2010, on the first Sunday of spring each year a parade is held for the Nain Rouge, where he confronts the city and is symbolically driven out of town. Half Mardi Gras parade, half Burning Man (though nowhere near as large or elaborate or well attended), the Marche du Nain Rouge is a strange, if entertaining, way to spend a Sunday morning in March. Fire jugglers accompany a float made to look like a giant cockroach, on top of which stands the Nain Rouge himself—or at least an actor portraying him, in full black leather and an appropriately demonic red mask. From his perch he mocks the crowd to the strains of Black Sabbath's "War Pigs," shouting, "You think you can defeat me! You'll never be able to defeat me!"; "You thought you got rid of me but I'm back!"; "You won't succeed, Detroit! I'll make you fail!"

Parade goers wave signs blaming the Red Dwarf for their troubles (NAIN BROKE MY TIRE, read one) or in support of the antagonist (DON'T DREAD THE RED!; SUPPORT THE SHORT!; STOP NAIN SHAMING!), while he claims credit for petty annoyances: "I fed your dog chocolates!" or "I cc'ed the wrong e-mail to everyone you know!" But even here there can be a harder edge beneath the veneer. "I put all the toxins in the air and the lead in the soil," he taunts. "I raised the parking ticket to $45." He seems to ally himself with the Republicans in control of the state government ("I support right to work"; "I gerrymandered Michigan!") as well as the new influx of white hipsters ("I think gentrification is excellent urban planning"; "I'm working on the new hipster political correctness"). The crowd on hand is overwhelmingly white, and young; participating in a public shaming of themselves, these gentrifiers perhaps hope to absolve themselves of some guilt. A carnivalesque scapegoat, the Nain Rouge can function as a release valve for pent-up annoyances and anxieties, which is the most you can hope for from any ghost.

It's hard to know for sure what lies in store for a city like Detroit, one that has so much promise and potential and so many dedicated citizens but that still has so many obstacles standing in its way. It's hard to know how much longer the Nain Rouge will return to pester the citizens and frustrate their dreams. From the rooftop of the massive Masonic Temple, the ghost of the building's architect, George Mason, looks down on the city, watching. Once, years before, he was allowed to rest in peace, but then he was resurrected, not unlike the Nain Rouge, and remade into a symbol of the city's tragic fortunes.

Perhaps, in the years to come, he may be able to rest in peace once more.

CHAPTER SIXTEEN

HILLSDALE, USA

The road to Hill House leads through Hillsdale. In Shirley Jackson's *The Haunting of Hill House*, Eleanor Vance is given detailed instructions on getting to the eponymous mansion and is advised explicitly not to ask about the mansion once she gets to the small town closest to her haunted destination. "I am making these directions so detailed," Dr. Montague writes to her in a letter, "because it is inadvisable to stop in Hillsdale to ask your way. The people there are rude to strangers and openly hostile to anyone inquiring about Hill House." And it's true: the people of Hillsdale feel an immediate distrust of this mousy Eleanor Vance who's preparing to spend several months at the haunted mansion.

In Jackson's novel Hill House's creator, Hugh Crain, materializes almost from nowhere, without a backstory and certainly not as a citizen of Hillsdale—his decision for choosing Hillsdale remains a mystery. Though Crain builds Hill House for his wife and family, his wife dies minutes before first laying eyes on it, as the carriage taking her to her new home overturns in the driveway. Bringing up his two children alone in the murky mansion, Crain eventually marries twice more, though both subsequent wives also come to untimely ends: the second from a fall, the third from consumption. It's not clear why things go so horribly wrong, only that Crain's house unleashes some unspeakable evil, or is itself that evil—an evil that lingers long after he himself is dead. Stuck with a darkness on the edge of town, the people of Hillsdale must contend with this new architectural evil perpetually on their periphery.

Why do the poor townspeople hate the haunted mansion? Well, because they're poor. They can't afford to move away, to uproot their families, even after some rich eccentric has uncorked some terrible spirit just outside town. "People *leave* this town," a Hillsdale resident tells Eleanor, "they don't *come* here." The archetypal haunted house story is fundamentally about class: new money who doesn't understand the land or the people or the history blunders into the landscape, attempting to buy his way into a community, blithely oblivious to the locals. A legend goes unheeded, a terrible secret is unearthed, sacred land is disturbed, and so forth. The townspeople grow resentful because, by the force of economics, they are imprisoned by the rich and their folly.

Shirley Jackson never specifies exactly where Hillsdale is, or even in which state it can be found. Take "Route 39 to Ashton," Dr. Montague's letter instructs Eleanor, "and then turn left onto Route 5 going west"—that's about it. For a long time I'd assumed it was in New England; Jackson was living in Vermont when she wrote the novel, and that's where director Robert Wise sets *The Haunting*, his adaptation of the novel: in "the most remote part of New England." But while there are about a dozen Ashtons throughout the country, none are in New England. There is, however, an Ashton, Illinois, right near the intersection of State Route 5 and State Route 38.

So Hill House might actually be in the Land of Lincoln. If you look closely, though, every state has its Hillsdale: a town beset by a local haunting, a paranormal real estate problem, a conflict between the haves and have-nots that plays out in supernatural terms.

As Salem has taught us, nothing brings out ghosts like property disputes. Events played out similarly sinister in Nyack, New York, a few decades ago. Helen Ackley had advertised her house as haunted for more than a decade before she put it up for sale in 1989; for years she had opened it up for local walking tours of haunted Nyack, and it had once been featured in *Reader's Digest*. But it was only *after* Jeffrey Stambovsky bought the house that he became aware of the rumors and the house's reputation. Stambovsky, who'd lived in New York City and wasn't up to speed on local lore, argued that the presence of ghosts lowered the value of the house, and he sued Ackley for failing to inform him of its haunted past.

West Virginia's Greenbrier Ghost would not be the last instance of the supernatural entering into American case law, and *Stambovsky v. Ackley* worked its way slowly through the courts. After a lower court dismissed Stambovsky's claim under the principle of caveat emptor (as the buyer of the home, it was his responsibility to do his due diligence), he appealed, and in a New York state appellate opinion, Justice Israel Rubin finally agreed with him.

Rubin's decision began by more or less sidestepping the question of whether or not the house was actually haunted: "Whether the source of the spectral apparitions seen by defendant seller are parapsychic or psychogenic," Rubin wrote, was irrelevant, since Ackley had repeatedly advertised her house as having ghosts: "defendant is estopped to deny their existence and, as a matter of law, the house is haunted."

Rubin recognized Stambovsky's predicament: though it was reasonable to expect the buyer to check for termites, water damage, and other possible faults, it struck him as unreasonable to expect a buyer to check for paranormal problems. "From the perspective of a person in the position of plaintiff herein, a very practical problem arises with respect to the discovery of a paranormal phenomenon: 'Who you gonna call?'" Rubin wrote, clearly having fun with his decision. Imagining prospective buyers having to hire not just a structural engineer and a pest-control consultant but also a ghost hunter, the court concluded that "the notion that a haunting is a condition which can and should be ascertained upon reasonable inspection of the premises is a hobgoblin which should be exorcised from the body of legal precedent and laid quietly to rest." Narrowly tailoring his decision, Rubin did reject Stambovsky's claim that Ackley had acted fraudulently, arguing that any attempt to recover actual damages from Ackley hadn't "a ghost of a chance." But, "moved by the spirit of equity," Rubin ordered the contract voided, awarding Stambovsky his original down payment.

Almost twenty years later the Pennsylvania Supreme Court would take on many of the same issues, though they would reach a significantly different outcome. In 2008 Janet Milliken sued the previous owners of her home in Thornton. The home had been the scene of a gruesome murder-suicide; it was subsequently bought cheaply at auction by Kathleen and Joseph Jacono, who renovated it and then resold it to Milliken. Milliken, who'd moved from California with her two young children after her husband's death, had no idea of the house's gruesome past and soon found her family beset with a number of ghostly encounters. After finally learning the true history of her house, she brought suit against the Jaconos, claiming that they'd purposefully withheld information that materially affected the value of the house.

Milliken v. Jacono went all the way to the Pennsylvania Supreme Court, and as part of her case Milliken brought in Randall Bell, a California appraiser whose specialty was consulting on properties that were "psychologically stigmatized." He'd first come to fame assisting with the sale of the condo where Nicole Brown Simpson and Ronald Goldman had been murdered. He'd also consulted on the house where Sharon Tate and four others were murdered by the Manson family, JonBenet Ramsey's former house, and the Rancho Santa Fe mansion where thirty-nine members of the Heaven's Gate cult committed suicide, as well as other places that bore the stain of a violent, sensationalized past. Bell himself doesn't believe in ghosts, but he recognizes that the perception of ghosts or a history involving violence can affect a home's resale value. "A haunted house is a perception," he's said. "If a property is perceived as haunted, it's haunted. If you don't think it's haunted, it isn't." Bell, along with Milliken's lawyers, argued that whether or not ghosts were really haunting the house was irrelevant; what mattered was that the house's history was affecting its price, and that the Jaconos had been obligated to disclose this during the sale.

Ultimately the court sided with the Jaconos, not Milliken. "One cannot quantify the psychological impact of different genres of murder, or suicide," it wrote in its opinion. Psychological stigma, no matter its subjective effect on some, presented the court with such a slippery slope of possibilities that there was no way for them to contemplate it as a material defect: "Does a bloodless death by poisoning or overdose create a less significant 'defect' than a bloody one from a stabbing or shooting? How would one treat other violent crimes such as rape, assault, home invasion, or child abuse? What if the killings were elsewhere, but the sadistic serial killer lived there? What if satanic rituals were performed in the house?" Unlike the New York court, the Pennsylvania justices put the onus entirely on the buyer: caveat emptor—buyer beware.

If *Milliken v. Jacono* was expected to settle, definitively, the question of whether ghosts can affect property values, it most assuredly has not, and the belief that a building's reputation as haunted can have a legitimate impact on its value has resurfaced over the years in sometimes unexpected ways. In Brooklyn the former Caledonian Hospital, overlooking the south side of Prospect Park, was transformed in 2014 into a luxury rental property, and almost immediately the ghosts moved in. Stories of strange smells, unexplained sounds, and other haunted phenomena began to emerge, and three doormen quit over the course of six months. One doorman who'd quit reportedly told a neighbor that 123 on the Park, as the building's now known, is "a messed-up place to work because it's haunted." The managing director of the property group that manages the building confirmed to local papers that there was high staff turnover and that there have been issues in renting units.

But these unexplained spirits may have a more predictable origin. Writing for *Gothamist*, Lauren Evans wondered whether the ghosts were themselves "understandably perturbed by the gentrification of their longtime home" and had "organized to retaliate." When she poked around the property trying to verify the haunting, she was told by employees that the ghost rumors had been started by neighbors, who were concerned that the high-priced apartments would drive up their own rents. Meanwhile, prospective renters at 123 on the Park have themselves apparently tried to use the ghosts as a bargaining chip, asking for reduced rents since their apartments already have occupants. In landscapes such as New York City, where real estate and issues of gentrification are already fraught, it doesn't much matter if the ghosts are real or not; what matters is the financial leverage they may provide.

I'd felt this myself firsthand when my wife and I were searching for our first home, in 2008, when the country's real estate market was in free fall. In many of the strange houses we looked at, I felt the hints of lives left behind by the foreclosure crisis, and the odd, haunting feeling such traces could engender. But nowhere did I feel it as strongly as in the one house we came to call the Happy Murder Castle.

Standing midway up the side of a hill off Alvarado Boulevard in Los Angeles's Echo Park neighborhood, even from a distance it stood out against the other homes. Driving up to it, we could see the faux flagstone that had been painted on some, but not all, of its walls. It was just up the street from an elementary school and might have once doubled as an unlicensed day care; perhaps the castle look had seemed inviting to children at one point. The citrus trees on the property were untended and filled with ripe and rotting fruit, and from those trees rose the back bedroom, complete with plywood crenellations to complete the medieval tower aesthetic. Meanwhile, the front of the house still bore the evidence of its former life as a 1920s bungalow. This was an architectural version of *The Fly*: two incompatible species gratuitously grafted together, resulting in an utter monstrosity.

As we walked in, we found another couple on their way out. They smiled grimly and said merely, "Hope you brought your mask," on their way past us. The owners, we learned, had left the taps dripping, so that pools of black mold festered beneath the sinks, but that was only the be-ginning. The house had once been half its current size, and the additions boggled the mind: the only door to the backyard was through a bath-room, and off the kitchen was something too wide to be a hallway, too small to be a room. This "room," in turn, led to that back bedroom tower, which amazingly had a ceiling painted with a marginal trompe l'oeil: scarf-draped cherubs blowing trumpets amid wispy clouds. It was hard to imagine how anyone could have made a home here, but we walked through it anyway, drinking in its distorted weirdness, its history mea-sured out in garish juxtapositions. We were about to leave when our real estate agent noted something we'd overlooked: scrawled in pencil on the living room wall were the words A MURDERER LIVED HERE.

The feeling I got from the house stayed with me for weeks, even after we'd ended our search. (We didn't put in an offer on the house, unsurpris-ingly.) The Happy Murder Castle was disquieting, uncanny, possessed of an uneasy sense I've rarely felt in any structure; I'll admit there are times I'm tempted to call it haunted. We tell ourselves ghost stories perhaps because we truly believe in the paranormal—or perhaps because we just need a word, a term, a story for that vague feeling that would be too silly to admit in other terms.

After our trip to the Happy Murder Castle, I Googled the address, along with "murderer," "killer," "child molester," every combination I could think of. I came up with nothing. Unlike in Pennsylvania, in Cali-fornia a real estate agent has to notify you if a death has occurred in a house within the past three years, but that wouldn't include a murderer who lived there and did his or her killing elsewhere or a murderer who was never caught. It's possible, I suppose, that a murderer really did live there. But the truth is likely far more obvious, more quotidian, more bit-ing. These were homeowners who bought at an inflated price before the market crashed and now found themselves underwater; they finally lost their home like so many thousands of others. Those penciled words were, like the black mold, likely an attempt to make their home as unappealing as they could, an albatross around the neck of the bank that had taken it from them. Forced out, the home's previous owners' memories linger in that house—bitter and spiteful spirits, mingling with a sense of melancholy and regret.

Wherever they are now, who can say. But this, too, you could say, is part of the American story, as we have always been people who move on, leaving behind wreckage and fragments in our wake. We will continue, despite our best intentions, to make haunted houses and cities, for we are endlessly mobile, leaving a pockmarked landscape of abandoned places in our wake. Like hermit crabs, Americans tend to abandon one home for the next, leaving behind a former dwelling to be either repurposed by its next occupant or left as detritus.

"We left the valley with reluctant feet, looking backward at every turn in the steep grade, much as our first parents must have lingered on the confines of Eden," a correspondent for the *Cincinnati Enquirer* wrote in 1875, signing her dispatch with only the name "Abigail." A travelogue through eastern California out of the Sierra Nevadas, Abigail's short article offers an early perspective on the changing nature of the country in the wake of the early mining booms. "We ate our first lunch under a great Sequoia tree, named 'Illinois,' and sped down into the Valley of the Stanislaus, and up to Sonora, through the deserted mining towns, like the ghosts of their departed prosperity. The country is ruined now for all agricultural purposes for ages, every inch of soil having been washed away, only the unsightly piles and ridges of stone and washed gravel left. The gold was dearly purchased at such a price."

Abigail's article, according to the Oxford English Dictionary, is the earliest use of the word "ghost" to denote an abandoned town. "Ghost town" would find increasing favor in the lexicon, particularly starting in the 1920s, as the last vestiges of the boomtown West dried up. In his 1931 popular history of mining in California and Nevada, *Here They Dug the*

Gold, George F. Willison wrote, "Today all lie ghost towns smelling of the long slow processes of ruin and decay," cementing the term as an idiom that has since become ubiquitous. As more and more of these towns dried up, confronting us with a strange new landscape, a term was needed, and the language of ghosts presented itself.

Many ghost towns, naturally, also claim to be haunted. The ruined town of Garnet, Montana, is one, named for the rich vein of gold, the Garnet lode, that birthed it. Its population peaked at a thousand residents in 1895, but within ten years it had dwindled to less than two hundred. A fire destroyed the business district in 1912, and the last resident died in 1947. Given over to the elements, the remaining buildings gradually fell to ruin until preservationists, along with the Bureau of Land Management, stabilized the remains and opened the town to visitors. When the tourists are gone, though, the ghosts appear—so says resident ghost historian Ellen Baumler. Officially employed as the interpretive historian for the Montana Historical Society, Baumler writes books on Montana's haunted past on the side, and she cites Garnet as among many ghost towns that now have spirits. "Sometimes, in the deep winter quiet, a piano tinkles in Kelley's Saloon and the spirits dance to ghostly music," she writes in her *Montana Chillers*. "Men's voices echo in the empty rooms. But the moment a living, human hand touches the building, the noises stop."

Ghost towns feel haunted because, even if they will never again host living society, they remain filled with hints of those who once lived there. Our imaginations cannot help but project onto these ruins the ghosts of the people who've left indelible traces, and these spirits can spring to life with just a shift in the wind, a creaking board, or a distant animal call. Far more comforting, after all, to believe that someone—even if not someone living—is still making use of these shacks, saloons, and general stores.

Americans aren't the only people to leave behind ghost towns, but we are particularly adept at it, as our peripatetic nature drives us from claim to claim, stake to stake, leaving behind not much but rubble and clapboard houses. The ghost town has become a defining feature of the West and its mythology, and as the country's manufacturing economy fell on hard times, it became the defining feature of an emptied-out rust belt. In the early years of a new century, we're poised to see more and more ghost towns emerge. As places like Manhattan and San Francisco become uninhabitable to all but the richest 0.01 percent, driving out even their own service workers, internal migration will continue and new places will become abandoned. A 2014 article in the *New York Times* suggested that as global warming increases, Americans will empty out the Southwest in favor of places like Maine, Oregon, and Alaska. Spurred by a global warming dust bowl, we'll move north, and in time Phoenix, Sacramento, and Los Angeles may come to be as ghost-haunted as Detroit seems now.

We live among the undead, in cities of ghosts. The buildings that used to have meaning and purpose—not only houses but banks and government buildings—have been emptied of what they once meant, and yet they remain, haunting us. Those of us who can, leave, moving on to new cities that we hope are not yet beset by the dead. Those of us who can't, like the residents of Hillsdale, Illinois, remain behind, haunted by forces larger than ourselves, imprisoned by the folly of the rich who have unleashed some unspeakable dread from which we cannot escape.

GHOSTS OF A NEW MACHINE

Allendale, CA

When Jessamyn West and her sister, Kate, moved into their father's home in Westport, Massachusetts, after his death in 2011, they didn't expect to find it haunted. Their father, Tom West, had been a hardware developer and program manager who'd achieved a certain measure of fame when his work was documented in Tracy Kidder's Pulitzer Prize–winning *The Soul of a New Machine*. Kidder's 1981 book followed West and his team as they developed a new computer for Data General: the Eclipse MV/8000. As a result of Kidder's book, riding as it did the early wave of the 1980s computer revolution, Tom West came to be seen as something of a symbol for the burgeoning tech economy, a standard-bearer of a brave new future.

And yet he left behind ghosts. When Jessamyn, who works as a community technology librarian, and Kate, an administrative officer in the Massachusetts State Police, moved into what they came to call the Museum of Dad, lights would turn themselves on and off without reason or human input—as though their father's spirit was still there with them, moving through the house, making his appointed rounds. A motion sensor set up in the driveway would go off randomly, even when no one was near the house, signaling the imminent return of something only it could see. Jessamyn told me, "I often thought the house was lonely without my dad in it."

There was, of course, an easy explanation for this, even if not an easy solution. Tom West, always on the cutting edge of technology, had wired the house with an X10 automated lighting system and a series of other automated systems, all of which were set up to follow his rhythms without having to have him lift a finger. In many rooms outlets and light switches had been replaced by nodes embedded in the walls that were driven by a configuration file on his laptop.

West's house was an early incarnation of what's now called the Internet of Things: a future in which not just phones and computers are connected to the Internet but light switches and refrigerators and security alarms and laundry machines—all connected via Wi-Fi and Bluetooth, automating our homes in myriad ways. The Internet of Things was still at a relatively primitive stage when West wired his house in 2010, and so mostly he only was able to automate the lighting and plumbing, but this was more than enough to create strange and unsettling effects after his death.

Jessamyn and Kate noticed at one point that their electricity bills had spiked. After some sleuthing they found an irrigation pump that had come on mysteriously—a pump that, as far as Jessamyn could determine, hadn't worked for several years. In the basement a Shop Vac would turn on by itself mysteriously at random hours. The toilet water became inexplicably hot at one point, breeding bacteria in the toilets that left the bathrooms with foul odors.

These are the kinds of freak occurrences that lead people to think a place is haunted, but in the case of West's house, it was more obviously a complicated electronic protocol that was gradually falling apart, without a clear blueprint that would allow either daughter to understand the problem. Jessamyn found herself trapped in the garage one day when she realized that the only way to open the door was through a remote that had gone missing; ultimately she had to dismantle the door manually. The toilet problem, the women learned, was the result of a water pump in the basement whose existence—let alone purpose—was unknown to them until it failed.

Even knowing that the lights in West's house weren't being controlled by spirits, they still posed problems. Some of the lights were timed in ways that made sense, such as coming on at five in the evening; others followed Tom's more idiosyncratic routines—routines that were never spelled out in a will or passed on to his heirs. The lights abruptly turning off at ten at night were meant to urge West to go to bed, a feature that was infuriating to anyone not on a similar schedule. To compound the confusion, the hard drive on the laptop that held the data crashed, making it difficult (though by no means impossible) to reprogram the house. Jessamyn and Kate debugged the most egregious programs and hired electricians to work through the rest. What remains, they've since learned to live with—the back porch still doesn't have a light switch.

When West worked for the microcomputer manufacturer Data General, he was known for a saying he'd written on a whiteboard in his office: *not everything worth doing is worth doing well*. When Tracy Kidder asked him for a translation, he offered, "If you can do a quick-and-dirty job and it works, do it." Now, after his death, his daughters are living with the strange ramifications of this philosophy as it relates to West's own house, where an idiosyncratic and sometimes jury-rigged home infrastructure is now gradually falling apart.

A house that more or less operates under its own control, automated and animated and no longer requiring input from its living inhabitants—in such a strange new dwelling lies one glimpse of the future of hauntings. The house was set up for Tom West himself—his rhythms and habits, his patterns and haunts. With him gone, the house continues in many ways to respect those patterns of being, asserting them on its new occupants as though they, too, are obliged to adopt their father's modes of being. And should the house be sold, Jessamyn admitted, the next occupants will have to reckon, one way or another, with these same protocols, since there's no way to rid the house entirely of them, short of gutting its electrical and plumbing systems altogether. Which is to say, the house is cursed—benignly cursed, but cursed all the same. The spirit of Tom West is going to inhabit it for a long time to come.

Ray Bradbury had already imagined the Internet of Things in a 1950 short story that's turned out to be one of the more prescient stories of all time: "There Will Come Soft Rains." Set in the year 2026, the story follows a day in the (artificial) life of a fully automated house in the possibly fictional town of Allendale, California, a house that goes about its domestic duties—washing dishes, cleaning rooms, reciting poetry for entertainment—all the while unaware that its inhabitants, the McClellan family, are all dead, atomized in a nuclear explosion. It's a rare science fiction story that, aside from the nuclear holocaust part, has so far accurately predicted the future—an automated home so fully integrated that it can essentially function without us. If we're not there yet, this is certainly the dream of futurists, designers, and advertisers, and 2026 seems a pretty reasonable date.

Often characterized as science fiction, Bradbury's story is also a ghost story: a story of a haunted house. Sentient, the house acts of its own accord, an inanimate place animated, its poltergeists moving about. "Bridge tables sprouted from patio walls. Playing cards fluttered onto pads in a shower of pips. Martinis manifested on an oaken bench with egg-salad sandwiches. Music played. But the tables were silent and the cards untouched. At four o'clock the tables folded like great butterflies back through the paneled walls." Bradbury gives us the kind of house one expects from Disneyland's Haunted Mansion, where unseen ghosts flit about, frolicking and enjoying themselves as though still living. The story's title comes from a Sara Teasdale poem, which describes how nature will be unaffected by humanity's destruction, how the frogs and birds and trees will remain oblivious to humanity's final wars, apathetic and unmoved by the end of us—which Bradbury in turn extends to our technological marvels, continuing, undead and ghosted, after our own dear departures.

But in Bradbury's futuristic ghost story, who is haunting whom? The house, after all, is mostly self-sufficient, and the real ghosts are its missing occupants. The only remaining traces of the McClellan family are the ghostly traces on the walls outside:

> The entire west face of the house was black, save for five places. Here the silhouette in paint of a man mowing a lawn. Here, as in a photograph, a woman bent to pick flowers. Still farther over, their images burned on wood in one titanic instant, a small boy, hands flung into the air; higher up, the image of a thrown ball, and opposite him a girl, hands raised to catch a ball which never came down. The five spots of paint—the man, the woman, the children, the ball— remained. The rest was a thin charcoaled layer.

No longer living inhabitants, the McClellan family haunt their own house. Their lives, their hobbies and relations and jobs and desires and loves, are evident everywhere in the house, but they themselves are not. The true protagonist is the house itself, and it is the house's own life-and-death struggle that we witness, its former inhabitants now merely the specters that haunt its walls. In this way, too, Bradbury might have been onto something: With the coming of the Internet of Things, automated houses may mean not that the houses themselves are haunted but that we ourselves become the ghosts, mere guests obligated to the thing that once represented security.

Which isn't to say there aren't scientists working to disabuse us once and for all of our belief in spirits, proving them to be nothing more than phantasms of the mind that can be easily controlled and replicated in the laboratory. In 2014 researchers from the École Polytechnique Fédérale de Lausanne, in Switzerland, figured out a way to manufacture ghosts, thus suggesting that they're really all in our minds. A participant in their experiment would control a robot directly behind her or him, causing the robot to touch the participant's back when commanded. But sometimes the robot would delay its actions by a half second, sometimes not. The confusion caused by the expectation of a reaction and the slight delay interrupted participants' sense of their own sensorimotor input enough that they thought their own actions were that of another person—creating the "feeling of presence" in the subjects: a ghost behind them who wasn't really there.

"Our brain possesses several representations of our body in space," researcher Giulio Rognini explained. "Under normal conditions, it is able to assemble a unified self-perception of the self from these representations. But when the system malfunctions because of disease—or, in this case, a robot—this can sometimes create a second representation of one's own body, which is no longer perceived as 'me' but as someone else, a 'presence.'" For skeptics, studies like these can be powerful ammunition to convince those who've "felt something" that what they're really feeling are just manifestations of their own minds.

Even if science can help explain to us how our brains concoct ghosts, it won't explain their importance in our lives, and it will do little to dispel our belief of them. For even though communication technologies have made mammoth strides since the days when the telegraph inspired Spiritualists, the same technological static and gremlins are still with us. YouTube videos, with their often low resolution, shuttering frame rates, and other technical glitches, seem to some to evidence the paranormal. The conspiracy-minded and those looking for proof of spirits scour online videos for such static to interpret. A video of a young Japanese girl titled "Look at Her Face, Scary," in which her face dissolves slightly as she delivers a classroom presentation, has more than sixteen million views.

On the contrary, as technology changes our world at a speed so fast we can barely keep pace, it may be the case that our world will become increasingly haunted. Take the well-known phenomenon of the "Uncanny Valley" as one example: as computer-generated images and robots become more and more lifelike, they will paradoxically become more, not less, creepy. The closer they are to human, the more tiny faults—dead eyes, jerky movements—become magnified and unsettling. Japanese roboticist Masahiro Mori has been credited with first theorizing the problem, known as far back as 1970, but the idea didn't really gain traction until after 2000, when digital animation advanced sufficiently to make it a reality. And though designers and animators have made progress since first diagnosing the problem, what the Uncanny Valley reveals is that technological innovation often creates ghosts as fast as it dispels them.

Part of the reason that ghosts stay with us is that they remain a compelling mechanism to explain so much that is unknown in our lives. They enter and reenter our lexicon to explain the unexplainable, to represent the unrepresentable, to give a word to that which we don't understand. If scientists truly believe they are capable of dispelling the ghosts from our lives, then we'll have to replace them with some viable cultural conversation that offers an equally meaningful way of understanding death and the past.

And then there is social media, which has also created its share of ghosts. For several months in 2009, Facebook urged me to "reconnect" with a friend I hadn't spoken to in a while—but what Facebook was asking was impossible, since she had died earlier that year. To see her profile show up occasionally on my Facebook feed was never not jarring, particularly since Facebook's algorithms could not tell (and seemed to have no interest in learning) that she was dead. Because your online life lives on after you (unless you leave specific instructions on deactivating it) and because these sites depend on constant engagement, those who've left us have become cyber revenants.

This return of the dead happens more often than we think, and often with disturbing resonances. Images of Rehtaeh Parsons, a seventeen-year-old Canadian girl who committed suicide after a campaign of cyberbullying, began appearing after her death online as part of ads that beckoned: "Meet Canadian girls for friendship, dating or relationships. Sign up now!" The algorithm that crawled the Web, grabbed these images, and repurposed them for advertising had no idea—was never programmed to have an idea—about Parsons's life, her backstory, her death, or how her image's sudden reappearance could be so traumatic for those suddenly faced with it. This is how ghosts will continue to haunt us in the coming years: the unintended return of the dead via sites and algorithms that aren't yet programmed to let the dead rest.

Social media sites like Facebook, Twitter, and Instagram have in many ways replaced (or at least complemented) the cafés, parks, and bars where we gather; it's little wonder, then, that they've also become populated with ghosts. Physical places become haunted because of creaky doors, odd construction, and other quirks of architecture that get transformed in our minds into the paranormal. Online it's still a question of architecture: coding and algorithms with unintended consequences, like an uncanny hallway, which open up unexpected nightmares. And, as with physical architecture, it's unlikely that we'll ever dispel these ghosts in the machine entirely; coding, after all, is a human endeavor, and like architecture, it's prone to a thousand variables that can never be fully controlled.

Our belief (or lack thereof) in ghosts ultimately reflects the way we face death. Those of us who fear mortality can often find comfort in a belief in life after death, and those whom we fail to mourn properly may return to haunt us. If we can't find a way to design our cyber temples of the future in such a way as to accommodate the departed, we can expect their return in ways as surprising as they are unsettling.

Ghost stories are about how we face, or fail to face, the past—how we process information, how we narrate our past, and how we make sense of the gaps in that history. During my conversation with Eric Meharry about the ghost of Thelma Taylor, he mentioned that we may see fewer ghosts like Taylor's in the future, simply because we're so inundated with information, particularly about gruesome killings and other tragedies that tend to be fodder for ghost stories. "Lack of information is part of the recipe," Meharry told me, and today's ubiquitous news coverage—an endless online stream of updates, gossip, and posts by citizen journalists—is making that air of mystery more scarce. "Information," he said, "is killing ghost stories."

When I asked him if this was a good thing or not, he replied, "I don't know. The romantic idea of a lonely person haunting a place is slowly disappearing . . . the idea is becoming a ghost, I guess."

Then again, the glut of facts and the preponderance of evidence create as many gaps as they fill, leading to a swirling cacophony of information. There will never be a complete record, particularly when it comes to scenes of great emotional complexity. We can, for example, expect ghosts to continue to follow national tragedies—ghosts such as the mysterious woman who appeared in the Fresh Kills, New York, landfill in the days following September 11, 2001. Dressed in a World War II Red Cross outfit, holding a tray of sandwiches, the spectral aid worker appeared to a number of individuals, who claimed to be able to see her only from a distance and who said she vanished as they approached.

Besides, even if we could dispel them once and for all, we need them too badly. The language of ghosts is a means of coping with the unfamiliar, and if they sometimes require that we overlook the truth, that may be a price we're willing to pay. In some ways we don't want to know too much about the true story, since whatever happens, we can't break the spell— because the ghost is too important.

ACKNOWLEDGMENTS

This book could not have been written without help. Thanks to everyone who shared with me a ghost story or who directed me to a haunted house, hotel, prison, park, cemetery, or other haunted place. I'm also grateful to everyone who accompanied me on various ghost tours and ghost-hunting adventures, particularly: Elise Blackwell, Emily Mandel, Elizabeth Harper, Chelsey Johnson, Eric Bebernitz, Alex Dickey, Karl Erickson, and Gretchen Larsen. Thanks to all of the ghost hunters, historians, and tour guides who spoke with me for this project. In particular, thanks to Robert Kirkbride, Michele Yu, Kim Cooper, Richard Schave, Ben Miller, Margaret McGovern, Erik Meharry, and Jessamyn West, whose ideas gave me much-needed perspective throughout the process of writing this book.

Special thanks to Paulette Jarrett for sharing her stories with me.

Suzanne Fischer helped me work out the structure and format of this book through our early conversations, and I'm grateful for her feedback and her friendship. This book also benefited immensely from talks with Michelle Legro, Franz Potter, Kara Thompson, and Evan Kindley. Special thanks to Liberty Hardy for her unwavering support of this project and her all-around excellence. Thanks to Brenna Murray for research assistance.

Some of the first ideas of this book were worked out at lectures I presented at Machine Project in Los Angeles, Acme Studio in Brooklyn,

Odd Salon in San Francisco, and Death Salon Philadelphia at the Müt-ter Museum. Thanks to these venues and their staffs, particularly Mark Allen, Annetta Black, and Rachel James. Thanks to Dan Piepenbring at the *Paris Review* and Jane Friedman at the *Virginia Quarterly Review* for publishing early essays that would go on to become parts of this book. Thanks also to Fred Ramey and everyone at Unbridled Books.

I've also been fortunate to have surrounded myself with several differ-ent communities of writers, artists, and scholars who've helped nurture this project from its very beginning. At the Morbid Anatomy Museum, thanks to Tracy Hurley Martin, Joanna Ebenstein, Tonya Hurley, Laeti-tia Barbier, and Cristina Preda, without all of whom this book might not have happened. Thanks also to Caitlin Doughty, Megan Rosenbloom, Sarah Troop, and everyone at the Order of the Good Death for their constant support and inspiration. And thanks especially to the fabulous people at Betalevel: Jason Brown, Heather Parlato, Sean Deyoe, Amar Ravva, Dave Eng, Ariana Kelly, and Amina Cain.

A writer could not ask for a better agent than Anna Sproul-Latimer, whose enthusiasm for this project, along with her constant insight and expertise, made it happen. I am overwhelmed with gratitude for the sup-port I've received from her and everyone else at the Ross Yoon Agency. At Viking, my editor, Melanie Tortoroli, shaped and refined this manu-script and made it far better than I could have on my own. Thanks also to everyone else at Viking who's worked so hard on this book.

Thanks to my parents for taking me to the Winchester Mystery House so many times when I was a child and for supporting my youthful Stephen King obsession. Above all, thanks to Nicole, for having come so far with me through all the strangeness and for making the journey so much fun.

NOTES

AUTHOR'S NOTE

xiii   "All argument is against it; but all belief is for it": James Boswell, *The Life of Samuel Johnson, LL.D.* (London: Wordsworth Classics of World Literature, 1999), 635.

INTRODUCTION: ANATOMY OF A HAUNTING (NEW YORK, NY)

2   **Samuel Lenox Tredwell, Gertrude's brother:** Stories of the ghosts at the Merchant's House Museum have been collected in Andrew Bellov, *Some Say They Never Left: Tales of the Strange and Inexplicable at the Merchant's House Museum* (New York: Merchant's House Museum, 2007).

3   **"in the form of an old man":** Pliny the Younger, *The Letters of Caius Plinius Caecilius Secundus,* trans. William Melmoth, ed. Rev. F. C. T. Bosanquet (London: George Bell and Sons, 1905), 250.

3   **"made a sign with his hand":** Ibid., 251.

3   **45 percent of Americans:** Lee Speigel, "Spooky Number of Americans Believe in Ghosts," *Huffington Post,* February 8, 2013.

4   **The house was bought by Seabury Tredwell:** The best history of the Merchant's House Museum is Mary L. Knapp, *An Old Merchant's House: Life at Home in New York City, 1835–65* (New York: Girandole Books, 2012).

6   **known as a "memory palace":** On memory palaces, see Frances A. Yates, *The Art of Memory* (London: Routledge, 2001).

7   **"a representation of the unrepresentable":** Thomas W. Laqueur, *The Work of the Dead: A Cultural History of Mortal Remains* (Princeton, NJ: Princeton University Press, 2015), 69.

8   **changed shape through the decades:** See Judith Richardson, *Possessions: The History and Uses of Haunting in the Hudson Valley* (Cambridge: Harvard University Press, 2003), 103–9.

8   **a 2002 book containing the Leeds legend:** See Dennis William Hauck, *Haunted Places: The National Directory* (New York: Penguin, 2002), 297.

9   **"the return of the repressed":** Sigmund Freud, *Introductory Lessons on Psycho-Analysis*, trans. James Strachey (New York: W. W. Norton, 1989), 29.

10   **"allow access to dissonant knowledge":** Quoted in Tiya Miles, *Tales from the Haunted South: Dark Tourism and Memories of Slavery from the Civil War Era* (Chapel Hill: University of North Carolina Press, 2015), 10.

I: THE UNHOMELY

16   **"This house, which seemed somehow":** Shirley Jackson, *The Haunting of Hill House*, in *Novels and Stories* (New York: Library of America, 2010), 265.

17   **"the present writer must plead guilty":** Sigmund Freud, *The Uncanny*, trans. David McLintock (London: Penguin, 2003), 124.

18   **"shelters daydreaming" and "allows one to dream":** Gaston Bachelard, *The Poetics of Space*, trans. Maria Jolas (Boston: Beacon Press, 1994), 68.

18–19 **"Every corner in a house":** Ibid., 136.

19   **"The places in which we have *experienced*":** Ibid., 6.

19   **"When we concentrate on a material object":** Vladimir Nabokov, *Transparent Things* (New York: Vintage International, 1989), 1.

CHAPTER ONE: THE SECRET STAIRCASE (SALEM, MA)

21   **"Houses of any antiquity in New England":** Nathaniel Hawthorne, *Mosses from an Old Manse* (New York: Modern Library, 2003), 14.

22   **"Oh, there are subjects enough":** Quoted in James R. Mellow, *Nathaniel Hawthorne in His Times* (Baltimore: Johns Hopkins University Press, 1998), 175.

23   **it's "a rusty wooden house":** Nathaniel Hawthorne, *The House of the Seven Gables*, in *Collected Novels* (New York: Library of America, 1983), 355.

23   **"a great many times":** Ibid., 424.

24   **"form a patina, a part of the thing itself":** Lorinda R R. Goodwin, "Salem's House of the Seven Gables as Historic Site," in Dane Anthony Morrison and Nancy Lusignan Schultz, *Salem: Place, Myth, and Memory* (Boston: Northeastern University Press, 2015), 300.

24   **"what appears to be a teenage girl":** Ghost sightings at the House of the Seven Gables have been collected at www.graveaddiction.com/sevengab.html.

26   **"convince mankind—or, indeed":** Hawthorne, *House of the Seven Gables*, 352.

26   **"when no man shall build":** Ibid., 510.

27   **"pinching and pricking" her "dreadfully":** There are numerous accounts of the Salem witch crisis of 1692; the two I found to be most helpful are Mary Beth Norton, *In the Devil's Snare: The Salem Witchcraft Crisis of 1692* (New York: Vintage

Books, 2003), and Bernard Rosenthal, *Salem Story: Reading the Witch Trials of 1692* (Cambridge: Cambridge University Press, 1993).

28   **"by his warrant hath caused":** Quoted in Rosenthal, *Salem Story*, 195.

28   **"with a ghastly look":** Hawthorne, *House of the Seven Gables*, 358. See also Rosenthal, *Salem Story*, 87.

29   **"you are a lyer":** Quoted in Rosenthal, *Salem Story*, 87.

29   **According to the nineteenth-century historian Thomas Hutchinson:** Thomas Hutchinson, *The History of Massachusetts from the First Settlement Thereof in 1628, Until the Year 1750* (Boston: 1795), 2:56.

30   **"My first visit to the House":** Caroline O. Emmerton, *The Chronicles of Three Old Houses* (Salem, MA: House of Seven Gables Settlement Association, 1985), 29.

30   **"To console me my friends":** Ibid., 34.

31   **"pine tree sixpence and a book":** Ibid., 29.

31   **"Of what use for smuggling":** Ibid., 18.

31   **"Can there be any doubt":** Ibid., 15–16.

32   **"Thinking it over," Emmerton writes:** Ibid., 39.

32   **"For it seems to me":** Ibid., 38.

33   **any legal or financial obligation to the victims' descendants:** The 1957 bill named only Ann Pudeator and "certain other persons"; it wasn't until 2001 that the last five women were cleared by name. "Massachusetts Clears 5 from Salem Witch Trials," *New York Times*, November 2, 2001.

33   **The town seems caught between past and present:** See Frances Hill, "Salem as Witch City," in Morrison and Schultz, *Salem: Place, Myth, and Memory*, 283–98.

34   **"the crimes for which they had been arrested":** J. K. Rowling, "History of Magic in North America," Piece Two, "Seventeenth Century and Beyond," www.pottermore.com.

CHAPTER TWO: SHIFTING GROUND (ST. FRANCISVILLE, LA)

37   **"unable to defeat Satan":** Norton, *In the Devil's Snare*, 226.

37   **"The pavements of the Main-street":** Nathaniel Hawthorne, "Main Street," in *Tales and Sketches* (New York: Library of America, 1982), 1028.

39   **either mostly or wholly fictitious:** See Miles, *Tales from the Haunted South*, chapter 2.

40   **she soon found herself beset by paranormal events of all kinds:** Frances Kermeen, *The Myrtles Plantation: The True Story of America's Most Haunted House* (New York: Grand Central Publishing, 2005). Despite the book's subtitle, the copyright page lists Kermeen's book as a work of fiction.

42   **When the Lutzes bought their dream home:** Jay Anson, *The Amityville Horror* (New York: Pocket Star Books, 2005).

42   **"as an enclosure for the sick":** Ibid., 122.

42   **"the Shinnecock did not use this tract":** Ibid.

42   Johnson-Meyers channeled the spirit: William Grimes, "Hans Holzer, Ghost Hunter, Dies at 89," *New York Times*, April 29, 2009.

43   provided the couple with salient details: See Ric Osuna, *The Night the DeFeos Died: Reinvestigating the Amityville Murders* (Bloomington, IN: Xlibris, 2002).

43   a massive legal battle against the Maliseet: Renée L. Bergland, *The National Uncanny: Indian Ghosts and American Subjects* (Hanover, NH: University Press of New England, 2000), 162–9.

44   "Honey, do we *own* this?": Stephen King, *Pet Sematary* (New York: Pocket Books, 1983), 26.

44   "Now the Micmacs, the state of Maine": Ibid., 244.

44   "Who does own it": Ibid., 260.

44   "the Indians chose that spot": Kermeen, *Myrtles Plantation*, 2.

45   At the end of the last ice age: See Richard Campanella, *Bienville's Dilemma: A Historical Geography of New Orleans* (Lafayette, LA: Center for Louisiana Studies, 2008), 77.

46   "past small sandy islands": Quoted in Campanella, *Bienville's Dilemma*, 78.

46   In 1968 a guard: Michael F. P. Doming, "The Tale of the Tunica Treasure," *Harvard Crimson*, October 13, 1983.

47   "I found the thing": "Court Denies Claim to Items Found on Indian Burial Site," *New York Times*, December 31, 1986.

CHAPTER THREE: THE ENDLESS HOUSE (SAN JOSE, CA)

50   The basic facts of how the house got started: The definitive biography of Sarah Winchester is Mary Jo Ignoffo, *Captive of the Labyrinth* (Columbia: University of Missouri Press, 2010).

50   "expected that someday Hill House": Jackson, *Haunting of Hill House*, 315.

51   "There's the psychological aspect of the place": Steven Henry Madoff, "Guns and Ghosts: The Winchester Witch Project," *New York Times*, February 27, 2005.

51   "At one séance": Quoted in the press release "Rose Red: The Stephen King Mini-Series on ABC Inspired by a Real-Life Ghost Story," www.winchestermystery house.com, January 27, 2002.

55   In 1857 he had bought: For a history of the Winchester Repeating Arms Company, see R. L. Wilson, *Winchester: An American Legend* (New York: Chartwell Books, 2004).

57   San Francisco's population grew: Susan Craddock, *City of Plagues: Disease, Poverty, and Deviance in San Francisco* (Minneapolis: University of Minnesota Press, 2000), 30.

57   "Nor is sickness that scourge of humanity": Quoted in Susan Craddock, *City of Plagues*, 25.

57   by 1900 one-fourth of all migrants to California: Ibid., 23.

58   its great Electric Light Tower: See Linda S. Larson, *San Jose's Monument to Progress: The Electric Light Tower* (San Jose, CA: San Jose Historical Museum Association, 1989).

58   **"For the first time the citizens":** Quoted in ibid., 9.

58   **"California was a hot-bed":** Quoted in Kevin Starr, *Americans and the California Dream: 1850–1915* (New York: Oxford University Press, 1973), 110.

59   **"I am constantly having to make an upheaval":** Sarah Winchester to Jennie Bennett, June 11, 1898, Bennett Family Papers, Connecticut Historical Society.

59   **"If I did not get so easily tired out":** Ibid.

59   **"I hope some day":** Sarah Winchester to Jennie Bennett, May 14, 1898.

60   **"they did not want to encourage young girls":** Sara Holmes Boutelle, *Julia Morgan, Architect* (New York: Abbeville Press, 1988), 30.

61   **"I began to understand that everything":** Charles Dickens, *Great Expectations* (London: Penguin, 1996), 60.

64   **By 1895 unemployment:** See Samuel Rezneck, "Unemployment, Unrest, and Relief in the United States During the Depression of 1893–97," *Journal of Political Economy* 61, no. 4: 324.

64   **"dark, mysterious, crafty, wicked":** Quoted in David A. Zimmerman, *Panic!: Markets, Crises, and Crowds in American Fiction* (Chapel Hill: University of North Carolina Press, 2006), 65.

64   **"It is probably safe to say":** H. P. Robinson, "The Humiliating Report of the Strike Commission," *Forum* 18 (September 1894–February 1895): 523; quoted in Rezneck, "Unemployment, Unrest, and Relief in the United States during the Depression of 1893–97," 335.

64–65 **"result of rural rumors":** "Only Gossip: No Truth in the Story of the Winchester Palace," *San Jose Evening News*, October 11, 1897.

66   **"appraised as of no value":** Ignoffo, *Captive of the Labyrinth*, 206.

67   **"The whole thing is beautifully inlaid":** *Oregon Daily Journal*, November 3, 1924.

67   **"as sane and clear headed a woman":** Quoted in Ignoffo, *Captive of the Labyrinth*, 165.

CHAPTER FOUR: THE RATHOLE REVELATION (GEORGETOWN, NY, AND BULL VALLEY, IL)

69   **"found that if he put his chisel":** "Brown's Free Hall—Inspiration and Will," *Banner of Light*, January 18, 1879.

70   **they had been communicating with the spirit of a dead man:** There are many good histories of the Fox sisters; among them is Frank Podmore, *Modern Spiritualism: A History and a Criticism* (London: Methuen and Company, 1902), especially volume 2.

70   **"I then asked if Mr. ———":** Quoted in ibid., 181.

71   **in Philadelphia there were another:** Podmore, I:183.

71   **"his wonderful persistence has well-nigh conquered":** "Brown's Free Hall—Inspiration and Will," *Banner of Light*, January 18, 1879. Italics in original.

72   **one more "paroxysm of humbug":** John Dix, *Transatlantic Tracings* (London: W. Tweedie, Strand, 1853), 244.

72   Emerson called it the "rathole revelation": Quoted in Daniel Conway Moncure, *Emerson at Home and Abroad* (London: Trübner & Co., 1883), 189.

72   "have mistaken flatulence for inspiration": Ralph Waldo Emerson, *The Journals and Miscellaneous Notebooks of Ralph Waldo Emerson, 1854–1861*, ed. Susan Sutton Smith and Harrison Hayford (Cambridge, MA: Belknap Press, 1978), 254.

72   "I hate this shallow Americanism": Ralph Waldo Emerson, "Success," in *The Complete Works of Ralph Waldo Emerson*, ed. Edward Waldo Emerson (New York: AMS Press, 1904), vol. 7, 290.

73   "It is the secret of the world": Ralph Waldo Emerson, "Nominalist and Realist," in *Essays and Lectures* (New York: Library of America, 1983), 584.

73   our attitudes toward death were changing: On the changing social role of the dead body, see Ruth Richardson, *Death, Dissection and the Destitute* (London: Phoenix Press, 1988).

74   In short order Spiritualism became dominated by women: An excellent history of Spiritualism that traces its feminist roots is Ann Braude, *Radical Spirits: Spiritualism and Women's Rights in Nineteenth-Century America* (Bloomington: Indiana University Press, 2001).

74   "the only religious sect in the world": Quoted in ibid., 2.

74   "have always assumed that woman": Quoted in ibid., 3.

76   "This fellow had been taught": Quoted in Ignoffo, *Captive of the Labyrinth*, 209.

77   most economical shape for a stall is a wedge: J. C. Loudon, *An Encyclopaedia of Cottage, Farm, and Villa Architecture and Furniture* (London: Longman, Brown, Green, and Longmans, 1846), 375–76.

78   In 1995 the village clerk: Christine Winter, "Bull Valley Home Haunted Only by Reputation," *Chicago Tribune*, September 27, 1995.

78   "There's never been anything to those stories": Ibid.

78   "It's just something creepy that kids like to say about the place": Ibid.

79   "walking toward a group of pine trees": Carri Williams, "The Demon Walking Near the Stickney Mansion," www.trueghosttales.com/paranormal/the-demon -walking-near-the-stickney-mansion, April 13, 2011.

79   "put fear aside, and you may well encounter the divine there": MotherEarthPrayers, "Spirit House Society," YouTube video, February 28, 2011.

80   according to one study: Kathleen Weldon, "Paradise Polled: Americans and the Afterlife," *Huffington Post*, June 17, 2015.

CHAPTER FIVE: THE FAMILY THAT WOULD NOT LIVE (ST. LOUIS, MO)

82   The Lemp family story: A history of the Lemp family and their brewing empire can be found in Rebecca F. Pittman, *The History and Haunting of the Lemp Mansion* (Loveland, CO: Wonderland Productions, 2015).

82   His marriage to Lillian fell apart: See Pittman, *The History and Haunting of the Lemp Mansion*, 237–39.

83   **Tradition holds that Charles:** Ibid., 347–53.

85   **Media and medium were two sides of the same coin:** See Jeffrey Sconce, *Haunted Media: Electronic Presence from Telegraphy to Television* (Durham, NC: Duke University Press, 2000).

86   **"Here is night brothers, here the birds burn":** Quoted in ibid., 88.

86   **"Secret reports . . . it is bad here":** Quoted in ibid., 91.

86   **"to empirically provable reality with a factual background":** Konstantin Raudive, *Breakthrough: An Amazing Experiment in Electronic Communication with the Dead* (New York: Lancer Books, 1971), 2.

90   **"I will take it with me now":** See Pittman, *History and Haunting of the Lemp Mansion,* 229–30.

90   **according to historian Davidson Mullgardt:** See Jeannette Cooperman, "The Last Lemp," *St. Louis Magazine,* May 15, 2015.

91   **"Our desire and passion is to let the wonderful people":** Quoted in Cooperman, "The Last Lemp."

91   **just one more example of someone trying to capitalize:** See ibid.

II: AFTER HOURS

95   **If the guidebooks are to be believed:** Legends of the hauntings at the Stanley Hotel can be found in, among other places, Sherri Granato, *Haunted America and Other Paranormal Travels* (Bloomington, IN: LifeRich, 2015).

96   **"heat, light, and cook meals exclusively with electricity":** A short but reliable history of the Stanley is in Phyllis Perry, *It Happened in Rocky Mountain National Park* (Guilford, CT: Morris Book Publishing, 2008), 38–41.

96   **"We found ourselves the only guests":** Quoted in Gary A. Warner, "Guests and Ghosts: Relax at the Colorado Hotel That Inspired *The Shining,*" *Victor Valley Daily Press,* December 14, 2002.

97   **"I don't know why this person":** Quoted in Gregory Lee Sullivan, "Visiting the Oldest Bookstore in America—And Its Resident Ghost," *Guardian,* February 25, 2016.

97   **A former employee delightfully named Putt-Putt:** Dan Koeppel, "Ghost Sightings Aren't Spooking Sales at Toys 'R' Us," *Chicago Tribune,* June 23, 1991.

98   **"He's a classic case":** Sylvia Browne, *Visits from the Afterlife: The Truth About Haunting Spirits and Reunions with Lost Loved Ones* (New York: New American Library, 2004), 75.

99   **As if to prove the point:** Stories of other Toys "R" Us stores that are reputedly haunted have been collected at http://ghosts.org/haunted-toys-r-us-sunnyvale-ca.

99   **independent analyses of her work:** Sylvia Browne's record has been analyzed in Joseph Gomes, "Prophet Motive," *Brill's Content,* November 27, 2000.

99   **"go to the light of God":** Browne, *Visits from the Afterlife,* 76.

CHAPTER SIX: A DEVILISH PLACE (RICHMOND, VA)

103   **There are ghosts everywhere:** For the best collections of the various hauntings in Shockoe Bottom, see Pamela Kinney, *Haunted Richmond* (Atglen, PA: Schiffer Publishing, 2007), and Scott Bergman and Sandi Bergman, *Haunted Richmond: The Shadows of Shockoe* (Charleston, SC: Haunted America, 2007).

104   **Virginia was home to the earliest settlements in North America:** Interview with the author, April 26, 2015.

105   **"delightfully situated on eight hills":** Charles Dickens, *American Notes,* quoted in Jack Trammell, *The Richmond Slave Trade: The Economic Backbone of the Old Dominion* (Charleston, SC: History Press, 2012), 74–5.

106   **"The exposure of ordinary goods":** Frederick Law Olmsted, *A Journey in the Seaboard Slave States, with Remarks About Their Economy,* quoted in Trammell, *Richmond Slave Trade,* 77–8.

106   **"were taken from the cars":** Solomon Northup, *Twelve Years a Slave* (New York: Penguin Books, 2012), 33.

107   **"a large yellow man, quite stout":** Ibid., 35.

107   **"In this building Lumpkin was accustomed":** James B. Simmons, "Lumpkin's Slave Jail," in Charles H. Corey, *A History of the Richmond Theological Seminary: Reminiscences of Thirty Years' Work among the Colored People of the South* (Richmond, VA: J. W. Randolph Company, 1895), 76.

108   **"On the floor of that room":** Quoted in Ned Sublette and Constance Sublette, *The American Slave Coast: A History of the Slave-Breeding Industry* (Chicago: Lawrence Hill Books), 586.

108   **"the epicenter of some of the most profound":** Bergman and Bergman, *Haunted Richmond,* 11.

108   **"The area surrounding the Shockoe Valley":** Ibid.

108   **"We have been able to find very little":** Ibid., 18.

109   **"If a premature exit from this world":** Ibid., 11.

109   **There the president is heard:** Accounts of Thomas Jefferson's ghost can be found in Charles A. Stanfield, *Haunted Presidents: Ghosts in the Lives of the Chief Executives* (Mechanicsburg, PA: Stackpole Books, 2010).

110   **"we have the wolf by the ears":** Quoted in Philip J. Schwarz, *Slave Laws in Virginia* (Athens: University of Georgia Press, 2010), 36.

110   **"not a fear of ghosts":** Miles, *Tales from the Haunted South,* 40.

110   **The only way to keep alive the white world:** As historian Philip J. Schwarz notes, Jefferson "believed that conformity to the law of slavery constituted a civic duty, protected him from some of the dangers inherent in slavery, preserved his liberty to hold humans in bondage, and even, secondarily, gave some personal security to the enslaved." He saw himself, in other words, as having a moral obligation to preserve the order of things, even if the order was itself immoral. And yet, Schwarz adds, it wasn't just his "deep attachment to the mores of his society" that

led him to defend slavery: "his 'conspicuous consumption,' and his chronic debt problem held him captive to bondage." Schwarz, *Slave Laws in Virginia*, 35.

111 **"It is better to buy none in families"**: Quoted in Edward E. Baptist, *The Half Has Never Been Told: Slavery and the Making of American Capitalism* (New York: Basic Books, 2014), 102.

111 **This was not unintentional**: Ibid., 188.

111 **also of their memory in death**: See Vincent Brown, *The Reaper's Garden: Death and Power in the World of Atlantic Slavery* (Cambridge: Harvard University Press, 2008).

111 **"the new zombie body of slavery"**: Baptist, *The Half Has Never Been Told*, 147.

112 **"Not a house in the country"**: Toni Morrison, *Beloved* (New York: Plume, 1988), 5.

113 **"John May come back"**: Jane Arrington, *Born in Slavery: Slave Narratives from the Federal Writers' Project, 1936–1938, North Carolina Narratives*, Vol. 11 (Federal Writers' Project, United States Work Projects Administration; Manuscript Division, Library of Congress, digital ID: mesn 111/048044), 46.

113 **"One night we was driving"**: George Bollinger, *Born in Slavery: Slave Narratives from the Federal Writers' Project, 1936–1938, Missouri Narratives*, Vol. 10 (Federal Writers' Project, United States Work Projects Administration; Manuscript Division, Library of Congress, digital ID: mesn 100/041036), 36.

113 **A woman named Florida Clayton**: Florida Clayton, quoted in *Born in Slavery: Slave Narratives from the Federal Writers' Project, 1936–1938, Florida Narratives*, Vol. 3 (Federal Writers' Project, United States Work Projects Administration; Manuscript Division, Library of Congress, digital ID: mesn 030/065062), 62–63.

114 **"place where there is a high fence"**: Thomas Lewis, *Born in Slavery: Slave Narratives from the Federal Writers' Project, 1936–1938, Indiana Narratives*, Vol. 5 (Federal Writers' Project, United States Work Projects Administration; Manuscript Division, Library of Congress, digital ID: mesn 050/127123), 126–27.

114 **"When the nights were still"**: "Slave and Negro Lore," *Born in Slavery: Slave Narratives from the Federal Writers' Project, 1936–1938, Missouri Narratives*, Vol. 10 (Federal Writers' Project, United States Work Projects Administration; Manuscript Division, Library of Congress, digital ID: mesn 100/208203), 204.

114 **"How come I knows dey rides me?"**: "Foots Get Tired from Choppin' Cotton," *Born in Slavery: Slave Narratives from the Federal Writers' Project, 1936–1938, Alabama Narratives*, Vol. 1 (Federal Writers' Project, United States Work Projects Administration; Manuscript Division, Library of Congress, digital ID: mesn 010/435429), 430–31.

114 **One woman in Tennessee**: Recounted in Baptist, *The Half Has Never Been Told*, 148.

114–15 **A man identified only as Uncle Louis**: "Psychology of a Runaway Slave," *Born in Slavery: Slave Narratives from the Federal Writers' Project, 1936–1938, Alabama*

Narratives, Vol. 1 (Federal Writers' Project, United States Work Projects Administration; Manuscript Division, Library of Congress, digital ID: mesn 010/269263), 265–66.

115 **"The legacy of Wall Street":** Trammell, *Richmond Slave Trade*, 116.

116 **an archaeological team largely funded:** See Abigail Tucker, "Digging Up the Past at a Richmond Jail: The Excavation of a Notorious Jail Recalls Richmond's Leading Role in the Slave Trade," *Smithsonian Magazine*, March 2009.

117 **"I started weeping and couldn't stop":** Ibid.

117 **"It doesn't escape me for one moment":** Caitlin Dewey, "Transcript: Lupita Nyong'o's Emotional Oscars Acceptance Speech," *Washington Post*, March 2, 2014.

CHAPTER SEVEN: BABY (RENO, NV)

119 **that of Bella Rawhide and Timber Kate:** Bella and Kate's story is recounted in a number of places, including James Reynolds, *Ghosts in American Houses* (New York: Paperback Library, 1955), and Ken Summers, *Queer Hauntings: True Tales of Gay and Lesbian Ghosts* (Maple Shade, NJ: Heritage Press, 2009).

123 **"a seedy biker bar":** Alexa Albert, *Brothel: The Mustang Ranch and Its Women* (New York: Ballantine, 2001), 12.

125 **In 2013 investigators from the reality show:** "Mustang Ranch," *Ghost Adventures*, Travel Channel, October 18, 2013.

126 **"Baby apparently likes water":** Interview with the author, December 2, 2014.

128 **"This is the epitome of caregiving":** Interview with the author, December 1, 2014.

CHAPTER EIGHT: PASSING THROUGH (LOS ANGELES, CA)

132 **"There are many stories about ghostly presence":** Quoted in Dennis Romero, "Laura Finley's Death at Old Biltmore Hotel in Downtown L.A. Perplexes Investigators: A Commenter Suggests the Place Is Haunted," *LA Weekly*, October 27, 2010.

133 **"not a superstitious man":** Wilkie Collins, *Miss or Mrs?, The Haunted Hotel, The Guilty River* (Oxford: Oxford University Press, 1993), 172.

133 **"How many times":** Interview with the author, August 3, 2012.

134 **"We're two different people":** Interview with the author, August 12, 2012.

136 **"I think he's a corrupt cop":** Interview with the author, August 2, 2012.

137 **unusual repetition, or "involuntary repetition":** Freud, *The Uncanny*, 145.

137 **"The uncanny is home defamiliarized":** Wayne Koestenbaum, *Hotel Theory* (New York: Soft Skull Press, 2007), 116.

138 **"an old hotel that had once been exclusive":** Raymond Chandler, "Nevada Gas," in *Collected Stories* (New York: Alfred A. Knopf, 2002), 238.

139 **Amateur sleuths became obsessed with the video:** Josh Dean's "American Horror Story: The Cecil Hotel" (on the Web site *Matter*, October 27, 2015)

recounts the history of the Internet's fascination with Lam's death, as well as the subsequent police investigation.

140 **"ghost ship floating adrift"**: Quoted in Lynnea Chapman King, *The Coen Brothers Encyclopedia* (Lanham, MD: Rowan and Littlefield, 2014), 7.

142 **"It does not wish to be a part of the city"**: Frederic Jameson, *Postmodernism: Or, The Cultural Logic of Late Capitalism* (Durham, NC: Duke University Press, 2003), 42.

142 **"You are likely to move around"**: Charles Willard Moore, *A City Observed, Los Angeles: A Guide to Its Architecture and Landscapes* (New York: Random House, 1984), 16.

146 **"We want proof"**: LA Ghost Patrol, "LAGP on Fox News 11 at Suicide Bridge," YouTube video, March 10, 2012.

147 **"paranormal archaeology"**: Interview with the author, August 3, 2012.

III: CIVIC-MINDED SPIRITS

153 **"a generous, whole-souled man"**: Lloyd C. Henning, quoted in Leland J. Hanchett, *The Crooked Trail to Holbrook: An Arizona Cattle Trail* (Phoenix, AZ: Arrowhead Press, 1993), 217.

153 **"Hundreds of persons"**: Ibid., 215.

154 **that reflected his dark sense of humor**: Both funeral announcements can be found in, among other places, ibid., 216–17.

156 **"Smiley exhibited great coolness"**: Holbrook *Argus,* January 13, 1900, quoted in Linda Kor, "New Marker Recognizes Smiley's Place in Navajo County History," *Arizona Journal,* July 24, 2015.

156 **But according to Marita R. Keems:** See Antonio R. Garcez, *Arizona Ghost Stories* (Moriarty, NM: Red Rabbit Press, 2012).

CHAPTER NINE: MELANCHOLY CONTEMPLATION
(MOUNDSVILLE, WV)

159 **The husband's name was Erasmus Stribbling Trout Shue:** Shue's biography is recounted in Katie Letcher Lyle, *The Man Who Wanted Seven Wives: The Greenbrier Ghost and the Famous Murder Mystery of 1897* (Charleston, SC: Quarrier Press, 1999).

160 **"stretched out perfectly straight"**: Quoted in ibid., 9.

160 **"slight discoloration on the right side"**: Ibid.

161 **"It was no dream"**: Ibid., 118.

162 **"Because of lack of ventilation"**: *Crain v. Bordenkircher,* 342 S.E.2d 422, Supreme Court of Appeals of West Virginia, 1986.

162 **Adkins had been one of three men:** Stan Bumgardner and Christine Kreiser, "'Thy Brother's Blood': Capital Punishment in West Virginia," *West Virginia Historical Society Quarterly,* http://www.wvculture.org/history/wvhs/wvhs941.html.

162 **according to one employee I spoke to:** Benjamin Miller, interview with the author, November 1, 2015.

163 **"frightening yet intriguing"**: Margee Kerr, *Scream: Chilling Adventures in the Science of Fear* (New York: Public Affairs, 2015), 54–5.

163   **"leave you there or drop you"**: Ibid., 64.

164   **"Its good design"**: "Report of the Commissioners Appointed to Superintend the Erection of the Eastern Penitentiary, Near Philadelphia, on the Penal Code," in Samuel Hazard, ed., *The Register of Pennsylvania, Devoted to the Preservation of Facts and Documents, and Every Other Kind of Useful Information Respecting the State of Pennsylvania* (Philadelphia: W. F. Geddes, 1828), vol. 1, 264.

164   **"to impress so great a dread"**: Ibid.

164   **"The style of architecture of a prison"**: Quoted in Elmer Barnes, *The Evolution of Penology in Pennsylvania: A Study in American Social History* (Indianapolis, IN: Bobbs-Merrill, 1927), 143.

165   **a sense of awe and "melancholy contemplation"**: Charles C. Western, *Remarks Upon Prison Discipline* (London: James Ridgway, 1821), 22.

165   **"The design and execution impart"**: John Wilkes, *Encyclopaedia Londinensis* (London: G. Jones, 1826), vol. 21, 421–2.

167   **Joseph Tomlinson discovered it in 1770**: For a history of the Grave Creek Mound from its rediscovery to the present, see Delf Norona, *Moundsville's Mammoth Mound* (Moundsville: West Virginia Archeological Society, 1954).

167   **"Around the base of this column"**: Quoted in ibid., 34.

170   **"One of the most famous murder cases in Australia"**: Quoted in Lyle, *Man Who Wanted Seven Wives*, 159.

CHAPTER TEN: THE STAIN (DANVERS, MA, AND ATHENS, OH)

175   **"the present state of insane persons"**: Quoted in Andrew Scull, *Madness in Civilization: A Cultural History of Insanity, from the Bible to Freud, from the Madhouse to Modern Medicine* (Princeton, NJ: Princeton University Press, 2015), 192.

175   **"All experience"**: Quoted in ibid., 207.

176   **"laboratory for the purification of culture"**: Benjamin Reiss, *Theaters of Madness: Insane Asylums and Nineteenth-Century American Culture* (Chicago: University of Chicago Press, 2008), 79.

177   **One opponent, Hervey B. Wilbur**: See Carla Yanni, *The Architecture of Madness: Insane Asylums in the United States* (Minneapolis: University of Minnesota Press, 2007), 165.

178   **A report from 1939**: "The Commonwealth of Massachusetts Annual Report of the Trustees of the Danvers State Hospital for the Year Ending November 30, 1939, 11. Found online at http://abandonedasylum.com/yahoo_site_admin1/assets/docs/danvers1939.14582704.pdf.

179   **"If you think back to the beginnings"**: Quoted in Michael Puffer, "The Lore, and Lure, of Danvers State Hospital," *Danvers Herald,* October 29, 2003.

179   **Dr. Henry Cotton, who from 1907 to 1930**: See Andrew Scull, *Madhouse: A Tale of Megalomania and Modern Medicine* (New Haven: Yale University Press, 2005).

180   **In such a setting emerged a ghost story**: Carolyn M. Zimmermann, Ünige A. Laskay, and Glen P. Jackson, "Analysis of Suspected Trace Human Remains from

an Indoor Concrete Surface," *Journal of Forensic Sciences* 53, no. 6 (November 2008): 1437–42.

182   **"A disorderly patient is stripped naked":** *The Trial of Ebenezer Haskell, in Lunacy, and His Acquittal Before Judge Brewster, in November, 1868, Together with a Brief Sketch of the Mode of Treatment of Lunatics in Different Asylums in This Country and in England* (Philadelphia, 1869), 43.

183   **"a fantastic château, much dilapidated":** Edgar Allan Poe, "The System of Doctor Tarr and Professor Fether," in *Poetry and Tales* (New York: Library of America, 1984), 699–716.

184   **"These are America's castles":** Interview with the author, July 5, 2015.

185   **cost the state more than $30 million:** William Westhoven, "Greystone Fading into Black," *Daily Record,* October 10, 2015.

CHAPTER ELEVEN: AWAITING THE DEVIL'S COMING
(CHARLESTON, SC, AND DOUGLAS COUNTY, KS)

187   **"The Souls of the Dead appear frequently":** Joseph Addison, *The Spectator,* No. 90, June 13, 1711.

188   **Her father, Dr. Edmund Ravenel:** Ravenel's life and career is discussed in Lester D. Stephens, *Science, Race, and Religion in the American South: John Bachman and the Charleston Circle of Naturalists, 1815–1895* (Chapel Hill: University of North Carolina Press, 2000).

189   **Poe knew Ravenel while stationed at Sullivan's Island:** See Arthur Hobson Quinn, *Edgar Allan Poe: A Critical Biography* (Baltimore, MD: Johns Hopkins University Press, 1998), 130.

189   **"well-educated, with unusual powers":** Poe, "The Gold Bug," in *Poetry and Tales,* 561.

190   **We should not be dissuaded:** Some have suggested that Annabel may not have been Edmund Ravenel's daughter but perhaps a niece or other relative. But the exhaustive Ravenel genealogical records reveal no such plausible candidate; there are very few Annabels, Annabelles, Annas or Annes, and all either died in childhood or were born after Poe himself died.

190   **"If you would see Charleston's greatest attraction":** Edward Hepple Hall, *Appleton's Hand-Book of American Travel* (New York: D. Appleton & Co., 1866), 353.

191   **graveyards were as centrally located:** On the history and evolution of the graveyard, see Colin Dickey, "Necropolis," *Lapham's Quarterly* 3, no. 4 (Fall 2010).

191   **In 1744 a story circulated:** See John McManners, *Death and the Enlightenment: Changing Attitudes to Death Among Christians and Unbelievers in Eighteenth-Century France* (Oxford: Oxford University Press, 1985), 313.

191   **Fully 73 percent of Colma's land:** Carol Pogash, "Colma, Calif., Is a Town of 2.2 Square Miles, Most of It Six Feet Deep," *New York Times,* December 9, 2006.

192   **"the emanations of the dead":** Quoted in Christopher Vernon, *Graceland Cemetery: A Design History* (Amherst: University of Massachusetts Press, 2011), 26.

192   **and finally Graceland:** On the history of Graceland, see ibid.

192   **"neglected" and in an "actually repulsive condition":** Quoted in ibid., 28.

193   **described as the "most perfect expression":** Wilhelm Miller, quoted in ibid., 177.

193   **For much of English history:** A concise history of the etymology of "graveyard" and "cemetery" can be found in Laqueur, *Work of the Dead,* 118–21.

194   **"more efficient instrument to elevate Ambition":** Joseph Story, *An Address Delivered on the Dedication of the Cemetery at Mount Auburn, September 24, 1831* (Boston: Joseph T. and Edwin Buckingham, 1831), 14.

195   **"it was a little black relic":** Dutton Cook, *On the Stage: Studies of Theatrical History and the Actor's Art* (London: Sampson Low, Marston, Searl, and Rivington, 1883), vol. 1, 224.

195   **Additionally, Cooke's skull was stolen:** Ibid., 224–5.

196   **"haunted by legends of diabolical, supernatural happenings":** Jain Penner, "Legend of Devil Haunts Tiny Town," *University Daily Kansan,* November 5, 1974.

196   **"All of a sudden I heard a noise":** Ibid.

197   **"in awkward positions on the floor":** Tom Ramstack, "Devil Bypasses Cemetery," *University Daily Kansan,* March 22, 1978.

198   **"whatever lurks in the church":** Michelle Worrall, "Ghostly Tales Haunt Town's Graveyard," *University Daily Kansan,* April 16, 1985.

198   **"The real evil," the paper proclaimed:** Elicia Hill, "Vandalism at Stull's Mythical 'Gate to Hell' Frustrates Residents," *University Daily Kansan,* November 1, 1990.

198   **"When I used to patrol out there":** Tom Dehart, "Rumors, Urban Legends Surround Stull Cemetery," *University Daily Kansan,* October 31, 2013.

199   **"A lot of history fell":** Richard Gintowt, "Hell Hath No Fury," www.lawrence.com, October 26, 2004.

199   **"One man wrote and said a relative of mine":** Ibid.

199   **"This story about it being haunted":** Ibid.

200   **Inez was only six years old:** On the ghost of Inez Clarke, see Tom Ogden, *Haunted Cemeteries: Creepy Crypts, Spine-Tingling Spirits, and Midnight Mayhem* (Guilford, CT: Globe Pequot Press, 2010), 21; and Jeff Morris and Vince Shields, *Chicago Haunted Handbook: 99 Ghostly Places You Can Visit in and Around the Windy City* (Covington, KY: Clerisy Press, 2013), 21–2.

200   **a sample of the carver's work to drum up business:** An exhaustive search into the history of the statue can be found in John J. Binder and William G. Willard, "The Mysterious Statue of Inez 'Clarke,'" *Chicago Genealogist* 44, no. 1, 3–7.

CHAPTER TWELVE: OUR ILLUSTRIOUS DEAD (SHILOH, TN)

203   **In Cold Harbor, Virginia:** There are many books about ghosts of Civil War battlefields, including Beth Brown, *Haunted Battlefields: Virginia's Civil War Ghosts* (Atglen, PA: Schiffer Publishing, 2008); Mark Nesbitt, *Civil War Ghost Trails: Stories from America's Most Haunted Battlefields* (Mechanicsburg, PA: Stackpole Publishing, 2012); and Daniel Cohen, *Civil War Ghosts* (New York: Scholastic, 1999).

203   **"He was lying down on the moss":** Alan Brown, *Tales from the Haunted South* (Jackson: University Press of Mississippi, 2004), 239.

204   **The creation of the Civil War battlefield cemeteries:** On the creation of the Civil War battlefield monuments, see Drew Gilpin Faust, *This Republic of Suffering: Death and the American Civil War* (New York: Vintage Books, 2008), chapter 7.

204   **"Shall we permit their honored graves":** James F. Russling, "National Cemeteries," *Harper's New Monthly Magazine* (August 1866), 311–12.

205   **"arguably the most elaborate federal program":** Faust, *This Republic of Suffering*, 219.

206   **"the body, by the fact of its physical location":** Laqueur, *Work of the Dead*, 54.

206   **"though lost, still just":** Quoted in Faust, *This Republic of Suffering*, 245.

207   **"Sometimes we would meet one or two people":** Quoted in Gladys-Marie Fry, *Night Riders in Black Folk History* (Chapel Hill: University of North Carolina Press, 1975), 137.

207   **Stories circulated of an incident:** Wyn Craig Wade, *The Fiery Cross: The Ku Klux Klan in America* (New York: Oxford University Press, 1987), 36.

207   **"A spirit from the other world":** Walter Lynnwood Fleming, *Documentary History of Reconstruction: Political, Military, Social, Religious, Educational & Industrial, 1865 to the Present Time* (Cleveland: Arthur H. Clark, 1907), vol. 2, 361.

208   **"they had come from Manassas Gap":** Quoted in Fry, *Night Riders*, 137.

208   **"What do you all want to whip me for":** Quoted in Fleming, *Documentary History of Reconstruction*, 371–3.

208   **"bones rattling together":** Wade, *Fiery Cross*, 33.

209   **simple stage magic trickery:** Ibid., 35–36.

209   **"the Klan legends of terrified 'darkies'":** Ibid., 36–7.

210   **"it has been suggested that blacks":** Ibid.

210   **"The concept of returning Confederate dead":** Fry, *Night Riders*, 136.

210   **"The Klux is the living dead":** Edward H. Dixon, *The Terrible Mysteries of the Ku-Klux-Klan* (New York: n.p., 1868), 43.

210   **"The fraudulent ghost," Fry writes:** Fry, *Night Riders*, 73.

CHAPTER THIRTEEN: THE WIND THROUGH CATHEDRAL PARK (PORTLAND, OR)

213   **In the video there is first the image:** GuerrillaFilms1, "Amateur Ghost Hunting in Cathedral Park," YouTube video, November 3, 2010.

214   **"Oh yeah," one diner owner told the local news:** Tim Becker, "Thelma Taylor: Phantom in Cathedral Park?" www.koin.com, October 29, 2015.

214   **"visit the area and see":** Andy Weeks, *Haunted Oregon: Ghosts and Strange Phenomena of the Beaver State* (Mechanicsburg, PA: Stackpole Books, 2014), 20.

215   **"Inanimate materials, such as stone":** Donna Stewart, *Ghosthunting Oregon* (Cincinnati: Clerisy Press, 2014), 22.

215   **"The question is not whether people see ghosts":** T. C. Lethbridge, *Ghost and Ghoul* (London: Routledge and Kegan Paul, 1961), 36.

215–16 **"are no more than mental pictures":** Ibid., 151.

216   **a haunted house has "photographed" a past tragedy:** Oliver Lodge, *Man and the Universe: A Study in the Influence of the Advance in Scientific Knowledge upon Our Understanding of Christianity* (London: Methuen and Co., 1908), 194.

216   **"Is it a remnant spirit":** Interview with the author, March 9, 2015.

217   **"a vague, scary story that circulated":** Jim Speirs, "Speaking of Ghosts," deathinspadesandmore.blogspot.com, July 9, 2010.

218   **"I just felt *bad* for her":** Interview with the author, March 2, 2015.

218   **"According to John Mbiti":** James W. Loewen, *Lies Across America: What Our Historic Sites Get Wrong* (New York: Touchstone, 2000), 24.

219   **"Not primarily motivated by loss or grief":** Ibid.

219   **"It is not the passion":** Jean Baudrillard, *For a Critique of a Political Economy of the Sign*, trans. Charles Levin (St. Louis: Telos Press, 1981), 92.

221   **in the city of the sasha dead:** Kevin Brockmeier, *The Brief History of the Dead* (New York: Vintage, 2006).

221   **Having awakened memories decades old:** See Speirs, "Speaking of Ghosts," deathinspadesandmore.blogspot.com, July 9, 2010.

222   **"So she pulls it out of her mouth":** Interview with the author, January 10, 2016.

IV: USELESS MEMORY

228   **a dumb anecdote to entertain friends:** A user named "niki-mullins" commented on the Virtual Tourist Web site, "Also some say the water was cursed by Indians. And that if you drink it, that you'll be stuck here no matter how hard you try to leave. As far as for me I didn't grow up here, THANK GOD, but the curse seems to be holding up no matter what." Another user on the same page, "matt 999tye," concurs: "Honestly, I am not superstitious or anything, but this curse may be true. All my drive and passion for leaving Binghamton has vanished. Binghamton is not a recommended tourist area." See https://www.virtualtourist.com/travel/North_America/United_States_of_America/New_York_State/Binghamton-837475/Warnings_or_Dangers-Binghamton-TG-C-1.html.

230   **"A few stories came across as fairly light":** Elena Gormley, "Ghost Tours Turn Women's Abuse into Family Friendly Entertainment," Broadly.vice.com, October 10, 2015.

230   **"may have committed suicide":** Ibid.

231   **"white tourists always made smart comments":** Ibid.

231   **"The city's very obsessed with its brand":** Interview with the author, November 5, 2015.

231   **"By limiting the universe of speakers":** "Savannah Tour Guides Say City Uses Testing to Control Speech," Associated Press, August 15, 2015.

231   **the story is probably fictionalized:** See Miles, *Tales from the Haunted South*, chapter 1.

232   **Stephen Bader, however, contends:** Jamie Caskey, "Stephen Bader Responds (TAPS at Sorrel-Weed)," http://hauntedsavannah.blogspot.com/2005/11/stephen-bader-responds-taps-at-sorrel.html, November 15, 2005.

CHAPTER FOURTEEN: THE WET GRAVE (NEW ORLEANS, LA)

233   **"a song which rises like slow smoke":** Jeanne deLavigne, *Ghost Stories of Old New Orleans* (Baton Rouge: Louisiana State University Press, 2013), 3.

233   **"actually resembles no other city":** Lafcadio Hearn, *American Writings* (New York: Library of America, 2009), 670.

234   **"spectral, mysterious, inexplicable":** Ibid., 680.

234   **The wealthy Frenchman who lived here:** This story is told, among other places, in deLavigne's *Ghost Stories of Old New Orleans*, under the title "The Golden Brown Woman."

235   **"It's just a city that everybody loves":** Interview with the author, February 4, 2015.

236   **the building was operating:** Paul Oswell, *New Orleans Historic Hotels* (Charleston, SC: The History Press, 2014), 136.

236   **already being advertised as a haunted house:** The best history of the Lalaurie Mansion and its notorious owner is Carolyn Morrow Long, *Madame Lalaurie: Mistress of the Haunted House* (Gainesville: University Press of Florida, 2012).

237   **"no spirits wander through its wide halls":** Henry C. Castellanos, *New Orleans as It Was: Episodes of Louisiana Life* (Baton Rouge: Louisiana State University Press, 1978), 62.

237   **"barbarous treatment of her slaves contrary to law":** Quoted in Long, *Madame Lalaurie*, 79.

238   **"There are those who would be better employed":** Quoted in ibid., 90.

238   **"several wretched negroes":** Ibid.

238   **"seven slaves, more or less horribly mutilated":** Ibid.

238   **"with the intention of terminating the sufferings":** Ibid.

239   **"at least two thousand persons visited":** Ibid., 91.

239   **"justice will be done and the guilty be brought to punishment":** Ibid.

240   **"this bewitching and engaging creature":** Herbert Asbury, *The French Quarter: An Informal History of New Orleans* (New York: Alfred A. Knopf, 2003), 248.

240   **"Madame Lalaurie, under her soft and beautiful exterior":** deLavigne, *Ghost Stories of Old New Orleans*, 257.

241   **"memory operates as both quotation and invention":** Joseph Roach, *Cities of the Dead: Circum-Atlantic Performance* (New York: Columbia University Press, 1996), 33.

242   **"This is a higher crime area"**: Quoted in Anna Hartnell, "Katrina Tourism and a Tale of Two Cities: Visualizing Race and Class in New Orleans," *American Quarterly* 61, no. 3: 725.

242   **"site of translation"**: Ibid., 723.

242   **"spatial apartheid"**: Quoted in ibid., 732.

243   **"The house stands, and is meant to stand"**: Harriet Martineau, *Retrospect of Western Travel* (London: Saunders and Otley, 1838), vol. 1, 263.

243   **"The house is very still"**: George Washington Cable, "The 'Haunted House' in Royal Street," in *Strange True Tales of Louisiana* (New York: Charles Scribner's Sons, 1889), 195.

244   **"admirable firmness and propriety"**: Quoted in Long, *Madame Lalaurie*, 158.

246   **"Wait here until night"**: deLavigne, *Ghost Stories of Old New Orleans*, 13.

247   **"I was in my sleeping bag"**: Janet Yee, "Guardsmen Sense Ghostly Presence in New Orleans," KPIX, CBS5, San Francisco, September 23, 2005.

247   **"One of the many lessons"**: Ceci Connolly, "A Grisly but Essential Issue," *Washington Post*, June 9, 2006.

247   **"Even cities feel trauma"**: Andrew Buncombe, "Hurricane Katrina 10th Anniversary: New Orleans Is Haunted by the Death of Vera Smith," *The Independent*, August 24, 2015.

248   **"mammoth temple of burger worship"**: Sarah Baird, "Review: Charcoal's Gourmet Burger Bar," *Gambit*, October 13, 2014.

249   **"I saw a bloodied corpse weeping body fluids"**: Chris Rose, "Vera Smith's Makeshift Garden District Grave Endures as a Most Unlikely—and Poignant— Katrina Memorial," *Times-Picayune*, October 25, 2009.

250   **"symbol of the quiet suffering people endured"**: "Vera Smith's Death After Hurricane Katrina Still Haunts New Orleans Neighborhood," Associated Press, August 19, 2015.

250   **"She was not a sad woman"**: "New Orleans Restaurant Reportedly Haunted by Hurricane Katrina Victim," www.aol.com, August 24, 2015.

251   **"Our message to Vera"**: Kenny Lopez, "Hurricane Katrina Victim Haunting New Orleans Burger Joint?," wgno.com, December 10, 2013.

CHAPTER FIFTEEN: AMONG THE RUINS (DETROIT, MI)

253   **"the figure of a man, white and terrible"**: See Amy Elliott Bragg, *Hidden History of Detroit* (Charleston, SC: History Press, 2011), 120.

254   **"America, you have it better"**: Johann Wolfgang von Goethe, "Den Vereinigten Staaten," in *Goethes Werke: I. Abtheilung, 5 Band* (Tokyo: Sansyusya, 1975), 137.

256   **"In the ruin history has physically merged"**: Walter Benjamin, *The Origin of German Tragic Drama*, trans. John Osborne (London: Verso, 2009), 178.

256   **"deep and ample joy"**: Gustave Flaubert, *The Letters of Gustave Flaubert, 1830–1857*, ed. and trans. Francis Steegmuller (Cambridge, MA: Belknap Press, 1980), 71.

256 **"a ruin is a sacred thing"**: William Gilpin, *Observations, Relative Chiefly to Picturesque Beauty, Made in the Year 1772, on Several Parts of England, Particularly the Mountains and Lakes of Cumberland and Westmoreland*, 3rd ed. (London: T. Caddell and W. Davies, 1808), vol. 2, 183.

257 **"The ideas that ruins awaken in me"**: Denis Diderot, quoted in Michael S. Roth with Claire Lyons and Charles Merewether, *Irresistible Decay: Ruins Reclaimed* (Los Angeles: Getty Research Institute for the History of Art and the Humanities, 1997), 59.

257 **"Is it unseemly now or ever"**: Sarah Boxer, "Even in a Moonscape of Tragedy, Beauty Is in the Eye," *New York Times*, May 23, 2002.

258 **"At first you're really flattered"**: Quoted in Dora Apel, *Beautiful Terrible Ruins: Detroit and the Anxiety of Decline* (New Brunswick, NJ: Rutgers University Press, 2015), 20.

259 **"Mr. Mason went slightly overboard"**: Claire Moore, "Top Ten Most Haunted Places in Michigan," www.awesomemitten.com/ten-haunted-places-in-michigan, October 20, 2012.

261 **"a woman of unusual height"**: Marie Caroline Watson Hamlin, *Legends of Le Détroit* (Detroit: Thorndike Nourse, 1884), 25–30.

262 **"seen scampering along the shore"**: Charles M. Skinner, *Myths and Legends of Our Own Land* (Auckland, NZ: Floating Press, 2013), 460.

263 **"Detroit might be depopulated"**: Thomas J., Sugrue, "Notown: Good News: A Few Hipsters Are Rediscovering Detroit. Bad News: Everything Else," *Democracy: a Journal of Ideas*, Spring 2013, no. 28.

CHAPTER SIXTEEN: HILLSDALE, USA

267 **"I am making these directions so detailed"**: Jackson, *Haunting of Hill House*, 252.

268 **"People *leave* this town"**: Ibid., 259.

268 Take **"Route 39 to Ashton"**: Ibid., 252.

268 **"the most remote part of New England"**: *The Haunting*, directed by Robert Wise, 1963.

269 **"Whether the source of the spectral apparitions"**: *Stambovsky v. Ackley*, 169 A.D.2d 254, Appellate Division of the Supreme Court of New York, First Department, 1991.

270 **In 2008 Janet Milliken**: On the history of the house in Thornton, Pennsylvania, see Will Hunt and Matt Wolfe, "The Ghosts of Pickering Trail," *Atavist Magazine*, read.atavist.com/the-ghosts-of-pickering-trail.

270 **"If a property is perceived as haunted"**: Quoted in ibid.

271 **"One cannot quantify the psychological impact"**: *Milliken v. Jacono*, J-87-2013, Supreme Court of Pennsylvania, 2014.

271 **"a messed-up place to work because it's haunted"**: Frank Rosario, Chris Perez, and Jennifer Gould Kell, "Ghosts Scare Staff Away from Luxury Rental Building," *New York Post*, May 18, 2015.

271   **"understandably perturbed by the gentrification"**: Lauren Evans, "Anti-Gentrification Ghosts Haunt Luxury Flatbush Development," *Gothamist,* May 19, 2015.

274   **"We left the valley with reluctant feet"**: Abigail, "Pacific Coast Letter," *Cincinnati Enquirer,* July 2, 1875.

275   **"Today all lie ghost towns"**: George F. Willison, *Here They Dug for the Gold* (New York: Brentano's, 1931), 71.

275   **"Sometimes, in the deep winter quiet"**: Ellen Baumler, *Montana Chillers: 13 True Tales of Ghosts and Hauntings* (Helena, MT: Farcountry Press, 2009), 61.

276   **A 2014 article in the *New York Times***: Jennifer A. Kingson, "Portland Will Still Be Cool, but Anchorage May Be the Place to Be," *New York Times,* September 22, 2014.

EPILOGUE: GHOSTS OF A NEW MACHINE (ALLENDALE, CA)

278   **"I often thought the house was lonely"**: Interview with the author, January 3, 2016.

279   **"If you can do a quick-and-dirty job"**: Tracy Kidder, *The Soul of a New Machine* (New York: Back Bay Books, 1981), 119.

280   **"Bridge tables sprouted from patio walls"**: Ray Bradbury, "There Will Come Soft Rains," in *The Martian Chronicles* (New York: Simon & Schuster, 2012), 224.

281   **"The entire west face of the house"**: Ibid., 222.

282   **"Our brain possesses several representations"**: Sheila M. Eldred, "Do Ghosts Live in Our Brains?" *Discovery News,* November 6, 2014.

282   **A video of a young Japanese girl**: See Matthew Battles, "Distributed Ghosts in the Machine," *The Atlantic,* March 28, 2011.

283   **Images of Rehtaeh Parsons**: Katherine Jacobsen, "Facebook Mystery: How Did Rehteah Parsons Image End Up on Dating Ad?" *Christian Science Monitor,* September 18, 2013.

285   **"Lack of information is part of the recipe"**: Interview with the author, March 2, 2015.

285   **the mysterious woman who appeared**: Patricia Pearson, "The 9/11 Survivors Who Were Guided to Safety by Spirits," *Daily Mail,* May 19, 2014.

INDEX